On Becoming
a Better
Therapist

On Becoming a Better Therapist

**Evidence-Based Practice
One Client at a Time**

SECOND EDITION

BARRY L. DUNCAN

AMERICAN PSYCHOLOGICAL ASSOCIATION • *Washington, DC*

Published by
American Psychological Association
750 First Street, NE
Washington, DC 20002
www.apa.org

To order
APA Order Department
P.O. Box 92984
Washington, DC 20090-2984
Tel: (800) 374-2721; Direct: (202) 336-5510
Fax: (202) 336-5502; TDD/TTY: (202) 336-6123
Online: www.apa.org/pubs/books
E-mail: order@apa.org

In the U.K., Europe, Africa, and the Middle East, copies may be ordered from
American Psychological Association
3 Henrietta Street
Covent Garden, London
WC2E 8LU England

Typeset in Goudy by Circle Graphics, Inc., Columbia, MD

Printer: United Book Press, Inc., Baltimore, MD
Cover Designer: Naylor Design, Washington, DC

The opinions and statements published are the responsibility of the authors, and such opinions and statements do not necessarily represent the policies of the American Psychological Association.

Library of Congress Cataloging-in-Publication Data

Duncan, Barry L.
  On becoming a better therapist : evidence-based practice one client at a time / Barry L. Duncan. — Second edition.
    pages cm
  Includes bibliographical references and index.
  ISBN-13: 978-1-4338-1745-8
  ISBN-10: 1-4338-1745-4
  1. Psychotherapy. 2. Psychotherapists. I. American Psychological Association. II. Title.
  RC480.D857 2014
  616.89'14—dc23
                                        2013048651

British Library Cataloguing-in-Publication Data
A CIP record is available from the British Library.

Printed in the United States of America
Second Edition

http://dx.doi.org/10.1037/14392-000

CONTENTS

FOREWORD TO THE FIRST EDITION

MICHAEL J. LAMBERT

Outcome research in the last 2 decades has extensively focused on the effects of specific treatments for specific disorders, so-called clinical trials. Researchers employing this methodology typically attend to the individual therapist as an important factor to be controlled before undertaking their primary analysis of treatment effects. Such research uses considerable resources to diminish variability in outcomes that could be attributed to the therapist. This is typically accomplished through careful selection of therapists, extensive training, and supervision of therapists who are using treatment manuals to guide their interventions. The intent of such procedures is to maximize the likelihood of finding effects due to treatments, independent of the therapists who offer them. In a field dedicated to the understanding of human behavior, it is a paradox that half the human element of therapy, the therapist, has largely been relegated to the category of an extraneous variable in clinical trials. This has resulted in an "oddly personless" view of psychotherapy (Norcross, 2002, p. 4).

Such designs don't necessarily ignore the importance of the therapist's capacity to both build a relationship with the client and flexibly tailor therapeutic treatment (techniques) to meet the needs of the individual client, but they do reduce variability in these important capacities, which are so central in service delivery in everyday practice. Considering the therapist and the client as central elements in the process of therapy does not detract from psychotherapy itself as having important healing ingredients but expands the possibilities for understanding the human encounter as connected with, rather than incidental to, therapeutic techniques. It makes little practical sense in routine care to ignore or minimize the interpersonal nature of psychotherapy and the therapist's contribution to patient improvement.

On Becoming a Better Therapist redirects our attention from specific treatments to our behaviors and attitudes as therapists, offering a refreshing look at improving treatment that operates outside the contemporary solution of providing the "right psychological treatment for the right disorder." This book provides simple but elegant solutions for becoming a more effective therapist.

In *On Becoming a Better Therapist*, Barry Duncan emphasizes the therapist and the therapist's contribution to patient well-being, extending the usual solutions provided in graduate education and challenging therapists in two important ways. The first requires therapists to systematically monitor their clients' treatment response and the therapeutic alliance (as rated by the client) and to discuss these phenomena with the client. The second challenge is for therapists to examine their effectiveness over time and use this information to become more effective. The discourse is on the one hand highly personal, anecdotal, passionate, and persuasive, and on the other, evidence-based. Barry Duncan is one of a handful of individuals advocating and implementing client progress information as an integral method of helping while learning from our patients.

Duncan makes improving patient outcomes the private and primary business of therapists, rather than policymakers and researchers. In this persuasive book he shows therapists how they can empower themselves and change their identities from providers of brand-name treatments to effective providers. This is truly ambitious and even revolutionary. To quote his words:

> In this book I have suggested that you step up to the plate with two things: attaining systematic client feedback and taking your development as a therapist to heart. . . . Routine collection of client feedback allows you to monitor your outcomes and plot your *cumulative career development*, so you know about your effectiveness, can determine whether you are improving, and most important, can reflect about what you can do to grow as a therapist. Tailoring your services to client feedback and preferences encourages you to let loose of any grip on the certainty of any particular ideology or practice and stimulates your expansion of your *theoretical breadth*.

Thus, *On Becoming a Better Therapist* provides new goals for our therapeutic efforts. These goals shift our attention from becoming experts in techniques to becoming knowledgeable about our effects on patients and our effectiveness. Rather than settling for getting certifications in techniques based on participation in workshops, the emphasis is on systematically measuring patient treatment response.

In fact, substantial evidence exists showing the degree to which tracking patient treatment response benefits clients (Lambert, 2010). It is becoming clearer that patients (particularly if they go off track) are advantaged when their response to treatment is formally measured and viewed by their therapist. But in this book Duncan goes beyond this reason for implementing formal tracking and feedback. It is a good idea if we want to understand our strengths and weaknesses and use this information to help us grow. If readers find Duncan persuasive and take up his challenge of systematically monitoring treatment response and alliance, it will be possible to estimate the extent to which we therapists actually become more effective with ongoing cases and over time. Duncan is confident that practicing with progress and alliance feedback will accelerate movement toward becoming a more effective therapist, and he provides evidence that this can be the case.

It is surprising that those most likely to instigate systematic monitoring are system administrators, not therapists. One would think that therapists would eagerly embrace the collection of important and empowering information through the easily applied methods advocated here, but this is not generally the case. Most investigations of therapist effects (Brown, Jones, Lambert, & Minami, 2005; Okiishi, Lambert, Eggett, et al., 2006; Okiishi, Lambert, Nielsen, & Ogles, 2003; Wampold & Brown, 2005) have been conducted by systems of care that have grasped the advantages of managing outcomes. The presence of variability in client outcome due to individual therapists allows systems of care to manage service delivery on the basis of effectiveness, not just processes. Duncan persuasively argues the advantages of monitoring and feeding back information for therapists, appealing to the basic motives of those who enter the helping professions—to make a difference by relieving suffering and maximizing human potential.

On Becoming a Better Therapist goes a long way toward expanding the potential of outcome monitoring by arguing that such methods are not only good for clients but also good for therapists—that such simple methods can affect the identity and well-being of therapists. This volume is yet another good read produced by Barry Duncan. Here he emphasizes the contributions of the therapist to client well-being and what has been learned from those who practice day-to-day with no fanfare. This book advocates becoming a better therapist by virtue of formally tracking our patients' treatment response and discussing progress and problems. The possibility and novelty of his ideas make this an important and provocative contribution to the field. It is time to make monitoring the consequences of day-to-day practice routine.

FOREWORD TO THE SECOND EDITION

DAVID N. ELKINS

I first became aware of Barry Duncan's scholarly work in the field of psychotherapy more than a decade ago. In recent years I have come to know him more personally, and I am honored to write this foreword for the second edition of *On Becoming a Better Therapist*. Duncan became involved with common factors as a full-time practitioner who was looking for ways to increase his effectiveness with clients. Disenchanted by the debates about which model and techniques were most effective, Duncan came to believe that the best way to increase effectiveness was to apply what was known about psychotherapy outcome. He proposed that clinicians spend time in therapy commensurate to each element's differential impact on outcome. Because the outcome research showed that client factors and the therapeutic alliance were the most potent determinants of outcome, Duncan called on therapists to spend less time on models and techniques, which had relatively little effect on outcome, and more time supporting the inherent strengths of clients and building a positive therapeutic relationship. More specifically, he called for a "client-directed" approach that focused on clients' strengths and resources, clients' ideas on how they can be helped, clients' hopes and expectations about the therapy, and clients' views on the nature and quality of the therapeutic relationship.

Duncan has published 16 books and dozens of articles, as well as conducting research on psychotherapy outcome. As a clinician who has spent more than 17,000 hours in direct client contact, Duncan's major contribution to the field is his ongoing effort to operationalize the common factors in therapeutic work. He believes that the client and the alliance are the "heart and soul" of change, a term he chose to name both the popular book about common factors as well as the organization he directs (see https://heartandsoulofchange.com).

Duncan's focus on the importance of the client culminated in the publication of this book and a client feedback process known as the Partners for Change Outcome Management System (PCOMS). To identify clients not responding to therapy, PCOMS solicits client feedback at each session about the outcome of therapy and the alliance. The feedback system helps clients, in collaboration with the psychotherapist, to find new and more helpful directions when the therapy is not going well. Duncan believes ongoing client feedback should be a "common factor" in all psychotherapies because of its proven effectiveness in helping clients to become more actively engaged in monitoring and improving their therapy experience, thus promoting more effective outcomes.

For those clinicians who, like Barry Duncan, are committed to becoming the best therapist possible, this book will be a breath of fresh air. Written in an accessible yet scholarly style, this updated second edition offers evidence-based and practical guidance on how to become a more effective therapist. In fact, the information presented in the following pages is so practical and "clinician friendly" that therapists can apply it immediately, beginning with the next client who walks in the door.

PREFACE

At times our own light goes out and is rekindled by a spark from another person. Each of us has cause to think with deep gratitude of those who have lighted the flame within us.

—Albert Schweitzer

I named a previous book *The Heroic Client* (Duncan, Miller, & Sparks, 2004) to showcase the more noble sides of human nature that accompany clients to our offices and to recast the drama of therapy, assigning clients their rightful central roles in therapeutic change. I could have called this one *The Heroic Therapist* to spotlight those individuals who are in the trenches, fighting the good fight with clients to transcend adversity, manage life, and find meaning in this crazy existence. I truly admire you, and I write this book for you, regardless of your discipline or whether you call yourself a psychotherapist, counselor, case manager, nurse practitioner, addiction specialist, or student. You are the spark that has rekindled my flame over the years.

I have been in the presence of many great therapists in my life, and none of them have been workshop stars or authors of definitive works about psychotherapy. No, these exceptional therapists whom I have been privileged to know are *you*—the folks who, in spite of downsides of the work that lead some to burn out and accept mediocrity, still manage to care deeply about clients and do incredible work. As I travel in my role as a trainer and consultant, I am continually inspired not only by the character of individuals who do this work but also by their commitment to improve their effectiveness. It seems to be part of their makeup, their very identity, to strive to be more helpful, to increase the numbers of clients who benefit from their services.

On Becoming a Better Therapist: Evidence-Based Practice One Client at a Time intends to help you be better at what you do—to both improve your outcomes now and accelerate your development—in a pragmatic and measurable way via the Partners for Change Outcome Management System (PCOMS). PCOMS solicits the consumer's real-time feedback about outcome and the alliance to enable more effective care that is tailored to client preferences. It allows a clinically friendly method to track outcome, something that has been sorely missing.

When I was in graduate school, the only discussion of outcome was in the context of psychotherapy efficacy studies. And that was unbelievably confusing given all the types of psychometric instruments, not to mention the complexity of the findings, leaving many of us with our heads reeling and the idea that measuring outcomes was about research, with no applicability to everyday practice. In the late 1990s, a new era was ushered in based largely on the pioneering work of Michael Lambert and the Outcome Questionnaire 45.2 (Lambert et al., 1996). Over time Lambert demonstrated that feedback enhanced client benefit and that outcome management could be a part of routine clinical work. In other words, measuring outcomes wasn't just for researchers anymore. With that inspiration, PCOMS was developed as a brief and feasible yet psychometrically sound alternative to longer outcome tools, to encourage routine use and bring the advantages of feedback to the in-the-trenches therapist. PCOMS is designed for use in everyday practice as a reliable, valid, and perhaps most important, doable method to partner with clients to track outcome—to identify at-risk clients while offering a way for therapists to monitor their effectiveness over the course of their careers. And just in time, too, because the Affordable Care Act calls for measurable outcomes, a call that is increasing in volume from many private and public funders.

Since the first edition of this book was published, PCOMS has been included in the Substance Abuse and Mental Health Services Administration's National Registry of Evidence-Based Programs and Practices. All three randomized clinical trials (RCTs) that enabled our application for and realization of evidence-based practice (EBP) status were conducted by Partners (my colleagues and me) of the Heart and Soul of Change Project (see https://heartandsoulofchange.com). We are committed to the values of consumer privilege, partnership, and service accountability, and we put our efforts into proving that a value-based outcome management system can really make a difference.

And it does. As demonstrated by the extensive research (including five RCTs) described in this book, PCOMS has the potential to improve your outcomes more than anything since the beginning of psychotherapy. Sounds like hyperbole, but it's not. PCOMS identifies clients who aren't responding so that you can proactively address the lack of progress and collaboratively develop a new plan. PCOMS allows you to recapture those clients destined for a negative outcome.

But PCOMS is not a specific treatment model for a particular client diagnosis; it's a horse of a different color. It is atheoretical and therefore may be added to or integrated with any model of practice, and it applies to all diagnostic categories. So, in effect, one size does fit all, allowing you to be evidence based across your clients. And, more important, PCOMS is evidence based at the individual client–therapist level. Collecting client feedback monitors whether *this* therapeutic approach provided by *this* therapist is benefiting *this* client. It provides a seemingly contradictory way to become evidence based across all your clients while tailoring services to the individual client's needs, preferences, and culture—or *evidence-based practice one client at a time*. Hence, the new subtitle of this second edition.

This book asserts that getting better at this work we love requires you to step up to the plate with two things: attain systematic client feedback via PCOMS and take your development as a therapist to heart. You are a significant ingredient of therapeutic change—in fact, in more ways than not, you *are* the treatment. Consequently, your perceptions of yourself and the work, your effectiveness, and your professional development are critical to your ongoing vitality as a helper. Pragmatically integrating the groundbreaking research about therapist growth of Orlinsky and Rønnestad (2005) with PCOMS, *On Becoming a Better Therapist* details a five-step plan to take charge of your development and accelerate it, with ways to keep your growth on the front burner, stave off the grim reaper of burnout and disenchantment, and remain a vital force for change in clients' lives. I'll show you how to track your outcomes and form a strategic plan that ensures that you learn from your experience and not just repeat it.

Finally, *On Becoming a Better Therapist* brings the lessons that I have learned from the best teachers of psychotherapy, my clients, some of whom were instrumental in shaping my career as well as my identity as therapist. But more important, this book shows you how to take advantage of the lessons tendered by your clients in a more systematic, session-by-session way. Beyond the cliché of clients being the best teachers, clients can, in real time, shape your therapeutic behavior, to create a better fit with their expectations, improve your outcomes, and enable you to do better work with more people. *On*

Becoming a Better Therapist demonstrates how harvesting the lessons learned from clients not only replenishes us but also encourages quantum leaps in our development.

Speaking of clients, the vignettes in this book are real, but all identifying information, including specific circumstances, have been removed or substantially altered to protect client confidentiality. In some, details are interchanged with other clients just to ensure that no one can be identified. But the accounts of the clinical process reflect what happened and are accurate depictions of the therapeutic events described.

Those of you familiar with the first edition will notice many changes. In addition to significant research updates and new clinical examples, the focus has been broadened with two new chapters, one demonstrating PCOMS with couples, families, and youth and the other presenting how to implement PCOMS on an organizational scale. And in writing the second edition, I quickly realized that, once you repaint one room, then the whole house looks in need of a new coat. So this edition also includes everything I've learned since the first edition from considering the many thoughtful questions that have been raised in my trainings and implementations.

Many people deserve special mention for their contributions to this book. I want to express my deepest gratitude to my partners in crime at the Heart and Soul of Change Project, for their scholarly contributions and expansions of my thinking and also for their spirit of collaboration and friendship—it has been a joy to surround myself with people whom I trust, who are selflessly committed to the ideals in this book. First, the Project Leaders: Jacqueline Sparks, Brian DeSantis, John Murphy, Mary Susan Haynes, Bob Bohanske, Anne-Grethe Tuseth, Jeff Reese, Luc Isebaert, and Sami Timimi. And the Certified Trainers: Morten Anker, Robyn Pope, Tor Fjeldstad, Pamela Parkinson, Dave Hanna, Barbara L. Hernandez, Alan Girard, Joan Biever, George Braucht, Mark DeBord, Geir Skauli, and Don Rogers. In addition to the readers of the first edition, I owe an incalculable debt to David N. Elkins (who also graciously wrote the foreword to the second edition), Jeff Reese, Morten Anker, and especially Jacqueline Sparks (who also substantially contributed to Chapter 4), who generously gave their time to give me feedback about this edition. Finally, I am appreciative of Susan Reynolds and Tyler Aune of the American Psychological Association. Susan has remained supportive of my work over the years and encouraged this second edition, and Tyler contributed expert editorial advice that significantly improved this book.

On Becoming
a Better
Therapist

1

SO YOU WANT TO BE
A BETTER THERAPIST

It's never too late to be who you might have been.

—George Eliot

A long time ago in a galaxy far way, I was in my initial placement in graduate school at the Dayton Mental Health and Developmental Center, the state hospital. While I often don't remember where I leave my glasses, I still vividly recall my first client, including her full name, but I'll call her "Tina." Tina was like a lot of the clients: young, poor, disenfranchised, heavily medicated, and in the revolving door of hospitalizations—and at the ripe old age of 22, she was called a *chronic schizophrenic*.

Although this practicum offered some group experience, it was largely devoted to assessment, and that's how I met Tina. I gathered up my Wechsler Adult Intelligence Scale—Revised, the first of the battery of tests I was attempting to gain competence with, and was on my merry but nervous way to the assessment office, a stark, run-down room in a long-past-its-prime, barrack-style building that reeked of cleaning fluids overused to cover up some other worse smell, the institutional stench. But on the way I couldn't help noticing all the looks I was getting—a smirk from an orderly, a wink from a nurse, and

http://dx.doi.org/10.1037/14392-001
On Becoming a Better Therapist, Second Edition: Evidence-Based Practice One Client at a Time, by B. L. Duncan
Copyright © 2014 by the American Psychological Association. All rights reserved.

funny-looking smiles from nearly everyone else. My curiosity piqued, I was just about to ask what was going on when the chief psychologist put his hand on my shoulder and said, "Barry, you might want to leave the door open." And I did.

I greeted Tina, a young, extremely pale woman with brown cropped hair (who might have looked a bit like Mia Farrow in the *Rosemary's Baby* era had Tina lived in friendlier circumstances) and introduced myself in my most professional voice. Before I could sit down and open my test kit, Tina started to take off her clothes, mumbling something indiscernible. I just stared in disbelief, in total shock, really. Tina was undaunted by my dismay and quickly was down to her underwear when I finally broke my silence, hearing laughter in the distance, and said, "Tina, what are you doing?" Tina responded not with words but with actions, removing her bra like it had suddenly become very uncomfortable. So, there we were, a graduate student, speechless, in his first professional encounter, and a client sitting nearly naked, mumbling now quite loudly but still nothing I could understand, and contemplating whether to stand up to take her underwear off or simply continue her mission while sitting.

Finally, in desperation, I pleaded, "Tina, would you please do me a big favor? I mean, I would really appreciate it." She looked at me for the first time, looked me right in the eye, and said, "What?"

I replied, "I would really be grateful if you could put your clothes back on and help me get through this assessment. I've done them before, but never with a client, and I am kinda freaked out about it."

Tina whispered, "Sure," and put her clothes back on. And although Tina struggled with the testing and clearly was not enjoying herself, she completed it.

I was so genuinely appreciative of Tina's help that I told her she really pulled me through my first real assessment. She smiled proudly, and ultimately she smiled at me every time she saw me from then on. I wound up getting to know Tina pretty well and often reminded her of how she helped me, and I even told her that I thought she looked like Mia Farrow, to her immense enjoyment. The more I got to know Tina and realized that her actions, stemming from horrific abuse, were attempts to take control of situations in which she felt powerless, the angrier I became about her being used as a rite of passage for the psychology trainees—a practice that I subsequently put a stop to in that institution.

I'll never forget the lessons that Tina taught me in the very beginning of my psychotherapy journey: Authenticity matters, and when in doubt or in need of help, ask the client, because you are in this thing together. Wherever you are, Tina, thanks for charting my course toward the power of real partnerships with clients.

I am a true believer in psychotherapy and in therapists of all stripes and flavors. In the 34 years and over 17,000 hours of my experience with clients since I saw Tina, I have been privileged to witness the irrepressible ability of human beings to transcend adversity—clients troubled by self-loathing and depression, battling alcohol or drugs, struggling with intolerable marriages, terrorized by inexplicable voices, oppressed by their children's problems, traumatized by past or current life circumstances, and tormented with unwanted thoughts and anxieties—with amazing regularity. As a trainer and consultant, I have rubbed elbows with thousands of psychotherapists across the globe, and the thing that strikes me most is their authentic desire to be helpful. Regardless of discipline, theoretical persuasion, or career level, they really care about people and strive to do good work. The odds for change when you combine a resourceful client and caring therapist are worth betting on, certainly cause for hope, and responsible for my unswerving faith in psychotherapy as a healing endeavor.

It's no secret, however, that this is a tough time to be a therapist. In public agencies, we're underpaid, overworked, and often held to unattainable productivity standards. We're subjected to a continual onslaught of paperwork and frequently face cutbacks and layoff threats. While some of us still thrive in private practice, most of us make far less than we did during the "golden age" of fee-for-service insurance reimbursement, and we endure oversight that challenges our patience. Furthermore, the nature of clinical work itself is sometimes frustrating, even anxiety provoking, exposing us to high levels of human suffering, stories that are at times tough to shake.

Adding insult to injury, the culture at large doesn't seem to admire therapists particularly, or understand what we do. This point is clear if you take a moment to think about popular portrayals of therapists, such as Dr. Marvin Monroe of *The Simpsons* or Jack Nicholson in *Anger Management* or Barbra Streisand in *Meet the Fockers*. Sure, good examples of competent clinicians exist, but they're far outweighed by those that cast us as self-indulgent crackpots endlessly mouthing psychobabble. Perhaps one sobering indication of how much we are valued is provided by the online salary database PayScale. com, which reveals that the two worst-paying master's degrees are in counseling and social work. It is amazing to think, in these hard economic times, that smart, creative individuals make the necessary sacrifices to attain advanced degrees only to earn far less money than those with comparable degrees in other fields. So, why *would* anybody choose to enter such a field?

To be sure, most of us didn't chose this work because we thought we'd acquire the lifestyles of the rich and famous—and we knew at the outset that devoting our lives to trying to assuage human misery wouldn't be a walk in the park. The fact of the matter is that the overwhelming majority of psychotherapists, as corny as it sounds, want to be helpful. Many of us, including me, even answered in graduate school applications "I want to help people" as the reason we chose to be therapists (see Figure 1.1). Often, some well-meaning

Figure 1.1. Barry just wanted to help people.

person dissuaded us from that answer because it didn't sound sophisticated or appeared too "co-dependent." Doing the required servitude without the promise of a rags-to-riches future only makes sense because being a psychotherapist is more of a calling than a job—a quest for meaningful activity and personal fulfillment (Orlinsky et al., 2005) and a desire to make a difference in the lives of those we serve.

But when the realities of everyday practice set in, answering the call to the work brings with it an immediate conundrum: We want to build on our original aspirations and get better over the course of our careers, but how do we make sense of the cacophony of "latest" developments, all the fully manualized treatments hot off the press, each promising increased effectiveness with this or that disorder? Call me cynical, but the field doesn't seem to know what professional development means or how we can get better at therapy.

We are often told that developing ourselves as psychotherapists requires that we become more self-aware through personal therapy. This makes a lot of intuitive sense, and gaining an appreciation of what it is like to sit in the client's chair seems invaluable. But a look at probably the best source, *The Psychotherapist's Own Psychotherapy* (Geller, Norcross, & Orlinsky, 2005) reveals that the cold, hard truth is that although therapists rave about its benefits, personal therapy has nothing to do with outcome.

And although the need and value of training seem obvious, it has long been known that professional training and discipline are not related to positive outcomes (Beutler et al., 2004). A more recent study only confirmed this conclusion. Nyman, Nafziger, and Smith (2010) reported that, as strange as it seems, it didn't matter to outcome if the client was seen by a licensed doctoral-level counselor, a predoctoral intern, or a practicum student; all levels of training achieved about the same outcomes. As for continuing professional education, despite its requirement in nearly every state, there is no evidence that therapists learn anything from such experiences or that their participation translates to better outcomes (Neimeyer, Taylor, & Philip, 2009).

What about experience? Surely, years of clinical encounters make a difference. But are we getting better, or are we having the same year of experience over and over? How would we even know whether experience really improved our outcomes? More bad news here: Experience just doesn't seem to matter much (Beutler et al., 2004). Results are mixed at best, with recent studies suggesting no effects on outcome of experience (Hill & Knox, 2013). In large measure, generic experience does not improve outcomes—experienced and inexperienced therapists achieve about the same outcomes. (I revisit the issue of experience later in the chapter.)

Does this mean that we should forget the whole thing? No, not at all. But getting better is not about learning the latest and greatest miracle technique, or a never-before-available way to unravel the mysteries of the human psyche, or the most recent breakthrough in brain neurochemistry. There will be no husky voiceover here declaring a winner of the battle of the psychotherapy brands or adding yet another fashion to the therapy boutique of techniques. Most of you have already been there and done that. Rather, this book is about you—this time it's personal, from one therapist to another. Contrary to my cynical portrayal of the state of the field's efforts to help you get better, this book describes an evidence-based method that will both improve your outcomes and accelerate your development. *On Becoming a Better Therapist* intends to help you answer your calling and remember why you became a therapist in the first place.

This chapter sets the stage. I start with a broad look at the field of psychotherapy and its problems, and then I present an evidence-based solution that provides a seemingly contradictory way to become evidence based across all your clients while tailoring services to the individual client's needs, preferences, and culture—evidence-based practice one client at a time. Two other relevant topics are addressed: First, those aspects of the work that really matter in therapeutic change, the so-called, but not so common, *common factors*, and the apparently never-ending controversy surrounding evidence-based treatments and evidence-based practice.

THE GOOD, THE BAD, AND THE UGLY

To exchange one orthodoxy for another is not necessarily an advance. The enemy is the gramophone mind, whether or not one agrees with the record that is being played at the moment.

—George Orwell

The good news is that the efficacy of psychotherapy is very good—the average treated person is better off than about 80% of the untreated sample (Duncan, Miller, Wampold, & Hubble, 2010; Lambert, 2013), translating to an effect size (ES) of about 0.8.[1] Moreover, these substantial benefits extend from the laboratory to everyday practice. For example, a large (N = 5,613) real-world study in the U.K. (Stiles, Barkham, Mellor-Clark, & Connell, 2008) comparing cognitive behavioral therapy (CBT), psychodynamic therapy (PDT), and person-centered therapy (PCT) as routinely practiced reported a pre–post ES of around 1.30. Moreover, three benchmarking studies have demonstrated that observed results in not only managed care (Minami et al., 2008) and university counseling settings (Minami et al., 2009) are comparable to those in randomized clinical trials (RCTs), but also to those attained in a public behavioral health setting (Reese, Duncan, Bohanske, Owen, & Minami, 2014). In short, there is a lot to feel proud about our profession: We know that psychotherapy works, even in the trenches.

But there's more to the story. The bad news is twofold: First, dropouts are a significant problem in the delivery of mental health and substance abuse services, averaging at least 47% (Wierzbicki & Pekarik, 1993). When dropouts are considered, a hard rain falls on psychotherapy's efficacy parade, both

---

[1]*Effect size* (ES) refers to the magnitude of change attributable to treatment, compared with an untreated group. The ES most associated with psychotherapy is 0.8 standard deviations above the mean of the untreated group. An ES of 1.0 indicates that the mean of the treated group falls at approximately the 84th percentile of the untreated one. Consequently, the average treated person is better off than approximately 80% of those without the benefit of treatment.

in RCTs and in clinical settings. Second, despite the fact that general efficacy is consistently good, not everyone benefits. Hansen, Lambert, and Forman (2002), using a national database of 6,072 clients, reported a sobering picture of routine clinical care in which only 35% of clients improved as compared with the 57% to 67% rates typical of RCTs. Whichever rate is accepted as more representative of actual practice, the fact remains that a substantial portion of clients go home without help.

And the ugly: Explaining part of the volatile results, variability among therapists is the rule rather than the exception. Not surprising, although rarely discussed, some therapists are much better at securing positive results than others. Moreover, even very effective clinicians seem to be poor at identifying deteriorating clients. Hannan et al. (2005) compared therapist predictions of client deterioration to actuarial methods. Though therapists were aware of the study's purpose, familiar with the outcome measure used, and informed that the base rate was likely to be 8%, they did not identify 39 out of the 40 clients who deteriorated. In contrast, the actuarial method correctly predicted 36 of the 40.

So, despite the overall efficacy and effectiveness of psychotherapy, dropouts are a substantial problem, many clients do not benefit, and therapists vary significantly in effectiveness and are poor judges of client deterioration. Perhaps the ugliest of the ugly is that most of us don't know how effective we really are. Do you know how effective you are? With dropouts considered, how many of your clients leave your office absent of benefit? Which clients in your practice now are at risk for dropout or negative outcome?

What is the solution to these problems? Sometimes our altruistic desire to be helpful hoodwinks us into believing that if we are just smart enough or trained correctly, clients would not remain inured to our best efforts. If we found the Holy Grail, that special model or technique, we could once and for all defeat the psychic dragons that terrorize clients. We come by this belief honestly. We hear it all the time, constantly reinforced on nearly all fronts. The warring factions carry on the struggle for alpha dogma status in the psychotherapy pack and claims of "miracle cures better than the rest" continue unabated. The subtext is that if we don't avail ourselves of these approaches we are doing our clients a reprehensible disservice. But these admonitions leave out a vital fact: None of the heralded models have reliably demonstrated superiority to any other systematically applied psychotherapy.

This, of course, is the famous *dodo bird verdict* ("All have won and all must have prizes"), taken from the classic Lewis Carroll (1865/1962) tale, *Alice in Wonderland*, first invoked by Saul Rosenzweig way back in 1936 to illustrate the equivalence of outcome among approaches (see Duncan, 2010b). The dodo verdict is a much-replicated finding encompassing a broad array of research designs, problems, populations, and clinical settings. For example, the study mentioned previously (Stiles et al., 2008), comparing CBT, PDT, and PCT as routinely practiced, once again found no differences among the approaches.

A more controversial illustration is provided by the treatments for the diagnosis du jour, posttraumatic stress disorder (PTSD). CBT has demonstrated its efficacy and is widely believed to be the treatment of choice, but several approaches with diverse rationales and methods have also been shown to be effective: eye-movement desensitization and reprocessing, cognitive therapy without exposure, hypnotherapy, psychodynamic therapy, and present-centered therapy (PRCT). A meta-analysis comparing these treatments found all of them about equally effective (Benish, Imel, & Wampold, 2007). Two of the treatments, cognitive therapy without exposure and PRCT, were designed to exclude any therapeutic actions that might involve exposure (clients were not allowed to discuss their traumas because that invoked imaginal exposure). Despite the presumed extraordinary benefits of exposure for PTSD, the two treatments without it, or in which it was incidental (psychodynamic), were just as effective (Benish et al., 2007).

Unfortunately, the mountain of evidence researchers have amassed has had little impact on the training of mental health or substance abuse clinicians or, sad to say, on professional attitudes. We spend thousands of dollars on workshops, conferences, and books to learn highly publicized methods of treatment. Instead of feeling hopeful or validated and experiencing the oft-promised better outcomes, we often wind up feeling demoralized. Why didn't the powerful sword slay the dragon of misery of the client in my office now? The answer all too often is to blame ourselves—we are just not measuring up. The Holy Grail seems just out of reach.

Don't get me wrong. There is nothing wrong with learning about models and techniques—in fact, it is a good thing, as I'll discuss throughout the book. You definitely want to bring the best to your client that the field has to offer, but becoming beholden to any approach is not a good idea, nor is believing that salvation will come from any of them. They are indeed false gods. Why?

First, given the robust findings supporting the dodo verdict, it is important to keep in mind that the much ballyhooed models have only shown themselves to be better than sham treatments or no treatment at all, or to less than equal opponents, which is not exactly news to write home to mom about. Think about it. What if one of your friends went out on a date with a new person, and when you asked about the guy, your friend replied, "He was better than nothing—he was unequivocally better than watching TV or washing my hair." (Or, if your friend was a researcher: "He was *significantly* better, at a 95% confidence level, than watching TV or washing my hair")? How impressed would you be?

And second, the idea that change primarily emanates from the model or techniques you wield is a siren call destined to smash you against the jagged rocks of ineffective therapy. That therapists might possess the psychological equivalent of a "pill" for emotional distress resonates strongly with many, and is nothing if not seductive, because it teases our desires to be helpful. A treatment for a specific "disorder," from this perspective, is like a silver bullet, potent and transferable from research setting to clinical practice. Any therapist need only to load the silver bullet into any psychotherapy revolver and shoot the psychic werewolf stalking the client. In its most unfortunate interpretation, clients are reduced to a diagnosis and therapists are defined by a treatment technology—both interchangeable and insignificant to the procedure at hand. This product or medical view of psychotherapy is most empirically vacuous because the treatment model itself accounts for so little of outcome variance, whereas the client and the therapist—and their partnership—account for so much more.

Fear is also a potent motivator for the ongoing search for the Holy Grail. Going well beyond subtext, we are told that not administering the "right" treatment is unethical (Chambless & Crits-Christoph, 2006) and even "prosecutable!" A *New York Times* article reported: "Using vague, unstandardized methods to assist troubled clients 'should be prosecutable' in some cases, said Dr. Marsha Linehan . . . " (Carey, 2005, p. 2). Given the lack of demonstrated superiority of dialectical behavior therapy (DBT) or any other approach and the relative contribution of model and technique to change (see below), such rhetoric seems a bit over the top.

Perhaps the most publicized study of DBT (Linehan et al., 2006) compared it with community experts (CE), examining suicidal behavior, emergency room and hospital admissions, and other variables. Results indicated that DBT led to significantly fewer suicide attempts and emergency room and hospital admissions, as well as reduced medical risk, but no differences were found with CE on the rest of the outcome measures: suicidal ideation, the Reasons for Living Inventory, and the Hamilton Rating Scale for Depression. DBT therapists received 45 hours of specialized training as well as weekly supervision and support; the CE therapists received none. Moreover, in addition to the individual treatment component of DBT, the DBT therapists administered 38 group therapy sessions of 2.5 hours' duration largely focused on keeping people out of the hospital, perhaps accounting for the reduced ER and hospital admissions. Although the study reports that the dose of treatment was comparable, an examination of the tables revealed that the 2.5-hour group sessions were counted only as 20 minutes of therapy, a somewhat curious way to record 95 hours of additional treatment. Given the unequal doses of treatment as well as the differential training and attention that the DBT therapists received, it is surprising that DBT didn't outperform CE on all measures.

In truth, we are easily smitten by the lure of flashy techniques and miracle cures. Amid explanations and remedies aplenty, therapists courageously continue the search for designer explanations and brand-name miracles—disconnected from the power for change that resides in the pairing of two unique persons, the application of strategies that resonate with both, and the impact of a quality partnership. Despite our herculean efforts to master the right approach, we continue to observe that clients drop out or, even worse, continue without benefit.

TO THE RESCUE: CLIENT FEEDBACK

> Great doubt: great awakening. Little doubt: little awakening. No doubt: no awakening.
>
> —Zen mantra

Dan Ariely (2008) tells a horrendous story of an explosion that left him with 70% of his body covered with third-degree burns. His treatment included a much-dreaded daily removal of his bandages. In the absence of skin, the bandages were attached to raw flesh and their removal was both harrowing to witness and excruciatingly painful. The nurses removed the bandages as fast as possible, quickly ripping them off one by one. Believing that a slower pace would be less painful, Ariely repeatedly asked the nurses to slow down the removal process. The nurses, however, asserted that finishing fast was the best approach, and continued to do so. This ordeal inspired Ariely to research the experience of pain as well as other phenomena. His investigation of pain demonstrated that a slow and less intense experience of pain over longer periods was far easier to tolerate than more intense pain over shorter time frames.

Consider this story and its relevance to psychotherapy. It is noteworthy that the nurses disregarded Ariely's response to their removal methods—his experience of his own pain did not hold much weight for them! But the nurses ignored his response as well as his pleadings to slow down not because they were evil or had any malevolent intentions—in fact, Ariely reports that he grew to love the nurses and believed that they loved him as well. Rather, the nurses assumed they knew more about his pain than he did and went full steam ahead for his own good! He also later learned that the nurses considered it easier *for them* to remove the dressings quickly. Clinical lore about the rapid removal of bandages, as well as what was convenient for the nurses, prevailed over Ariely's experience of his own pain.

When services are provided without intimate connection to those receiving them and to their responses and preferences, clients become cardboard cutouts, the object of our professional deliberations and subject to our whims. Valuing clients as credible sources of their own experiences allows us to critically examine our assumptions and practices—to support what is working and challenge what is not—and allows clients to teach us how we can be the most effective with them.

A relatively new research paradigm called *patient-focused research* (Howard, Moras, Brill, Martinovich, & Lutz, 1996) rescues us from the problems noted above (the bad and ugly) as well as Ariely's unfortunate circumstance. Howard et al. (1996) advocated for the systematic evaluation of client response to treatment during the course of therapy and recommended that such information be used to "determine the appropriateness of the current treatment . . . [and] the need for further treatment . . . [and] prompt a clinical consultation for patients who [were] not progressing at expected rates" (Howard et al., 1996, p. 1063).

Although several systems have emerged that answer Howard's original call (for a review, see Castonguay, Barkham, Lutz, & McAleavey, 2013; Lambert, 2010), only two have demonstrated treatment gains in RCTs and gained evidence-based-practice designation. The pioneering work of Michael Lambert and colleagues stands out—not only for the development of measurement systems and predictive algorithms but also for their groundbreaking investigations of the effects of providing therapists feedback about client progress in treatment.

In a meta-analytic review of the Outcome Questionnaire 45.2 (OQ) system, Shimokawa, Lambert, and Smart (2010) reanalyzed the combined data set ($N = 6,151$) from all six of the OQ feedback studies that compared the OQ system with treatment as usual (TAU; Harmon et al., 2007; Hawkins, Lambert, Vermeersch, Slade, & Tuttle, 2004; Lambert et al., 2001, 2002; Slade, Lambert, Harmon, Smart, & Bailey, 2008; Whipple, Lambert, Vermeersch, Smart, Nielsen, & Hawkins, 2003). When the odds of deterioration and clinically significant improvement were compared, those in the feedback (OQ) group had less than half the odds of experiencing deterioration while having 2.6 times higher odds of attaining reliable improvement than the TAU group.

The other RCT-supported method of using continuous client feedback to improve outcomes is the one presented in this book, the Partners for Change Outcome Management System (PCOMS; Duncan, 2010a, 2012; Duncan, Miller, & Sparks, 2004; Duncan & Sparks, 2002). Much of this system's appeal rests on the brevity of the measures and therefore its feasibility for everyday use in the demanding schedules of frontline clinicians. The Outcome Rating Scale (ORS) and the Session Rating Scale (SRS) are both four-item measures that track outcome and the therapeutic alliance, respectively. PCOMS was based on Lambert and colleagues' (1996) continuous assessment model using the OQ, but there are differences beyond the measures. First, PCOMS is integrated into the ongoing psychotherapy process and includes a transparent discussion of the feedback with the client (Duncan & Sparks, 2002). Session-by-session interaction is focused by client feedback about the benefits or lack thereof of psychotherapy. Second, PCOMS assesses the therapeutic alliance every session and includes a discussion of any potential problems. Lambert's system includes alliance assessment only when there is a lack of progress.

Moreover, unlike most other outcome instruments, the ORS is not a list of symptoms or problems checked by clients or others on a Likert scale. Rather it is an instrument that evolves from a general framework of client distress to a specific representation of the client's idiosyncratic experience and reasons for service; the ORS is individualized for each client. It therefore requires collaboration with clients as well as clinical skill and nuance in its application; the therapist is intimately involved and inextricably linked to its success.

Six studies have demonstrated the benefits of client feedback with PCOMS. The first (Miller, Duncan, Brown, Sorrell, & Chalk, 2006) explored the impact of feedback in a large ($N = 6,424$) culturally diverse sample utilizing a telephonic employee assistant program (EAP). Although the study's quasi-experimental design qualifies the results, the use of feedback doubled overall effectiveness and significantly increased retention. Several RCTs conducted by those affiliated with my organization, the Heart and Soul of Change Project (hereafter the Project), used PCOMS to investigate the effects of feedback versus TAU. Norwegian therapist and researcher Morten Anker and other colleagues from the Project (Anker, Duncan, & Sparks, 2009) randomized couples seeking couple therapy ($N = 410$) at an outpatient clinic in Norway to PCOMS or TAU; therapists saw both PCOMS and TAU clients to control for therapist effects. This study, the largest RCT of couple therapy ever done, found that nearly 4 times more feedback couples than non-feedback couples reached clinically significant change, and over doubled the percentage of couples in which both individuals reached reliable and/or clinically significant change (50.5% vs. 22.6%). At 6-month follow-up, 47.6% of couples in the feedback condition reported reliable and/or significant change versus 18.8% in TAU. The feedback condition not only maintained its advantage at 6-month follow-up but also achieved a 46% lower separation/divorce rate. Feedback improved the outcomes of 9 of 10 therapists in this study. It is noteworthy that the therapists in this study were naïve to feedback; they had not used PCOMS in their work prior to the study and therefore were not "true believers."

University of Kentucky professor and Project Leader Jeff Reese and colleagues (Reese, Norsworthy, & Rowland, 2009) found significant treatment gains for feedback when compared with TAU. This study was two small trials in one. Study 1 occurred at a university counseling center ($n = 74$) and Study 2 at a graduate training clinic ($n = 74$). Clients in the PCOMS condition in both studies showed significantly more reliable change versus TAU clients (80% vs. 54% in Study 1, 67% vs. 41% in Study 2). In addition, clients using PCOMS achieved reliable change in significantly fewer sessions than TAU. Reese, Toland, Slone, and Norsworthy (2010) replicated the Anker et al. (2009) study with couples and found nearly the same results. Finally, a meta-analysis of PCOMS studies (Lambert & Shimokawa, 2011) found that those in the feedback group had 3.5 higher odds of experiencing reliable change and less than half the odds of experiencing deterioration.

The applicability of PCOMS to other modalities and populations was recently demonstrated. Schuman, Slone, Reese, and Duncan (in press) conducted an RCT ($N = 263$) of group treatment of returning Iraq and Afghanistan veterans and active duty soldiers struggling with alcohol and drug problems that compared a minimal PCOMS intervention (only using the ORS) to TAU. Soldiers in the feedback condition achieved significantly more improvement on the ORS, higher rates of clinically significant change, and higher ratings of success by both clinicians and commanders, and they attended significantly more sessions compared to the TAU condition. Similarly, a recent RCT ($N = 85$) by Slone, Reese, Mathews-Duvall, and Kodet (2014) of group psychotherapy found that clients in the PCOMS condition achieved significantly higher gain on the ORS compared with TAU. Additionally, significantly more clients in the feedback condition experienced reliable (feedback: 31.8%; TAU: 17.0%) and clinically significant (feedback: 40.9%; TAU: 29.3%) change, attended significantly more sessions (feedback: 8.5 sessions; TAU: 6.0 sessions), and dropped out at a lower rate (feedback: 34%; TAU: 56%) than clients in the TAU condition.

Regarding children, using a cohort design comparing outcomes in the schools with 7-to-11-year-olds in Northern Ireland, University of Rhode Island professor and Project Leader Jacqueline Sparks and University of Strathclyde professor Mick Cooper and his team from the U.K. (Cooper, Stewart, Sparks, & Bunting, 2013) found that school-based counseling incorporating systematic feedback via PCOMS was associated with large reductions in psychological distress for children ($N = 288$). In addition, comparing caretaker and teacher ratings on the U.K. standardized measure, the Strength and Difficulties Questionnaire (SDQ) revealed an approximate twofold advantage in ES on the caretaker-completed SDQ when PCOMS was used and a small but significant advantage in effect on the teacher-completed SDQ.

These studies collectively support the effectiveness of PCOMS across various treatment sites, client populations, and therapeutic models, and they make a strong case for routine outcome management. Because of the

RCTs conducted by me and my colleagues from the Project, PCOMS is designated as an evidence-based practice by the Substance Abuse Mental Health Services Administration and listed in the National Registry of Evidence-based Programs and Practices. PCOMS, however, is not your average evidence-based practice: It is not a specific treatment model for a specific client diagnosis. First, it is a-theoretical and may be added to or integrated with any model of practice. PCOMS does not suggest how to understand client problems nor does it prescribe a treatment for them. Rather, it provides a vehicle to partner with clients around their views of benefit and the alliance, and the ability to identify when whatever chosen model is not helping. Second, PCOMS applies to all diagnostic categories. So, in effect, one size does fit all, allowing you to be evidence based across your clients in contrast to the ridiculous notion that you can learn an evidence-based approach for each of the seemingly ever-growing list of diagnoses. Finally, PCOMS is "evidence based" at two levels. It is evidence based by virtue of the RCTs that found significant benefits for both clients and therapists when feedback was part of the work, regardless of the theoretical orientations of the therapists or the diagnoses of the clients. More important, PCOMS is evidence based at the individual client–therapist level. Not just relying on the *past* evidence of efficacy in RCTs (e.g., Anker et al., 2009), or even past evidence of effectiveness in real clinical settings (e.g., Reese et al., 2014), PCOMS focuses you on the *present* evidence of effectiveness with the client in your office right now. In other words, it is *evidence-based practice one client at a time*.

PCOMS has the potential to significantly improve your outcomes, but it's not a miracle cure, nor does it explain human behavior. It also doesn't make you any smarter or better-looking or serve as a panacea for the complexity and difficulty of the psychotherapy process. It does, however, identify your clients who aren't responding to your therapeutic business as usual so that you can address the lack of progress in a positive, proactive way that keeps clients engaged while you collaboratively seek new directions. Think about this for a minute. Even if you are one of the la crème de la crème now (my looks at many data sets reveal that the best therapists are effective about two-thirds of the time), for every cycle of 10 clients you see, three will go home without benefit. Over the course of a year, this amounts to a lot of unhappy clients. You can recover a substantial portion of those folks who don't benefit by first identifying who they are, keeping them engaged, and tailoring your services accordingly.

That's it in a nutshell. PCOMS is your ticket to both better outcomes and to taking charge of your development. Knowing how effective you really are sets the stage for you to proactively get better at this work. Unfortunately, up to now, therapeutic outcomes have been hard to define and even harder to actually measure in everyday practice, leaving us to our own devices and judgment—which aren't so good. Consider a study (Dew & Riemer, 2003) that asked 143 clinicians to rate their job performance from A+ to F. Two thirds considered themselves A or better; not one therapist rated him- or herself as below average. More recently, Walfish, McAlister, O'Donnell, and Lambert (2012) surveyed practitioners and found that therapists likely inflate their effectiveness, reporting that 85% of their clients improve and seeing themselves as above average in effectiveness (90% saw themselves as above the 75th percentile). If you know anything about the Bell curve, you know this can't be true. We are not all above average—we are not from Lake Woebegon!

But of course it is not that we're naïve or stupid; it's simply hard, if not impossible, to accurately assess your effectiveness without some quantitative standard as a reference point; you need to measure outcomes. And the field has not been very useful to us in this regard. Until recently, measures of outcomes were only for researchers and totally impractical for everyday clinical use. But that has changed with PCOMS. Measuring outcomes allows you to cut through the ambiguity of therapy, using objective evidence from your practice to help you discern your clinical development without falling prey to that perennial bugaboo of the therapeutic endeavor: wishful thinking.

As this book details, measuring outcomes relates directly to both having an awareness about our development and doing something about it. PCOMS can help you survive—indeed thrive—in a profession that is under siege, yet still compelling; a profession that offers a lifetime training ground for human connection and growth, and frequently yields small victories that matter in the lives of those we see.

WHAT WORKS IN THERAPY: GUIDELINES FROM RESEARCH

Whoever acquires knowledge and does not practice it resembles him [sic] who ploughs his land and leaves it unsown.

—Sa'di, *Gulistan*

A story illustrates the sentiments that many practitioners feel about research. Two researchers were attending their annual conference. Although enjoying the proceedings, they decided to find some diversion to combat the tedium of sitting all day and absorbing vast amounts of information. They settled on a hot-air balloon ride and were quite enjoying themselves until a mysterious fog rolled in. Hopelessly lost, they drifted for hours until, finally, a clearing in the fog appeared and they saw a man standing in an open field. Joyfully, they yelled down at the man, "Where are we?" The man looked at them, and then down at the ground, before turning a full 360 degrees to survey his surroundings. Finally, after scratching his beard and what seemed to be several moments of facial contortions reflecting deep concentration, the man looked up and said, "You are above my farm."

The first researcher looked at the second researcher and said, "That man is a researcher—he is a scientist!" To which the second researcher replied, "Are you crazy, man? He is a simple farmer!" "No," answered the first researcher emphatically, "that man is a researcher and there are three facts that support my assertion: First, what he said was absolutely 100% accurate; second, he systematically addressed our question through an examination of all of the empirical evidence at his disposal, and then carefully deliberated before delivering his conclusion; and finally, the third reason I know he is a researcher is that what he told us is absolutely useless to our predicament."

In this book, I strive to present only research that is useful to conducting psychotherapy, and the common factors, I believe, represent the best of what empirical investigation has to offer "our predicament."

The common factors—what works in therapy—have a storied history that started with Rosenzweig's (1936) classic article "Implicit Common Factors in Diverse Forms of Psychotherapy." In addition to the original invocation of the dodo bird and seminal explication of the common factors of change, Rosenzweig also provided the best explanation for the common factors, still used today: namely, that given that all approaches achieve roughly similar results, there must be pantheoretical factors accounting for the observed changes beyond the presumed differences among schools (Duncan, 2010b). Rosenzweig's four-page article is still well worth the read (and available at https://heartandsoulofchange.com).

If Rosenzweig penned the first notes of a common factors chorus, Jerome Frank (1961, 1973; Frank & Frank, 1991) composed an entire symphony. He advanced the idea that psychotherapy orientations (and other forms of healing) are equivalent in their effectiveness because of factors shared by all: (a) a healing setting; (b) a rationale, myth, or conceptual framework that provides an explanation for the client's complaint and a method for resolving it; (c) an emotionally charged, confiding relationship with a helping person; and (d) a ritual or procedure that requires involvement of both the healer and client to bring about "cure" or resolution. Frank's work is particularly helpful, as noted below, in understanding the role of model and technique as the vehicle for providing the other factors.

Several others have identified these elements found in all therapies, but Brigham Young University's Michael Lambert deserves special mention. After an extensive analysis of decades of outcome research, Lambert (1986, 2013) identified four factors—and their estimated percentages of outcome variance—as the principal elements accounting for improvement: client/life variables (40%); relationship factors (30%); hope, expectancy, and placebo (15%); and model/technique (15%). Although these factors are not derived from a statistical analysis, he suggested that they embody what studies indicated about treatment outcome. Lambert's portrayal of the common factors bravely differentiated factors according to their relative contribution to outcome, opening a new vista of understanding models and their proportional importance to success—a bold challenge to the reverence many researchers and therapists feel toward their preferred models.

Inspired by Lambert's proposal and the integration movement, my colleagues and I (Duncan & Moynihan, 1994; Duncan, Solovey, & Rusk, 1992) proposed a "client directed" perspective to apply the common factors based on their differential impact on outcome. *Client directed* spoke to the influence of clients on outcome: their resources, strengths, and resiliencies, their view of the alliance, their ideas and theories of how they can be helped, and their hopes and expectations. The common factors, in other words, make the case that clients should direct the therapeutic process: Their views should be the privileged ones in the room. Intervention success was described as dependent on rallying client resources and as a tangible expression of the quality of the alliance. I have been attempting to operationalize the factors ever since (e.g., Duncan, 2010a, in press; Duncan et al., 2010; Sparks & Duncan, 2010). The common factors help us take a step back and get a big-picture view of what really works, suggesting that we spend our time in therapy commensurate to each element's differential impact on outcome.

Recent findings from meta-analytic studies (see below) point to the biggest omission of Lambert's portrayal of the common factors, namely, the profound impact of the therapist, and they paint a more complicated but satisfying representation of the different factors, their effects, and their relationship to each other. The "pie chart" view of the common factors incorrectly implies that the proportion of outcome attributable to each was static and could be added up to 100% of therapy effects. This suggested that the factors were discrete elements and could be distilled into a treatment model and that techniques could be created and then administered to the client. Any such formulaic application across clients, however, merely leads to the creation of another model. On this point, the jury has deliberated and the verdict has been rendered; model differences ultimately matter little in terms of outcome. In truth, the factors are interdependent, fluid, dynamic, and dependent on who the players are and what their interactions are like. Five factors comprise this meta-analytic perspective: client, therapist, alliance, model/technique (general and specific effects), and feedback.

Client/Life Factors

To understand the common factors, it is first necessary to separate the variance due to psychotherapy from that attributed to client/life factors, those variables incidental to the treatment model, idiosyncratic to the specific client, and part of the client's life circumstances that aid in recovery despite participation in therapy (Asay & Lambert, 1999)—everything about the client that has nothing to do with us. Calculated from the often-reported 0.80 ES of therapy, the proportion of outcome attributable to treatment (14%) is depicted by the small circle nested within the larger circle at the lower right side of the left circle in Figure 1.2. The remaining variance accounted for by client factors (86%), including unexplained and error variance is represented by the large circle on the left. Even a casual inspection reveals the disproportionate influence of what the client brings to therapy. More conservative estimates put the client's contribution at 40% (Lambert, 2013). As examples, persistence, faith, a supportive grandmother, depression, membership in a religious community, divorce, a new job, a chance encounter with a stranger, a crisis successfully managed all may be included. Although they are hard to research because of their idiosyncratic nature, these elements are the most powerful of the common factors—the client is the engine of change (Bohart & Tallman, 2010).

In the absence of compelling evidence for any specific variables that cut across clients to predict outcome or account for the unexplained variance, this most potent source remains largely uncharted. Client factors cannot be generalized because they differ with each client. These unpredictable differences can only emerge one client at a time, one alliance at a time, one therapist at a time, and one treatment at a time.

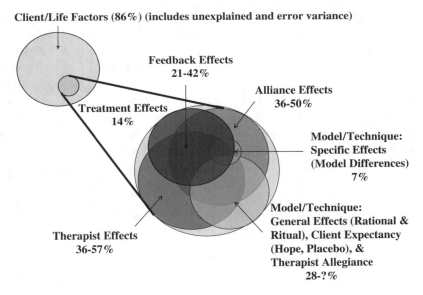

Figure 1.2. The Common Factors.

But we do know one thing for sure: If we don't recruit these idiosyncratic contributions to outcome in service of client goals, we are inclined to fail. Indeed, in a comprehensive review of 50 years of literature for the 5th edition of the *Handbook of Psychotherapy and Behavior Change*, Orlinsky, Rønnestad, and Willutzki (2004) observed that "the quality of the patient's participation . . . [emerges] as the *most* important determinant of outcome" (p. 324; emphasis added).

> **Bottom Line:** *Becoming a better therapist depends on rallying clients and their resources to the cause. PCOMS sets the context for client participation in the monitoring of therapy outcome and the alliance.*

Figure 1.2 also illustrates the second step in understanding the common factors. The second, larger circle in the center depicts the overlapping elements that form the 14% of variance attributable to treatment. Visually, the relationship among the common factors, as opposed to a static pie-chart depicting discreet elements adding to a total of 100%, is more accurately represented with a Venn diagram, using overlapping circles and shading to demonstrate mutual and interdependent action. The factors, in effect, act in concert and cannot be separated into disembodied parts (Duncan et al., 1992).

To exemplify the various factors and their attending portions of the variance, the tried-and-true Treatment of Depression Collaborative Research Program (TDCRP; Elkin et al., 1989) will be enlisted. The TDCRP randomly assigned 250 depressed participants to four different conditions: CBT, interpersonal therapy (IPT), antidepressants plus clinical management (IMI), and a pill placebo plus clinical management. The four conditions—including placebo—achieved about the same results, although both IPT and IMI surpassed placebo (but not the other treatments) on the recovery criterion (yet another example of the dodo verdict). Although the TDCRP is now over 20 years old, the data continue to be analyzed and remain relevant.

Therapist Effects

Therapist effects represent the amount of variance attributable not to the model wielded but rather to *who* the therapist is—it's no surprise that the participants in the therapeutic endeavor account for the lion's share of how change occurs. Depending on whether therapist variability is investigated in efficacy or effectiveness studies, a recent meta-analysis suggested that 5% to 7% of the overall variance is accounted for by therapist effects (Baldwin & Imel, 2013). This is a conservative finding, compared with earlier estimates that suggested that at least 8% of the variance is accounted for by therapist factors, including the TDCRP (Kim, Wampold, & Bolt, 2006) and a recent investigation by my Project colleagues and me (Owen, Duncan, Reese, Anker, & Sparks, in press). Therefore, in Figure 1.2, a 5% to 8% range is depicted or 36% to 57% of the variance (the 14%) attributed to treatment.[2] The amount of variance, therefore, accounted for by therapist factors is about 5 to 8 times more than that of model differences. In many respects, you *are* the treatment. This is why attention to your development is important.

The psychiatrists in the TDCRP illustrate—the clients receiving sugar pills from the top third most effective psychiatrists did better than the clients taking antidepressants from the bottom third, least effective psychiatrists (Kim et al., 2006). *Who* was providing the medication or sugar pill was far more important than *what* the pill contained. Although we know that some therapists are better than others, there is not a lot of research about what specifically distinguishes the best from the rest. Demographics (gender, ethnicity, discipline, and experience) don't seem to matter much (Beutler et al., 2004), and although a variety of therapist interpersonal variables seem intuitively important, there is not much empirical support for any particular quality or attribute (Baldwin & Imel, 2013). So what does matter? There are two preliminary possibilities and one absolute certainty.

One possibility—and building on the Orlinsky et al. (2004) quote above—is what Gassmann and Grawe (2006) called *resource activation v. problem activation*. They conducted minute-by-minute analyses of 120 sessions involving 30 clients treated for a range of psychological problems. They found that unsuccessful therapists focused more on problems while neglecting client strengths. Successful therapists attended more to identifying client resources and channeling them toward achieving client goals.

Another possibility is experience, but not the generic kind that we are often told that will make us better. A criticism often leveled at research investigating therapist experience is that it is not operationally defined and that a more sophisticated look may yield more positive findings (Beutler et al., 2004). For example, Kraus, Castonguay, Boswell, Nordberg, and Hayes (2011) found that therapist competencies can be domain specific, as some therapists were better at treating certain "conditions." Specificity, therefore, in the definition of experience may be important. My colleagues and I put this to the test in our examination of therapist effects in the study mentioned above (Owen et al., in press). Similar to other studies, demographics were not significant, but specific experience in couple therapy explained 25% of the variance accounted for by therapists. So, experienced therapists

---

[2]The percentages are best viewed as a defensible way to understand outcome variance but not as representing any ultimate truths. They are meta-analytic estimates of what each of the factors contributes to change. Because of the overlap among the common factors, the percentages for the separate factors will not add to 100%.

can take some solace that getting older does have its advantages—as long as it is specific to the task at hand.

And the absolute certainty: The client's view of the alliance is not only a robust predictor of therapy outcomes, but also is the best avenue to understand therapist differences. Marcus et al. (2009) noted:

> High levels of consensus in client ratings of their therapist indicate that clients of the same therapist tend to agree about the traits or characteristics of their therapist, suggesting that there is something about the therapist's manner or behavior that evokes similar response from all of his or her clients. (p. 538)

Baldwin, Wampold, and Imel (2007) found only modest therapist variability (2%) compared with other studies but reported that therapist average alliance quality accounted for 97% of that variability. Our study of therapist differences found that therapist average alliance quality accounted for 50% of the variability in outcomes attributed to therapists (Owen et al., in press). In general, research indicates that clients seen by therapists with higher average alliance ratings have better outcomes (Crits-Christoph et al., 2009; Zuroff, Kelly, Leybman, Blatt, & Wampold, 2010). There is really no mystery here. The answer to the oft-heard question about why some therapists are better than others is that tried-and-true but taken-for-granted old friend, the therapeutic alliance.

> **Bottom Line:** *Therapist differences loom large and may be related to the ability to mobilize client resources and participation and gain specific experience. More importantly, therapist variability is related to the ability to form strong alliances across clients. PCOMS by design engages clients in a partnership that increases participation and resource activation, while not leaving the alliance to chance.*

The Alliance

Researchers repeatedly find that a *positive alliance*—an interpersonal partnership between the client and therapist to achieve the client's goals (Bordin, 1979)—is one of the best predictors of outcome. Historically, the amount of variance attributed to the alliance has ranged from 5% to 7% of overall variance or from 36% to 50% of the variance accounted for by treatment (e.g., Horvath, & Bedi, 2002). More recently, Horvath, Del Re, Flückiger, and Symonds (2011) examined 201 studies and found the alliance to account for a slightly higher 7.5% of the variance. Putting this into perspective, the amount of change attributable to the alliance is about five to seven times that of specific model or technique. In addition, a recent meta-analytic longitudinal study examining the alliance outcome relationship found that it remained largely intact regardless of the type of investigation or analyses used (Flückiger, Del Re, Wampold, Symonds, & Horvath, 2012).

Krupnick et al. (1996) analyzed data from the TDCRP and found that the alliance, from the client's perspective, was predictive of success for all conditions; the treatment model was not. Mean alliance scores explained 21% of the overall variance (Wampold, 2001). Keep in mind that treatment accounts for, on average, 14% of the variance (see Figure 1.2). The alliance in the TDCRP, therefore, explained more of the variance than typically attributed to treatment, illustrating how the percentages are not fixed and depend on the particular context of client, therapist, alliance, and treatment model.

Some have suggested that the relationship between alliance and outcome could be a consequence of how much clients are benefiting from therapy (e.g., Barber, 2009). However, several recent studies have confirmed that there appears to be little evidence that controlling for prior change substantially reduces the alliance–outcome correlation (Crits-Cristoph, Connolly Gibbons, & Mukherjee, 2013; Horvath et al., 2011). Similarly, my colleagues and I (Anker, Owen, Duncan, & Sparks, 2010) found that the alliance at the third session significantly predicted outcome over and above early reliable change. The fact that the alliance is predictive beyond early benefit suggests a more causal relationship.

> **Bottom Line:** *The alliance makes significant contributions to psychotherapy outcome and therefore should be actively monitored and tailored to the individual client.*

Model/Technique: Specific and General Effects (Explanation and Ritual), Client Expectancy (Hope, Placebo), and Therapist Allegiance

Model/technique factors are the beliefs and procedures unique to any given treatment. But these specific effects—the impact of the differences among treatments—are very small, only about 1% of the overall variance (Wampold, 2001), or 7% of that attributable to treatment. But the *general effects* of providing a treatment (an explanation of the problem and solution for it) that harness both client expectancy and therapist allegiance are far more potent. Models achieve their effects, in large part, if not completely, through the activation of placebo, hope, and expectancy, combined with the therapist's belief in (allegiance to) the treatment administered.

When a placebo or technically "inert" condition is offered in a manner that fosters positive expectations for improvement, it reliably produces effects almost as large as a bona fide treatment (Baskin, Tierney, Minami, & Wampold, 2003). (There is some controversy surrounding how potent this effect is, hence the question mark in Figure 1.2.) As long as a <u>treatment makes sense to, is</u>

accepted by, and enhances the active engagement of the client, the particular approach used is unimportant. Said another way, therapeutic techniques are placebo-delivery devices (Kirsch, 2005). Placebo factors are also fueled by a therapist belief that change occurs naturally and almost universally—the human organism, shaped by millennia of evolution and survival, tends to heal and to find a way, even out of the heart of darkness (Sparks & Duncan, 2010).

Allegiance and expectancy are two sides of the same coin—the belief by both the therapist and the client in the restorative power and credibility of the therapy's rationale and related rituals. The TDCRP is again instructive. First, across all conditions, client expectation of improvement predicted outcome (Sotsky et al., 1991). And second, an inspection of the Beck Depression Inventory scores of those who completed the study (see Elkin et al., 1989) reveals that the placebo plus clinical management condition accounted for nearly 93% of the average response to the active treatments (Duncan, 2010a).

To punctuate the point about the more powerful general effects, consider present centered therapy mentioned earlier as a treatment that works for PTSD (see Wampold, 2007, for a full description). Researchers testing the efficacy of CBT for PTSD wanted a comparison group that contained curative factors shared by all treatments (warm, empathic relationship) while excluding those believed unique to CBT (exposure). This control treatment, PRCT, contained no treatment rationale and no therapeutic actions. Moreover, to rule out any possibility of exposure, even covert in nature, clients were not allowed to talk about the traumatic events that had precipitated therapy. PRCT was, of course, found to be less effective than CBT—it was really a sham treatment without "active" ingredients. However, when later a manual containing a rationale and condition-specific treatment actions was added to facilitate standardization in training and delivery, few differences in efficacy were found between PRCT and CBT in the treatment of PTSD (McDonagh et al., 2005). In fact, significantly fewer clients dropped out of PRCT than CBT. Thus, when PRCT was made to resemble a bona fide treatment, that is, it added placebo, expectancy, and allegiance variables, it was not only as effective but also more acceptable than CBT.

The act of providing treatment is the vehicle that carries allegiance and placebo effects in addition to the specific effects of the given approach. It pays, therefore, to have several rationales and remedies at your disposal that you believe in, as well as believing in the client's ideas about change. Keep in mind that the selection of the tasks of therapy, that is, model and technique, is also a critical component of the alliance, hence the overlap between model and alliance depicted in Figure 1.2. Finally, it is important to note that, in suggesting that specific effects are small in comparison with general effects and that psychotherapy approaches achieve about the same results, I do not mean that models and techniques are not important. On the contrary, while there is no differential efficacy on aggregate, there are approaches that are likely better or worse for the client in your office now and ones that better fit or match the client's view of what could be helpful. Once again, the TDCRP is helpful. Clients' perceptions of treatment match with their beliefs about the origin of their depression and what would be helpful (psychotherapy or medication) contributed to early engagement, continuation in therapy, and the development of a positive alliance (Elkin et al., 1999).

> **Bottom Line:** *The specifics of any approach are not as important as the cogency of the rationale and ritual to both the client and the therapist, and, most important, as the client's response to the delivered treatment.*

Feedback Effects

At first blush, feedback may seem like an odd addition to the list of factors that cut across all approaches. The process of attaining formal client feedback and using that input to tailor services, however, seems a worthy addition for several reasons. First, the effects of feedback seem largely independent of the measures used. Second, systematic feedback improves outcome regardless of the specific process used, whether in collaboration with clients (although collaboration tends to yield better results) or merely giving the feedback to therapists—over the phone or face-to-face, paper-and-pencil administrations versus electronic formats, matters not. Third, feedback increases client benefit across professional discipline, clinical setting, client population, as well as beginning or experienced therapists. Fourth, feedback significantly improves outcome regardless of the model practiced—the feedback process does not dictate what technique is used but, rather, is a vehicle to modify any delivered treatment for client benefit. Fifth, attaining informal client feedback about progress and the alliance is common practice among psychotherapists. Any approach that openly discusses the outcome of services or checks in about the relationship is incorporating informal client feedback into the therapeutic mix. Feedback speaks to an interpersonal process of give-and-take between the clinician and client and, at least to some extent, can be argued to be characteristic of many therapeutic encounters. Finally, the evidence regarding feedback continues to build. Feedback, then, similar to the concept of the alliance (see Gaston, 1990), was initially viewed as an important aspect of conducting effective psychotherapy and is garnering a growing evidence base that supports a more formal understanding and systematic inclusion.

Common-factors research provides general guidance for enhancing those elements shown to be most influential to positive outcomes. The specifics, however, can only be derived from the client's response to what we deliver—the client's feedback regarding progress in therapy and the quality of the alliance. An inspection of Figure 1.2 shows that feedback overlaps and affects all the factors; it is the tie that binds them together, allowing the other common factors to be delivered one client at a time. Soliciting systematic feedback is a living, ongoing process that engages clients in the collaborative monitoring of outcome, heightens hope for improvement, fits client preferences, maximizes alliance quality and client participation, and is itself a core feature of therapeutic change. Feedback embodies the lessons I learned from Tina, providing for a transparent interpersonal process that solicits the client's help in ensuring a positive outcome.

> **Bottom Line:** *Given its broad applicability, lack of theoretical baggage, and independence from any specific instrument, feedback can be understood as a factor that demonstrably contributes to outcome regardless of the model predilection of the clinician.*

EVIDENCE-BASED TREATMENTS AND EVIDENCE-BASED PRACTICE

Seek facts and classify them and you will be the workmen of science. Conceive or accept theories and you will be their politicians.
—Nicholas Maurice Arthus, *De l'Anaphylaxie à l'immunité*

All approaches have valid explanations and solutions for the problems that clients bring us. It only makes good clinical sense to expand our model/ technique horizons and learn multiple ways to serve client goals. Similarly, it also makes good clinical sense to be evidence based in our work. In truth, no one says, "Evidence, schmevidence! It means nothing to my work—I fly by the seat of my pants, meander willy-nilly through sessions, and rely totally on the wisdom of the stars to show the way." Saying you don't believe in the almighty evidence is tantamount to not believing in Mom or apple pie, or whatever your sacrosanct cultural icons happen to be. So what is the controversy about?

On the heels of the American Psychiatric Association's development of practice guidelines in 1993, to ensure their continued viability in the market, psychologists rushed to offer magic bullets to counter psychiatry's magic pills—to establish empirically supported treatments or what is now more typically called *evidence-based treatments* (EBTs). With all good intentions, a task force of Division 12 (Society of Clinical Psychology; Task Force on Promotion and Dissemination of Psychological Procedures, 1995) reviewed the available research and cataloged treatments of choice for specific diagnoses based on their demonstrated efficacy in RCTs. On the one hand, the Division 12 task force effectively increased recognition of the efficacy of psychological intervention among the public, policy makers, and training programs; on the other hand, it simultaneously promulgated gross misinterpretations—such as the idea that EBTs have proven their superiority over other approaches and, therefore, should be mandated and/or exclusively reimbursed. Unfortunately many people, including many state government funders, to paraphrase Orwell, now believe that some therapies are more equal than others.

The notion, however, that any approach is reliably better than another and should be exclusively practiced or funded is indefensible in light of the evidence that supports the dodo verdict, as well as the relative influence of factors other than model and technique. Efficacy over placebo, sham, or no treatment does not mean efficacy over other approaches. In the minority of studies that claim superiority over TAU or another approach, you need only to ask one question of the investigation (see Duncan & Reese, 2012, for a full discussion): Is it a fair contest? Is the study a comparison of two valid approaches that are intended to be therapeutic, administered in equal amounts by therapists who equally believe in what they are doing and are equally supported to do it? Recall the DBT example: Are the therapists from the same pool with equal caseloads or is the experimental group special—selected, trained, and supervised by the researcher/founder of the approach and with reduced caseloads? I have never seen a purported advantage of any approach over another (or TAU) that wasn't a lopsided contest that had its winner predetermined.

In the face of growing criticism, 2005 American Psychological Association (APA) President Ronald Levant appointed the APA Presidential Task Force on Evidence-Based Practice (hereafter Task Force). The Task Force defined *evidenced-based practice* (EBP) as: "the integration of the best available research with clinical expertise in the context of patient [sic] characteristics, culture, and preferences" (APA Task Force, 2006, p. 273). This definition transcends the "demonstrated efficacy in two RCTs" mentality of EBTs and makes common clinical sense.

In fact, the Task Force's EBP definition emphasizes the major themes of this book: The first part, "the integration of the best available research," includes the consideration of EBTs without privileging them, as well as the wide range of findings regarding the alliance and other common factors. Next, "with clinical expertise," in contrast to the EBT mentality of the therapist as an interchangeable part, brings you back into the equation—your interpersonal skill plus everything about you attained through education, training, and experience—highlighting what therapists bring is consistent with the growing research about the importance of clinician variability to outcome. This part of the EBP definition supports attention to your development. Moreover, the Task Force submitted:

> Clinical expertise also entails the monitoring of patient progress (and of changes in the patient's circumstances—e.g., job loss, major illness) that may suggest the need to adjust the treatment (Lambert, Bergin, &

Garfield, 2004). If progress is not proceeding adequately, the psychologist alters or addresses problematic aspects of the treatment (e.g., problems in the therapeutic relationship or in the implementation of the goals of the treatment) as appropriate. (APA Task Force, 2006, pp. 276–277)

So, attaining feedback, as described in this book, on yet another level is an EBP.

Next, "in the context of patient characteristics, culture, and preferences" rightfully emphasizes what the client brings to the therapeutic stage, as well as the acceptability of any intervention to the client's expectations and how well any model or technique resonates. In short, EBP now accommodates the common factors, reinforces the importance of your development of clinical expertise, and includes client feedback as a necessary component.

The two approaches, EBT and EBP, take radically different stances about defining and disseminating evidence. One seeks to improve clinical practice via the dissemination of treatments meeting a minimum standard of empirical support (EBT), and the other describes a process of research application to practice that includes clinical judgment and client preferences (EBP; see Littell, 2010, for a full discussion of the two approaches). In essence an EBT approach, as characterized by Division 12, depicts confidence in the available evidence and appeals to those who believe that more structure and consistency and less clinician judgment is needed to bring about positive outcomes. On the other hand, EBP reflects the understanding that scientific evidence is tentative and that outcome is dependent not only on applying the various types of empirical research but also on the participants. EBP appeals to those who value clinician autonomy and individualized treatment decisions based on unique presentations of clients. The APA Task Force on EBP exemplifies this approach to the evidence.

Finally, the Task Force (2006) said:

> The application of research evidence to a given patient always involves probabilistic inferences. Therefore, ongoing monitoring of patient progress and adjustment of treatment as needed are essential. (APA Task Force, p. 280)

Proponents from both sides of the EBT-versus-EBP aisle recognized that outcome is not guaranteed regardless of evidentiary support of a given technique or the expertise of the therapist. The APA definition, as does this book, supports an identity of plurality, essential attention to client preferences, a focus on therapist expertise, and the importance of feedback.

Bottom Line: APA's definition brings clinical common sense to the controversy. There is nothing wrong with EBTs. But the evidence doesn't justify mandates, exclusive reimbursement, or dictates about the way to address client problems. The only way to know what the "right" treatment is to measure the client's response to any delivered treatment—to conduct EBP one client at a time.

ABOUT THIS BOOK

Feedback is the breakfast of champions.
— Ken Blanchard and Spencer Johnson, *The One-Minute Manager*

On Becoming a Better Therapist intends to help you remember your original aspirations, continue to develop as a therapist, and achieve better outcomes more often with more clients. It draws on the experiences of the two most important people to psychotherapy outcome: the client and you: Client perspectives about the benefit and the alliance and your perceptions of your professional growth. Regardless of your approach, this book will help you continue what you are doing well while expanding your influence to those clients who do not respond to your usual efforts. Through a transparent process of attaining client feedback, you'll learn ways to deepen the therapeutic conversation, intensify the power of a collaborative alliance, and more effectively recruit clients' resources in the service of change. In short, you'll accelerate your development and learn how to become a better therapist—one client at a time.

Psychotherapy is not an uninhabited landscape of technical procedures. It is not the sterile, stepwise process of surgery, nor does it follow the predictable path of diagnosis, prescription, and cure. It cannot be described without the client and therapist, co-adventurers in a journey across what is largely uncharted territory. The common factors provide useful landmarks for this intensely interpersonal and idiosyncratic trip, and specific models and techniques provide well-traveled routes to consider, but feedback offers a necessary compass to provide bearings of the psychotherapy terrain and guidance to the desired destination.

This book has nine chapters. Chapter 2, "Becoming a Better Therapist With PCOMS," shows you how to get started using PCOMS to help clients help you do good work—not sometime, next month, or even next week, but with your next client. It begins with a discussion of the measures and then covers the first-session pragmatics, detailing all you need to know to start becoming a better therapist. Chapter 3, "How Being Bad Can Make You Better," describes how recapturing the clients who are not benefiting will make the difference between being an average therapist or a better one. Rather than only learning from failed cases, this chapter details how to turn them around before a negative outcome ensues. Chapter 4, "Getting Better With Couples, Families, and Youth," reviews the lessons from the five published couple studies that arose from the Norway Feedback Trial and details the clinical process of using PCOMS with youth, couples, and families. "Using PCOMS to Accelerate Your Development" is the topic of Chapter 5. Integrating the groundbreaking work of Orlinsky and Rønnestad (2005) regarding therapist development, Chapter 5 shows you how to take charge of your professional growth and ensure that you learn from your experience rather than repeat it. Building on Chapter 5's framework to track your development and outcomes, Chapter 6, "The Heart and Soul of Change," delineates strategies to improve your effectiveness based on the most potent common factors—the client and the therapeutic alliance. Chapter 7, "Wizards, Humbugs, or Witches," encourages you to reflect about your identity as a therapist and what it is that you do—to create a description of your work that you can believe in and that provides clinical flexibility. Next, Chapter 8 broadens the focus. "Becoming a Better Agency" addresses implementation of PCOMS in public behavioral health (PBH) and other organizations, detailing what it takes for success. In addition, Chapter 8 presents the results of our benchmarking study of a large PBH agency in Arizona. Contrary to earlier dire accounts of PBH effectiveness, this agency achieved outcomes comparable to benchmarks from RCTs of depression and feedback. How? This agency implemented PCOMS.

Each of the first eight chapters concludes with a story that documents key lessons that clients have taught me over my career—meaningful moments that reminded me of why I made the choice to become a therapist. These examples are not intended to depict everyday therapeutic encounters but, rather, the ones that made the most dramatic impact on my identity as a psychotherapist. Finally, Chapter 9, "For the Love of the Work," continues the focus on your development, exploring ways for continued reflection about the work you love. It concludes with my parting thoughts about the controversial issues of the day as they pertain to our identity as therapists, as well as what I think it takes to become a "master" therapist.

CLIENTS ARE THE BEST TEACHERS: THEIR STORIES DOCUMENT OUR DEVELOPMENT

At bottom every man [sic] knows well enough that he is a unique being, only once on this earth; and by no extraordinary chance will such a marvelously picturesque piece of diversity in unity as he is, ever be put together a second time.

—Friedrich Nietzsche

When I was an intern, I worked in an outpatient unit euphemistically called Specialized Adult Services (SAS). While it included a stress management program, SAS was really an aftercare facility devoted to working with clients labeled *severely mentally ill*. By that time, I had acquired experiences in two community mental health centers and an assessment stint in the state hospital. But the hospital experience lingered, leaving me with a bad taste in my mouth. I saw firsthand the facial grimaces and tongue wagging that characterize the neurological damage caused by antipsychotics and sadly realized that these young adults would be forever branded as grotesquely different, as "mental patients." I witnessed the dehumanization of people reduced to drooling, shuffling zombies, spoken to like children and treated like cattle. I barely kept my head above water as hopelessness flooded the halls of the hospital, drowning staff and clients alike in an ocean of lost causes. I could not even imagine what it would have been like to live there in the revolving-door fashion that many endured. Now, in my internship, my charge was to help people stay out of the hospital, and I took that charge quite seriously.

One of my first clients was Peter. Peter was not well liked at SAS. He sometimes said ominous things to other clients in the waiting room, or spoke in a boisterous way about how the fluorescent lights controlled his thinking through a hole in his head. When he wasn't speaking, he grunted and squealed and made other sounds like a pig. As a new intern, I was put under considerable pressure to address Peter's less-than-endearing behaviors, particularly because he sometimes offended the stress management clients, who were seen as coveted treasures not to be messed with. Actually, I found Peter to be a terrific guy with a very dry sense of humor, but a man of little hope who lived in constant dread of returning to the state hospital. His behaviors were mostly his efforts to distract himself from tormenting voices that told him people were trying to kill him and other scary things.

Peter would be routinely terrorized by these voices until he started taking actions that led him to ultimately wind up in the state hospital. He might empty his refrigerator for fear that someone had poisoned his food, creating a stench that would soon bring in the landlord and ultimately the authorities. Or, occasionally, he would start threatening or menacing others, those he believed were trying to kill him. Once he was hospitalized, his medications were changed, usually increased in dose, and he essentially slept out the crisis. These cycles occurred about every 4 to 6 months and had done so for the previous 8 years. Peter's treatment brought with it tardive dyskinesia and about a hundred pounds of extra weight.

Peter hated the state hospital, and I could truly commiserate, after my own less-than-inspiring experience there. I felt profoundly sad for this young man, who was about my age. I also felt completely helpless. Nothing in my training provided any guidance. I had no clue about what to do to be helpful to him. I was trying to apply strategies I had learned from my supervisor about addressing the voices, which were helpful to others but not with Peter. I knew he was ramping up for another admission—he told me that he had already emptied his refrigerator and left the contents on the kitchen floor. It seemed that nothing I said could convince Peter to get off the merry-go-round to the state hospital. The anguish in his eyes about his impending hospitalization haunted me.

Only because I had no clue about what to do, I asked Peter what he thought it would take to get a little relief from his situation—what might give him just a glimpse of a break from the torment of the voices and the revolving-door hospitalizations. After a long pause, Peter said something very curious: He said that it would help if he would start riding his bike again. This led to my inquiry about the word "again." Peter told me about what his life was like before the bottom fell out. Peter had been a competitive cyclist in college and was physically fit as only world class cyclists can be. I heard the story of a young man away from home for the first time, overwhelmed by life, training day and night to keep his spot on the racing team, and topped off by falling in love for the first time. When the relationship ended, it was too much for Peter, and he was hospitalized, and then hospitalized again, then hospitalized again, and so on until there was no more money or insurance—then the state hospitalization cycles ensued.

On a roll now and enjoying a level of conversation not achieved before, I asked Peter what it would take to get him going again on his bike. He said that his bike was in need of parts and what he needed was for me to accompany him to the bike shop. Peter was afraid to go out in public alone for fear of threatening someone and ending up in the hospital. I immediately consulted with my supervisor, who gave me an enthusiastic green light. The next day, I went with Peter to the bike shop, where I bought a bike as well. Peter and I started having our sessions biking together. Peter still struggled with the voices at times, but he stayed out of the hospital and they never kept him from biking. He eventually joined a bike club and moved into an unsupervised living arrangement.

You can read a lot of books about "schizophrenia" and its treatment, but you'll never find one that recommends biking as a cure. And you can read a lot of books about treatments in general, and you'll never read a better idea about a client dilemma than will emerge from a client in conversation with you—a person who cares and wants to be helpful.

2

BECOMING A BETTER THERAPIST WITH PCOMS

The only man I know who behaves sensibly is my tailor; he takes my measurements anew each time he sees me. The rest go on with their old measurements and expect me to fit them.

—George Bernard Shaw

First, let's put all the cards on the table about why you might be reluctant to systematically collect outcome feedback. Finding out how effective you really are can be risky business. What if you find out that you are not so good? What if you discover that you are—the kiss of death—just average? What if the data reveal that you are in the wrong profession? What if . . . ? You get the picture; you might learn something that you might not want to know. Measuring outcomes puts you in a vulnerable spot. But, still, you want to be a better therapist. The only way to get better is to know where you are now versus where you would like to be—to aspire for the best results, and take deliberate actions to get them. It does take courage. But so did walking into therapy, for the first time, with someone in distress, and so does doing it day in and day out. You have some guts, let's face it. And we know it works. Recall that in our large feedback study with couples, nine of 10 therapists improved their outcomes with feedback (Anker, Duncan, & Sparks, 2009).

http://dx.doi.org/10.1037/14392-002

On Becoming a Better Therapist, Second Edition: Evidence-Based Practice One Client at a Time, by B. L. Duncan
Copyright © 2014 by the American Psychological Association. All rights reserved.

Another thing that may be preventing you from betting on the Partners for Change Outcome Management System (PCOMS; Duncan, 2012) hand is the whole idea of "assessment" and the evil D word, "data." The thought of using standardized measures to monitor outcome may make your skin crawl and seem like just more of the same funder mandates. Moreover, the thought of numbers and—heaven forbid—"collecting data" may be almost enough to make you run out of the room screaming. But this is different—really different—because the measures are not used to unravel the mysteries of the human psyche, nor are they just another rendition of a "biopsychosocial" assessment. Rather, these measures invite clients into the inner circle of mental health and substance abuse services; they collaboratively involve clients in monitoring progress toward their goals, amplifying their voices in any decisions about their care. PCOMS does involve numbers, but they are simple and straightforward, and it doesn't take a stat consultant to interpret them.

Unlike other systems of feedback, all scoring and interpretation in PCOMS are done together *with* clients. This represents a radical departure from traditional assessment and also gives clients a new way to look at and comment on their experience of therapy. Assessment, rather than being an expert-driven evaluation of the client or an imposed requirement to fulfill funder mandates, becomes a pivotal part of the relationship and of change itself. PCOMS, then, provides the tools to level the therapeutic process, foster a true partnership with clients, and enable a kind of transparency about what we do that is rare.

Another reason that you might not embrace PCOMS is that you may think you already know the information it is designed to reveal. Many of us believe that we are attuned to the client's experience and that using the forms would be superfluous. In fact, in the Norway study (Anker et al., 2009), all 10 of the therapists indicated that they had already informally acquired outcome and alliance information and, moreover, that formal feedback would not improve their effectiveness. Nine of 10 *did* improve their outcomes, so only one of them was correct. And, a friendly reminder: It is the client's view of the alliance that predicts outcomes, not the therapist's.

There may also be the fear of what others might do with the data, that your supervisor, agency, or third-party payer may be like the card shark with aces up his or her sleeve, dealing from the bottom of the deck, and just waiting to use your "tell," your data, against you. PCOMS is not intended to be used in any punitive way whatsoever (see Chapter 8). It is not a way to reprimand or give performance bonuses. Such practices undermine the spirit of outcome management and ultimately damage therapist morale. Collecting real-time data to inform practice has only one purpose: improving the benefits that clients receive while increasing the effectiveness of therapists.

And perhaps the trump card of your reticence is the paperwork. You need more paperwork like you need a hole in the head—it is the bane of the frontline therapist's existence. We can get really worked up over anything that adds paperwork, especially when we don't see any clinical relevance. For example, in reaction to a managed care company's introduction of a 30-item version of the Outcome Questionnaire (OQ), the *New England Psychologist* (Hanlon, 2005) reported that providers complained about its length and frequent administration, that it cut into sessions and increased workload, and that some items were intrusive. The response by clinicians was so severe that the State Psychological Association president said, "I have never seen such negative reaction from providers" (p. 11). This is not an infrequent reaction in my experience (see below).

But attaining client feedback about progress and the alliance need not be cumbersome or intrusive. The measures take clients only a minute or less to complete, so it is not a tedious task or asking too much. In fact, the entire process of PCOMS only takes a few minutes, generally about 5 but never more than 10 for administering, scoring, discussing, and integrating into the work. It is a light-touch, checking-in process indistinguishable from the work itself. PCOMS works best as a way to gently guide whatever models and techniques you use toward the client's perspective and a focus on outcome. And it is all done within the therapeutic hour because it is part of the work, not outside of it.

Keep your concerns in the back of your mind as you read this chapter. It starts with a discussion about the most robust predictors of outcome available—namely, early change and the alliance—that make PCOMS possible. It also presents the history and development of PCOMS as well as the psychometrics of its measures. More important, this chapter provides the pragmatics of getting started: all you need to begin with your next client. It aims to address all your concerns or reluctance about giving client feedback a go.

EARLY CHANGE AND THE ALLIANCE

If a man (*sic*) will kick a fact out of the window, when he comes back he finds it again in the chimney corner.

—Ralph Waldo Emerson

To retain clients at risk for slipping through the proverbial crack, we need to embrace what we know about change in therapy: that both early client change and the therapeutic alliance are robust predictors of ultimate treatment outcome. The Emerson quote is apropos of the early change phenomenon. Time and again, from the pioneering work of the late Ken Howard

(Howard, Kopta, Krause, & Orlinsky, 1986) to current sophisticated investigations using the latest statistical methods (Baldwin, Berkeljon, Atkins, Olsen, & Nielsen, 2009), studies reveal that the majority of clients experience the majority of change in the first eight visits. This is a surprisingly consistent finding. For example, an inspection of the trajectories in the Treatment of Depression Collaborative Research Program (Lutz, Stulz, & Köck, 2009), Project Match (Project MATCH Research Group, 1997), and the Cannabis Youth Treatment Project (Dennis et al., 2004) indicate the same pattern. Moreover, an examination of these trajectories across studies demonstrates that early change is an important predictor of short- and long-term outcome in psychotherapy. In other words, clients who report little or no progress early on will likely show no improvement over the entire course of therapy, or will end up on the dropout list. Early change predicts engagement in therapy and a good outcome at termination (Brown, Dreis, & Nace, 1999). The research about early change is quite a gift; monitoring change provides a tangible way for us to identify folks who are not responding so that we can chart a new course.

But this fact, seemingly regardless of how often it reappears in the "chimney corner," rubs some the wrong way. Sometimes therapists think that the research demonstrating that most change happens early and that early change predicts outcome is somehow an indictment against long-term work with clients. This is simply not true. Long-term work is perfectly fine as long as clients are benefiting. Although as time moves on it may take more time for less gain, a longer course of sessions can sometimes make great clinical sense.

Similarly, some say that the early-change phenomenon does not apply to longer term clients—that some clients who do change take longer than others to do so, and their trajectory is different. It is true that some clients take longer than others to show a change. However, it is a myth that clients will show no change for long periods of time and then suddenly have an epiphany. Clients typically don't flatline and then spike. I am not saying it has never happened in the history of psychotherapy, just that it is not very common. The Baldwin study confirmed that change tends to start right away, even with clients who spend a long time in therapy and whose changes come very slowly (more flat if you are looking at a graph).

So the question still remains: When should you start getting worried if clients are not responding to your therapy? I vote for sooner rather than later. This of course doesn't mean that if a client reports early change, the problem is "cured" or completely resolved. Rather, it suggests that the client has a subjective sense that therapy has gotten under way and that she's on the right path. Early change, then, is a reflection of heightened client hope and engagement, both powerful common factors stacking the deck for a positive outcome.

Finally, when some therapists see the trajectories depicting that the majority of change happens in the first eight sessions, it just does not feel intuitively right to them. There is good reason for this reaction. Consider two data sets, one from a university counseling center (UCC; the Baldwin et al., 2009, study) and one from a public behavioral health (PBH) agency (Reese, Duncan, Bohanske, Owen, & Minami, 2014; see Chapter 8 for more about this study). Both data sets are big, with 4,676 clients at the UCC and 5,168 at the PBH agency. Seventy-seven percent of clients at the UCC attended eight sessions or fewer, and 62% attended eight or fewer at the PBH agency; it took 12 sessions to reach 77%. So, at both sites, the majority of clients attended eight sessions or fewer, and fewer than one client in four went longer than eight sessions at the UCC and 12 sessions at the PBH center. This just means that data suggesting that most clients attend eight or fewer sessions, that most change occurs in that time frame, and that change, if it happens, begins early, have a pretty good track record of fitting most clients.

However, if one client in four goes longer than eight sessions, this means that, over time, a therapist will likely develop a caseload dominated by the longer term clients, given that the shorter term clients cycle through much more quickly. So, intuitively, it seems as though most clients take longer. Consequently, when some therapists see the expected treatment response graphs depicting trajectories through eight sessions, they easily dismiss them as "not fitting my clients." Unfortunately, this also dismisses the importance of early change and how the lack of change can help to reliably identify clients at risk regardless of the length of therapy.

After much deliberation on this issue, a practical solution came to me: We could develop expected treatment responses or trajectories for those clients who attend more than eight sessions. I enlisted statistical whiz and University of Kentucky professor Michael Toland, and software magician and webmaster Bill Wiggin, to look at a massive data set with me. We looked at a total of 427,000 sessions (95,000 clients) and divided them into those who attended eight sessions or fewer and those who attended nine to 18 sessions (18 because that represented 97% of the data set and, as in the Baldwin et al., 2009, sample, 77% of the clients attended eight sessions or fewer). Toland worked his statistical magic, and Wiggin programmed the magic so we could see the algorithms in action.

We (Wiggin mainly) also compared the algorithm-based trajectories with the means of each intake score across sessions, to see if the trajectories made sense—the "smell" test—and they passed. We also compared the predictions with the data sets from the randomized controlled trials of PCOMS as well as the data from the PBH agency discussed above, and the amount of change predicted by the algorithms was confirmed. And voilà, the new algorithms were born and incorporated in the web-based systems to be discussed in Chapter 5.

They predict therapy outcomes based on length of stay (short-term vs. longer term therapy encounters), thereby addressing the needs of both clients who attend more sessions and clinicians leaning toward a longer term perspective. Of course, these trajectories also demonstrate that change happens early even for those clients who attend therapy longer.

A second robust predictor of positive change described in Chapter 1, solidly demonstrated by a large body of studies (Horvath, Del Re, Flückiger, & Symonds, 2011), is our old friend the therapeutic alliance. Clients who highly rate their partnership with their therapists are more apt to remain in therapy and benefit from it. Enlisting these robust predictors of outcome, PCOMS provides invaluable information about the prospects for treatment success or failure. Specifically, it tells us about the match among ourselves, our approach, and the client, providing an outcome management system that partners with clients while honoring the daily pressures of frontline clinicians.

> **Bottom Line:** *We know the usual trajectory of change—early change predicts continued change, and good alliances predict ultimate treatment outcome. You can therefore predispose therapy to success by implementing an early warning system—tools that measure change and the alliance, the Outcome Rating Scale and Session Rating Scale.*

PCOMS: MEASURE DEVELOPMENT AND VALIDATION

Although it took me a while to embrace the idea of starting off a session with an outcome measure, I started using the OQ (Lambert et al., 1996) in the late 1990s in my private practice as well as in consultations with mental health agencies (see Duncan & Miller, 2000). I liked the OQ and particularly resonated with the idea that the client's perspective of benefit could "direct" the therapeutic process. It seemed a way to systematically privilege the client's voice, a radical innovation that could finally give the client his or her due. During this time, I also supervised graduate students in a community clinic and attempted to use the OQ there as well. Despite its obvious strengths, many clinicians complained about the length of time needed to complete the measure. They also said that it did not seem to fit, because of its symptom focus, many of the concerns that clients brought to therapy.

It became apparent that, in spite of the quality of the measure, the benefits of outcome monitoring would not occur if clients saw it as a burden and therapists didn't use it. This sobering realization not only came from my attempts at implementation at the clinic which resulted in an abysmal 1-year compliance rate of 25%, but also thanks to a study I conducted (mainly with my student at the time, Jacqueline Sparks) that compared a feedback condition using the OQ and the Working Alliance Inventory (WAI; Tracey & Kokotovic, 1989) with a condition in which therapists were taught "checking-in" questions about outcome and the alliance. The checking-in questions were an attempt to see if a more client/clinician friendly process would achieve similar results as formal outcome management.

We learned that therapists, despite repeated encouragement, would not consistently use the OQ and, to our surprise, would also not reliably ask the checking-in questions. The study was abandoned because of both missing OQ data points and therapist nonadherence to the checking-in questions (16% adherence). This failed investigation confirmed that longer measures of outcome were not feasible for everyday practice and that teaching therapists checking-in questions did not result in the hoped-for routine discussions of outcome and the alliance. This study led to the development of the ORS/ SRS (Outcome Rating Scale/Session Rating Scale), a structured yet feasible way to systematically "check in" with clients about progress and the alliance.

Monitoring Benefit: The Outcome Rating Scale

The ORS emerged from a combination of the OQ and two ideas. The first idea was *scaling questions* (Berg & de Shazer, 1993) commonly used in solution-focused therapy to assess client perceptions of problems and goal attainment ("On a scale of 0 to 10, with 0 being the worst it's been with this concern and 10 being where you want it to be, where are things right now?"). Client-based scaling provides instant feedback and privileges the client's voice when assessing the effectiveness of therapy (Franklin, Corcoran, Nowicki, & Streeter, 1997). After the failed investigation, I suggested to my then colleague Scott Miller that we simply ask scaling questions based on the major domains from the OQ to enable a total outcome score.

Later, Miller suggested the use of a visual analog scale because of its demonstrated face validity instead of scaling questions, and the ORS (Miller & Duncan, 2000) was born. Thereafter, based in 2 years of private practice experience and that of the multiple teams that I supervised in the community clinic, the clinical process of using the ORS was developed and first detailed in Duncan and Sparks (2002). It became evident that families would be unable to participate in feedback protocols without a valid measure for children. With this as an impetus, the Child Outcome Rating Scale (CORS; Duncan, Miller, & Sparks, 2003) was developed, and the clinical process with children and families first presented in Murphy and Duncan (2007; all the measures discussed here are available for free download for individual use at https://heartandsoulofchange.com).

Figure 2.1 reveals that the ORS assesses four dimensions, expressed as: (1) *Individually*—personal or symptomatic distress or well-being,

Outcome Rating Scale (ORS)

Name _____ Age (Yrs):____ Sex: M / F
Session # ____ Date: _____
Who is filling out this form? Please check one: Self_____   Other_____
If other, what is your relationship to this person? _____

Looking back over the last week, including today, help us understand how you have been feeling by rating how well you have been doing in the following areas of your life, where marks to the left represent low levels and marks to the right indicate high levels. *If you are filling out this form for another person, please fill out according to how you think he or she is doing.*

Individually
(Personal well-being)

I---I

Interpersonally
(Family, close relationships)

I---I

Socially
(Work, school, friendships)

I---I

Overall
(General sense of well-being)

I---I

Figure 2.1. The Outcome Rating Scale. Copyright 2000 by S. D. Miller and B. L. Duncan. Reprinted with permission. For examination only. Download a free working copy at https://heartandsoulofchange.com.

(2) *Interpersonally*—relational distress or how well the client is getting along in intimate relationships, (3) *Socially*—the client's view of work/school and relationships outside of the home, and (4) *Overall*—a big-picture view or general sense of well-being. The ORS translates these four dimensions into a visual analog format of four 10 cm lines, with instructions to place a mark on each line with low estimates to the left and high to the right. The four 10-cm lines add to a total score of 40. The score is the summation of the marks made by the client to the nearest millimeter on each of the four lines, measured by a centimeter ruler or template (or web-based system). Because of its simplicity, ORS feedback is immediately available for use at the time the service is delivered. Rated at a seventh-grade reading level and translated into multiple languages, the ORS is easily understood by adults and adolescents and enjoys rapid connection to clients' day-to-day lived experience. The CORS, validated for children ages 6 to 12 and their caregivers, translates the ORS into child-friendly language, rated at a third-grade reading level (see Chapter 4 for a figure of the CORS).

There are no numbers on the ORS, and you may wonder why. We designed it that way because research with visual analog scales suggested that numbers influence how many will mark the scale. Numbers tend to influence people to score more on the average side of things and to round off to whole numbers as well. It sounds funny, but without numbers, you get more of an accurate representation of the client's subjective experience.

On par with its clinical usefulness and feasibility, the utility of the ORS as an outcome-management tool depends on its reliability and validity. In addition to the ORS/SRS manual (Duncan, 2011a), four validation studies of the ORS have been published (Bringhurst, Watson, Miller, & Duncan, 2006; Campbell & Hemsley, 2009; Duncan, Sparks, Miller, Bohanske, & Claud, 2006; Miller, Duncan, Brown, Sparks, & Claud, 2003). Across studies, average Cronbach's alpha coefficients (i.e., internal consistency or reliability) for the ORS were .85 (clinical samples) and .95 (nonclinical samples; Gillaspy & Murphy, 2011). Duncan et al. (2006) reported that internal consistency for the ORS/CORS was .93 for adolescents and .84 for children. As an indicator of treatment progress, the ORS/CORS have been found to be sensitive to change for clinical samples yet stable over time for nonclinical samples (Bringhurst et al., 2006; Duncan et al., 2006; Miller et al., 2003).

The concurrent validity of the ORS has primarily been examined through correlations with established outcome measures. The average correlation between the ORS and OQ across three studies (Bringhurst et al., 2006; Campbell & Hemsley, 2009; Miller et al., 2003) was .62 (range: .53–.74), indicating moderately strong concurrent validity (Gillaspy & Murphy, 2011). Campbell and Hemsley (2009) reported moderately strong relationships (.53–.74) between the ORS and the Depression Anxiety Stress Scale (Lovibond & Lovibond, 1995), Quality of Life Scale (Burckhardt & Anderson, 2003), and Rosenberg Self-Esteem Scale (Rosenberg, 1989). Duncan et al. (2006) found that the CORS also demonstrated moderate concurrent validity with the Youth Outcome Questionnaire (YOQ; Burlingame et al., 2001) for adolescents ($r = .53$) and children ($r = .43$). In addition, Miller et al. (2003) reported that pretreatment ORS scores distinguished clinical and nonclinical samples, providing further support for the construct validity of the ORS.

Like most outcome instruments, the ORS appears to measure global distress, which explains how such a brief instrument can measure up to much longer ones. You can use longer measures, then, but you don't have to. The brevity of the ORS really makes a difference because, as is news to no clinician on the front lines and especially in the public sector, the number of forms and other oversight procedures has exploded. Few have the time or inclination, as demonstrated above, to devote to the repeated administration, scoring, and interpretation of lengthy measures, and so feasibility is critical.

Clients quickly tire of measures that lack obvious face validity, require more than a few minutes to complete, or appear to take away from time spent with the counselor.

Intimately related to feasibility is the issue of the immediacy and utility of the feedback: whether the measure has an intended *clinical* use to improve effectiveness. Most outcome measures were developed primarily as pre–post and/or periodic assessments, or they become that way because they are too cumbersome to administer in each session. Such instruments provide an excellent way to measure program effectiveness but do not provide real-time feedback for immediate treatment modification before clients drop out or suffer a negative outcome. The ORS was designed first as a clinical tool to provide real-time feedback to both clients and providers to improve effectiveness—to get therapists to talk to clients about outcome—and evolved, via psychometric validation and empirical investigation, to a way to measure and improve outcomes at individual, program, and agency levels.

To be sure, because of its brevity, the ORS is weaker psychometrically and does not have the same breadth and depth of assessment as the longer scales. At the same time, a measure that goes unused is useless regardless of its strengths. In the real world of delivering services, finding the right outcome measure means striking a balance between the competing demands of validity, reliability, and feasibility. The development of the ORS and CORS reflects our attempt to find such a balance.

Jeff Reese and I (Duncan & Reese, 2013) recently exchanged views with Halstead, Youn, and Armijo (2013) about this balance, debating when a measure is too brief and when it is too long. First, regarding when a measure is too brief: There is no doubt that having 45 items, 30 items, or even 19 items is psychometrically better than four items and that the increased reliability and validity likely result in better detection, prediction, and ultimate measurement of outcome. But how much better is really the question. Are these differences clinically meaningful, and do they offset the low compliance rates and resulting data integrity issues from missing data? These are the questions that require empirical investigation to determine how brief is too brief, although from my experience, the verdict has already been rendered. But when is a measure too long? The answer is simple: When clinicians won't use it.

Monitoring the Alliance: The Session Rating Scale

Routine assessment of the alliance enables therapists to identify and correct potential problems before they exert a negative effect on outcome or result in dropout (Sharf, Primavera, & Diener, 2010). The development of the SRS followed a similar story line as the ORS. We were experimenting with using the 12-item WAI (Tracey & Kokotovic, 1989) and the 10-item SRS. And similarly, even though these instruments were pretty brief, they apparently were not brief enough; it was tough to get therapists to do either of them, and implementation rates were terrible. For example, the 1-year compliance rate was just 29% for the 12-item WAI (Duncan et al., 2003). Ultimately, the SRS (V.3) was developed (Miller, Duncan, & Johnson, 2002), pressed by a need for a brief alliance measure at the telephonic employee assistance program mentioned in Chapter 1, and guided by Bordin's (1979) classic definition of the alliance as well as research about alliance measures.

Recognizing the much-replicated findings regarding the alliance across modalities and client populations, we also developed the Child Session Rating Scale (CSRS; Duncan, Miller, & Sparks, 2003b), the Relationship Rating Scale (RRS) for peer services and self-help (Duncan & Miller, 2004), the Group Session Rating Scale (GSRS; Duncan & Miller, 2007), and the Group Child Session Rating Sale (GCSRS; Duncan, Miller, Sparks, & Murphy, 2011) as brief alternatives to longer research-based measures.

Figure 2.2 reveals that the SRS simply translates what is known about the alliance into four visual analog dimensions, based in Bordin's (1979) classic delineation of the components of the alliance: the relational bond and the degree of agreement between the client and therapist about the goals and tasks of therapy. First, the relationship dimension rates the meeting on a continuum from "I did not feel heard, understood, and respected" to "I felt heard, understood, and respected." Second is a goals and topics scale that rates the conversation on a continuum from "We did not work on or talk about what I wanted to work on or talk about" to "We worked on or talked about what I wanted to work on or talk about." Third is an approach or method dimension, requiring the client to rate the meeting on a continuum from "The approach is not a good fit for me" to "The approach is a good fit for me." Finally, the fourth scale looks at how the client perceives the encounter in total along the continuum: "There was something missing in the session today" to "Overall, today's session was right for me." Like the ORS, the instrument takes only a couple of minutes to administer, score, and discuss. The SRS is scored similarly to the ORS, by adding the total of the client's marks on the four 10-cm lines. Rated at a seventh-grade reading level and translated into multiple languages, the SRS is also easily understood. The CSRS translates the SRS into child-friendly language, rated at a third-grade reading level (see Chapter 4 for a figure of the CSRS). The GSRS adds a coherence dimension, a factor more predictive of outcome in group work than the alliance with the leader or facilitator (see Figure 2.3).

Session Rating Scale (SRS V.3.0)

Name _____ Age (Yrs):____
ID# _____ Sex: M / F
Session # ____ Date: _____

Please rate today's session by placing a mark on the line nearest to the description that best fits your experience.

Relationship

I did not feel
heard, understood,
and respected.

I--I

I felt heard,
understood, and
respected.

Goals and Topics

We did *not* work
on or talk about
what I wanted to
work on and talk
about.

I--I

We worked on and
talked about what I
wanted to work on
and talk about.

Approach or Method

The therapist's
approach is not a
good fit for me.

I--I

The therapist's
approach is a good
fit for me.

Overall

There was
something missing
in the session
today.

I--I

Overall, today's
session was right
for me.

Figure 2.2. The Session Rating Scale. Copyright 2002 by S. D. Miller, B. L. Duncan, and L. Johnson. Reprinted with permission. For examination only. Download a free working copy at https://heartandsoulofchange.com.

A factor analysis by Hatcher and Barends (1996) revealed that, in addition to the general factor measured by all alliance scales (i.e., strength of the alliance), two other factors were predictive: *confident collaboration* and *expression of negative feelings*. Confident collaboration speaks to the level of confidence that the client has that therapy and the therapist will be helpful. Although overlapping with the third scale on the SRS, the fourth dimension of the SRS directly addresses this factor. The other factor predictive beyond the general strength of the alliance is the client's freedom to voice negative reactions to the therapist. Clients who express even low levels of disagreement with their therapists report better progress (Hatcher & Barends, 1996). The entire SRS is based on encouraging clients to identify alliance problems, to elicit client disagreements so that the clinician may change to better fit client expectations.

Regarding psychometrics of the SRS, internal consistency estimates were reported in four studies with an average alpha of .92, range .88 (Anker,

Group Session Rating Scale (GSRS)

Name _____ Age (Yrs):____
ID# _____ Sex: M / F
Session # ____ Date: _____

Please rate today's group by placing a mark on the line nearest to the description that best fits your experience.

Relationship

I did not feel understood, respected, and/or accepted by the leader and/or the group.

I--I

I felt understood, respected, and accepted by the leader and the group.

Goals and Topics

We did *not* work on or talk about what I wanted to work on and talk about.

I--I

We worked on and talked about what I wanted to work on and talk about.

Approach or Method

The leader and/or the group's approach are/is not a good fit for me.

I--I

The leader and the group's approach are a good fit for me.

Overall

There was something missing in group today—I did not feel like a part of the group.

I--I

Overall, today's group was right for me—I felt like a part of the group.

Figure 2.3. The Group Session Rating Scale. Copyright 2007 by B. L. Duncan and S. D. Miller. Reprinted with permission. Download a free working copy at https://heartandsoulofchange.com.

Owen, Duncan, & Sparks, 2010; Duncan et al., 2003; Reese, Toland, Slone, & Norsworthy, 2010) to .96 (Duncan, 2011a; Gillaspy & Murphy, 2011). These alpha coefficients suggest that the SRS assesses a single, global alliance construct. This is consistent with research on other alliance measures such as the WAI (Horvath & Greenberg, 1989). The alpha coefficients for the GSRS ranged from .86 to .90, similarly suggesting a single alliance factor (Quirk, Miller, Duncan, & Owen, 2013). Three studies (Duncan, 2011a; Duncan et al., 2003; Reese et al., 2010) reported test–retest reliability of SRS scores from the first to second session. The average reliability coefficient was .59 (range: .54–.64), indicating adequate stability (Gillaspy & Murphy, 2011). The test–retest reliability coefficient for the GSRS ranged from .42 to .62 (Quirk et al., 2013).

Three studies have investigated the concurrent validity of the SRS. Duncan et al. (2003) reported a correlation of .48 between the SRS and the revised Helping Alliance Questionnaire (HAQ–II; Luborsky et al., 1996). Campbell and Hemsley (2009) found that SRS scores correlated .58 with the WAI (Tracey & Kokotovic, 1989). Reese et al. (2013) reported correlations with the WAI ranging from .57 to .65. These findings indicate moderate concurrent validity with longer alliance measures. In addition, Reese et al. (2013) also found evidence for discriminant validity of the SRS. A low correlation was found between the SRS and the Social Desirability Scale (Ballard, 1992; $r = .05$). Regarding the GSRS, correlation coefficients between the GSRS and the WAI ranged from .41 to .61; coefficients between the GSRS and the Group Climate Questionnaire (MacKenzie, 1983) and the Therapist Factor Inventory, Cohesiveness Scale (Lese & MacNair-Semands, 2000) ranged from .31 to .60 (Quirk et al., 2013). These data indicate that the GSRS adequately assesses similar constructs.

Finally, the predictive validity of the SRS was supported by Duncan et al. (2003). Early SRS scores (second or third session) were predictive of posttreatment ORS scores ($r = .29$), consistent with previous research linking early client perceptions of alliance with outcome (Horvath & Bedi, 2002). Similarly, Quirk et al. (2013) found that GSRS scores were predictive of change in the fourth session ($r = .23$).

> **Bottom Line:** The ORS and SRS are the instruments used in PCOMS. Both have just four items, making them feasible for everyday, every-session use with clients. Both reliable and valid, these brief measures tell you the most important things you need to know about your therapy: whether the client and the therapy are on the right track.

NUTS AND BOLTS OF PCOMS

Frothy eloquence neither convinces nor satisfies me. . . . You've got to show me.

—Willard Duncan Vandiver,
Speech at a Naval Banquet in Philadelphia

Given that, at its heart, PCOMS is a collaborative intervention, everything about the use of the measures and the results attained is shared with clients. Consequently, the client needs to understand what it's all about, and especially these two points: that the ORS will be used to collaboratively track outcome in every session to ensure the client benefits and that it is a way to make sure that the client's voice is not only heard but also remains central to therapy as it unfolds.

The ORS is given at the beginning of each session. In the first meeting, the ORS pinpoints where the client sees him- or herself, allowing for an ongoing comparison in later sessions. As noted, the ORS is not an assessment tool in the traditional sense. Rather, it is a clinical tool intimately integrated into the work itself. It requires that the therapist ensure that the ORS represents both the client's experience of his or her life and the reasons for service—that the general framework of client distress evolves into a specific account of the work done in therapy.

The SRS opens space for the client's voice about the alliance. It is given at the end of the meeting, but with enough time left for discussing the client's responses. The SRS is not a measure of a therapist's competence or ultimate ability to form good alliances, or anything else negative about therapists or clients. It is designed to facilitate a discussion about the partnership between the therapist and the client; any lower rating is an indication that the client feels comfortable to report that something is wrong. Appreciation of any negative feedback is a powerful alliance builder, as is the ongoing attention of the therapist to the client's experience of it.

There is a factor in PCOMS that is absolutely essential—you. If you don't authentically value clients' perspectives and believe that they should be active participants in therapy, PCOMS will fall flat. In addition, without your investment of yourself into the spirit of partnership of the feedback process, little gain is likely to happen. It's not enough to flick a form in a client's face—you have to use it clinically and allow yourself and the work to be influenced by it. Obviously, if you don't look at the feedback, use it, or expect it to add anything you don't already know, client feedback will not improve your outcomes (de Jong et al., 2012). Your task is to make PCOMS your own.

There are four steps to using the measures in the first session.

Step One: Introducing and Scoring the ORS

Clients need to be on board, and that is up to you. This means informing them about the nature of the partnership and starting to build a culture of feedback in which their voice is essential. In the first contact by you or an intake person, it is important to convey a commitment to improving the client's situation as well as to the highest quality of collaborative care:

> I am committed to your reaching your goals here, so I like to monitor whether my clients are benefiting through the use of two brief forms. These take only a couple minutes to fill out, but yield a great deal of information about how things are going and whether or not we should set a different course. I will give you one in the beginning of the session and one toward the end. This will allow us to keep an eye on whether you are getting what you came here to get and how well

we are working together. It's good to know these things sooner rather than later so we can do something about it—it also lets us know if you would be better served by someone else. I will explain this in greater detail when you arrive for your first session. Is this something you can help me out with?

I have never had anyone tell me that keeping track of progress is a bad idea. The above script is just a suggestion. Feel free to be creative in your explanation. Put it in your own words and natural way of communicating.

Continue building a culture of feedback in the first session and administer the ORS as an invitation into a collaborative partnership. Avoid technical jargon and instead explain the purpose of the measures and their rationale in a natural, commonsense way. Make the administration, scoring, and discussion part of a relaxed and ordinary way of having conversations and working. The specific words are not important. Your interest in the client's desired outcome speaks volumes about your commitment to the individual. Convey that there is no such thing as "bad news" on these forms because feedback improves the chance for success. Ensure that clients know that the measures are specifically designed to empower their voice in all aspects of therapy and include them in all decisions that affect their care, and the ORS will be used to monitor their progress to make sure that they are reaching their desired goals. Here are two examples from actual clients:

> When I work with people I like to start off with this very brief form, it's called the Outcome Rating Scale, and it is a way for me to get a snapshot of how you are viewing how things are going for you right now, and a way that you and I can check in each time to make sure that our work together is beneficial for you. So it's a way to track progress and it's also a way to make sure that how you are viewing things stays central to the way we are working together.

> When I work with folks, what I like to do to start things off is give this very brief form to fill out called the Outcome Rating Scale and this gives me a snapshot of how you are doing right now with things. It serves as an anchor point so we can track your progress so we both know how things are going so we can talk about that. It's also a way to make sure that your voice stays central to this process because sometimes client voice has a way of falling through the cracks. This is a way to make sure that your perspective of how you are doing stays central to all the works that's done. Would you mind doing that for me?

These excerpts are just examples, not mandates or research protocols. So put the introduction in your own words, the way that you talk and interact with clients. Remember, in most respects, you are the therapy—you account for most of the variance in any delivered treatment. Similarly, you are PCOMS!

Here are the provided instructions on the ORS:

> Looking back over the last week, including today, help us understand how you have been feeling by rating how well you have been doing in the following areas of your life, where marks to the left represent low levels and marks to the right indicate high levels. *If you are filling out this form for another person, please fill out according to how you think he or she is doing.*

Use your judgment about how much to explain the instructions. Most people understand the measures with minimal explanation, but you can't overexplain the measures, so do whatever it takes to ensure that the client understands what it is about. Given that the forms are intended to make sure the client's perspective is not lost in the shuffle (recall Dan Ariely, the burn patient, in Chapter 1), the whole point is missed if the client doesn't get what the measures and PCOMS are about.

The ORS has very good face validity—the domains make common sense, so clients very quickly apply their lived experience to the different areas of functioning and make their marks. Whatever explanation the client gives in his or her own words is okay. Some clients will say, "You mean like poor to well?" or "Like 1 on the left and 10 on the right?" Keep in mind it's their subjective experience we are interested in, so their understanding of the measure in the context of their lives is paramount. Your efforts to understand the meaning of the client's ratings also contribute to the client's ultimately "getting" what the ORS is all about.

Sometimes clients ask for clarification between scales or how they should rate two aspects of the same dimension. For example, regarding the *Interpersonally* line, which looks at close relationships such as partners and immediate family, clients may say something like, "I am doing great with my kids, but my relationship with my spouse stinks;" or on the *Socially* dimension, "My work is the only thing going right, but I have no friends—should I average this?"

Here you simply ask the client to rate the dimension relevant to his or her decision to seek therapy, because you want the measure to reflect progress in that area. So you say something like, "Are either of the topics related to why you are here?" (The client responds that he is here because of his relationship with his partner or she is here because of her troubles making friends.) "Okay, please rate the line to reflect your concerns there because we want to see when progress is made."

It's also okay to orient clients to how you would like them to rate the ORS. For example, at the couple clinic where the PCOMS feedback study was done, clients are asked to rate the *Interpersonally* dimension according to how things are going with their partners, given that is what the service is about. Similarly if you work in a substance abuse program, you might ask the client to score the ORS relative to their substance use. Think about what makes clinical sense to your practice. Some therapists like to orient clients in the first session to fill out the ORS relative to their reasons for therapy. That's okay too. My preference is for clients to complete the ORS without additional instructions and allow their reasons to emerge from how they filled it out. But that's just my preference. It's okay to provide more context if you find that more helpful.

Clients rarely say no to PCOMS when a sincere, authentic therapist conveys that the purpose of the ORS and the SRS is to ensure that the client's voice stays central and that the client will benefit. But the therapist has to believe that this is true and use the measures in a way that makes them meaningful to the work. If the ORS is treated as a perfunctory piece of paper that is not related to the therapeutic process, then clients will see it similarly.

Next, you have to score the client's marks. This is easy and only requires a centimeter ruler or template. But by all means practice it a few times. Many therapists will not try this because they are afraid they will look inept. They mostly worry about measuring the marks and adding up the scores. Keep in mind there are only four marks and four scores, so measuring the marks and adding the numbers is not quite like calculating regression equations (although using a calculator is fine). Just practice it a few times until you feel that you can do it without fumbling around too much.

And, however you do it, won't be as bad as I've done it—no kidding. When I am doing training, to ease the anxiety around using the measures for the first time, I show a video of me administering the measures in anything but a cool, expert, and professionally adept way. The agency where I was consulting used PCOMS and had the ORS on one side of a page and the SRS on the other. I didn't notice. So I explained the ORS to the mother and adolescent daughter who were very tense because of a very troubling, violent daughter-on-mother episode, while giving them the SRS to fill out. Imagine what they thought, reading "I felt heard, understood, and respected" ("Sure Barry, in the first minute this is going fine even though I haven't said anything yet!"). The clients dutifully filled out the SRS and gave it back to me, and I went on, totally unaware, with measuring the marks and adding the scores—and I still didn't notice that it was the SRS while I was giving them feedback about their ORS scores. What they must have thought! Finally I saw it and, laughing, I confessed what I had done and said I wouldn't blame them if they didn't want to talk with such a klutzy therapist. Then they started laughing too. My bumbling killed the tension, and it was a great session.

> **Bottom Line:** *Fold the administration and scoring of the measures into your natural way of talking and being with clients. Make sure clients get what the ORS is about: privileging their perspective and ensuring that they benefit. Don't stress so much about doing it right. Perhaps it is best to practice it a few times, but just do it.*

Step Two: Discussing the Client's Score and the Clinical Cutoff: Contextualizing and Making Sense of the Client's Score

By now, we have given the client the ORS, measured the marks, and tallied up a total score. Given that everything about PCOMS is 100% transparent, the task now is to discuss the number and make sense of it with the final authority—the client. The clinical cutoff provides a way to do this. *Clinical cutoff* is a statistical term that represents nothing ominous, nor does it say anything negative about the client. It is only the dividing line between people who typically do not find themselves in therapy and those who do, differentiating between a so-called clinical population from a nonclinical one. The clinical cutoff for the adult ORS is 25 (for adolescents, 28, and for children, 32). Recall that the ORS is really a measure of distress, so the number 25 out of 40 generally means that those under 25 are reporting the level of distress typically associated with being a client, and those over 25 are reporting a level of distress generally associated with not being a client. It's not magic. It is just the number that reliably distinguishes the two populations.

The average intake score of an outpatient psychotherapy setting is from 18 to 20, but anywhere between one fourth and one third of your clients will come in over the clinical cutoff. People who score under the cutoff are typically looking for change, something different in their lives, while those who score higher or over the cutoff tend to be folks who are more satisfied with the status quo and therefore may require a bit more context to understand what they are looking for from therapy.

So, once we have the score, it's time to say what the number means: to contextualize client scores using the cutoff as a jumping off point to promote understanding and best use. Discussing the cutoff allows you to check out whether the score makes sense to the client and fits what they were trying to convey in their marks; it is a way to make sure you have a good (i.e., true) rating. And, finally, addressing the cutoff allows you to validate the client and convey that he or she is in the right place.

There are only two choices here: The client's initial score on the ORS is either above or below the clinical cutoff. Scores that are under the cutoff may seem a bit more straightforward. The client is reporting distress at a level similar to those of other persons seeking mental health or substance abuse services—the lower the score, the higher the distress. These folks are looking for a change on the horizon, and a very low score is definitely saying that the sooner the change happens, the better. Here are two examples, to illustrate introductions to talking about the cutoff.

First is Connie, a bright, resourceful 31-year-old professional woman with a strong social network, who sought therapy because of difficulties in shaking a very painful divorce and a strong desire to make sense of what has happened to her, especially why her marriage failed. She scored a 19.8 on the ORS:

> *Barry:* *(Client gives her ORS to Barry.)* What I do is I just measure this up. It's four 10-cm lines and it gives a score from 0 to 40, and I just pull out this ruler and add up the scores, and then I will tell you about what this says and you can tell me whether it is accurate or not, and then we will have an anchor point to measure each time and see if you are getting what you came here to get. . . . Okay, you scored a 19.8. And what that means is that this scale, the Outcome Rating Scale, has a cutoff of 25 and people who score under 25 tend to be those who wind up talking to people like me; they're looking for something different in their lives, there's something in their lives that's not going so well. You scored about the average intake score of persons who enter therapy, so you're in the right place. And it's not hard to look at this and see pretty quickly that the family/close relationship area is what you are struggling with the most right now. Does that make sense?

> *Connie:* Yes, definitely.

> *Barry:* So what do you think would be the most useful thing for us to talk about today?

> *Connie:* Well, I am in the middle of divorce and struggling with figuring this out . . .

Then there was Harold, whom we'll follow into Chapter 3.

Harold was an incredibly energetic and community-involved 71-year-old retired engineer whose life had taken a downturn in the past year, when he started battling "chronic depression and panic attacks." Harold was coming off his third hospitalization in the past year and was feeling increasingly frail and hopeless. He especially was distressed about his propensity to ruminate about simple decisions, some of which evolved into panic attacks or bouts of isolating himself in bed or what the referral source called "debilitating depression." Harold scored a 14.2 on the ORS.

> *Barry:* *(Client gives his completed ORS to Barry.)* What I do is I just measure your marks on these four 10-cm lines with this ruler, which will give a score somewhere between 0 and 40. Then I'll tell you

what the number may mean and you can tell me whether it is accurate or not and then we will have a starting point to measure each time to if you are benefiting from our work together. Wow, your ORS score is 14.2 and that says things are really tough for you now. You are in the right place. Generally, a score under 25 indicates people who are in enough distress to seek help. Your total score of 14.2 is pretty low. The average intake score is usually about 18 to 20, so it says you are in quite a bit of distress. Does that fit your experience?

Harold: Yeah, it sure does. Nothing is the same anymore. Where do I start?

Barry: You might want to start with what led to you make the mark on the *Individually* Scale (*picking up the ORS*), the one you marked the lowest or you can start anywhere you'd like. What's going on?

Harold: I've been a personal wreck for the last year—I can't make a decision and can hardly get out of bed. . . .

That is all there is to it. Give the score, say what it might mean, and look for feedback to see if it fits. Keep in mind that it is the client who made the marks, so you are not going out on a limb when you discuss the score. If it doesn't fit for the client, then it's good that you found out so you take another pass and ensure a good rating, one that represents the client's experience of distress.

There are a couple of noteworthy things about these excerpts. First, the ORS is not burdensome for the client. Connie and Harold completed the ORS in 36 and 44 seconds, respectively. And, second, what you will find in 99 out of 100 administrations in the first meeting is that the scale clients mark the lowest is the one they are there to talk to you about. Connie and Harold both did just that. The initial ORS score is an instant snapshot of how the client views him- or herself. It brings an understanding of the client's experience to the opening minutes of a session that didn't previously exist, at least for me. With Harold, within 2 minutes, I knew that here was an individual in significant distress, well under the average intake cutoff, and I knew that of the domains of his life, he felt more impacted in his personal well-being. So I honed in on that right away.

What about folks over the clinical cutoff? Scores are usually above the cutoff for one or both of two reasons: (a) although most things are going well, there is a specific concern or issue for which the person desires help and/or (b) someone else has either suggested or required this person's participation in therapy.

Clients who are mandated (or coerced) to therapy from the courts, their employers, partners, or child protective services, etc. (and nearly all kids are mandated—they typically don't announce at the breakfast table over a bowl of Cheerios that they want to talk to a therapist) represent the lion's share of clients scoring over the cutoff. In these instances, it is very helpful to have clients complete the ORS twice, once as themselves, and once as if he or she were the referral person. If possible, it is preferable to get the referral person's actual rating. Although it is easy to obtain these two views with children and parents, it can be challenging with other mandated referrals, but not impossible. If you have a working relationship with the referral source, you can fax or e-mail the form so you have it as a point of comparison for discussion with the client. You can also call and administer the ORS over the phone (oral scripts are available at https://heartandsoulofchange. com) and ask referral sources if you can periodically check in to get their impressions of how the client is doing. This not only helps you track progress from the set of eyes that can make a difference for your client but also helps you identify what specifically the referral source is looking for as sign of improvement.

Consider Larry: He was referred by the courts because of his second DUI and was not very happy about that, nor was he happy to be sitting face-to-face with me in my office. Larry scored a 28.9 on the ORS.

Barry: Thanks for doing that for me. It helps me make sure that I pay attention to how you think about things. Okay, you scored a 28.9. The way this works is that the four lines there are 10 cm each and total up to 40. Twenty-five is considered the cutoff, which means that, generally, when people score above 25, things are going pretty well for them—not perfect, but pretty much okay. The score is more indicative of people who don't usually find themselves sitting in my office. Does that make sense in terms of how you marked it?

Larry: Yeah, it does, because I am doing fine and I don't really want to be here. The courts are making me.

Barry: Okay, good. I'm always glad when the ORS accurately reflects the client's experience.

Larry: You know, things are not perfect, but they are okay. I only had a few beers at a company picnic. It was the same cop that got me before—I think he was just waiting in my neighborhood to nail me. For Christ's sake, he must have been gunning for me. How could it be the same cop?

Barry: Does sound fishy, doesn't it? So things are okay except for this DUI business and that's why you are here to see me, because the courts have that hanging over your head, and that is what accounts for your lower rating on this first scale (*Barry points to the* Individually *Scale on the ORS*).

Larry: Yep, that's it. The PO thinks I have a drinking problem and that I need treatment.

Barry: You are on probation and your PO believes you to have a drinking problem. And you disagree with that.

Larry: You bet!

Barry: So it sounds like, and let me know if I'm getting this, that one thing we may need to do is convince your PO that you don't have a drinking problem and that you don't need to come here.

Larry: Yeah, that's it. That and let her know I can have my license back.

Barry: Okay, would you be willing to take another pass at that ORS for me? But this time fill it out like you were the PO rating you? Given she is the one we have to please, it might help us figure out a few things.

Larry: Sure. Okay. (*Barry gives Larry back his ORS and Larry completes it from the perspective of the PO.*)

Barry: Wow, this is really different. She would rate you a 16.8. Quite a difference between that and 28.9.

Larry: Yeah, she thinks I'm an alcoholic and that I need to go to AA.

Barry: I see. So what do you think you and I need to do to convince her that isn't true? Or (*picking up the ORS*), what needs to happen to bring her view of you more in line with your view of yourself?

The ORS, once again, sets the stage and focuses the work at hand. You may notice that I didn't enter into unnecessary clashes over the client's view of being set up by the police or how much he had to drink. Mandated clients are no different from voluntary clients with regard to the alliance. Attaining the client's rating as if he or she were the referral source is a great way to bring in the other view without challenging the client's perspective. Confirming my experience with every mandated client I have ever seen, the referral source rated Larry much lower than he did. I explored that with Larry to understand the difference. In a sense, the ORS allows the referral source's view to be externalized, represented by the form itself, making it easier to talk about, and not risking the alliance (few things are worth that risk).

One last thing of note about clients who enter therapy scoring over the cutoff: Even though the client may be reporting that things are going well, there will still be one scale that is lower than the rest, and that is often your invitation to collaborate.

Step Three: Connecting the Marks to the Client's Described Experience and Reasons for Service

This is the most important clinical nuance of PCOMS. The ORS and SRS are not like bread to a sandwich, separate from the real meat of the session. Rather, they are clinical tools intimately integrated into the work itself. Moreover, the ORS is not an emotional thermometer that rates how the client is feeling at the particular moment it is given, nor is it intended to be an ongoing account of how the client's life is going week to week. Rather, the ORS is designed to measure how things are going in the client's life relative to the reasons for therapy.

Because the ORS has face validity, as noted, clients usually mark the scale the lowest that represents the reason they are seeking therapy, and often connect that reason to the mark they've made. For example, Harold marked the *Individually* scale the lowest, with the *Socially* scale coming in a close second. As he was describing how he ruminates about minor decisions, often working himself into a real frenzy, he pointed to the ORS and explained that this problem accounted for his mark. With other clients, you may need to clarify the connection between the client's descriptions of the reasons for service and the client's marks on the ORS. This entails eliciting the client's perspective on what the marks mean, so that you are on the "same page" regarding what the marks say about the therapeutic work and whether the client is making any gains. This way, both you and the client know what the mark on the line represents to the client and what will need to happen so that the client will both realize a change *and* indicate that change on the ORS. At some point in the meeting, the therapist needs only to pick up on the client's comments and connect them to the ORS:

> Okay, it sounds like dealing with the loss of your job [or relationship with partner, sister's drinking, or anxiety attacks, etc.] is an important part of what we are doing here. Does the distress from that situation account for your mark here on the [____] scale on the ORS? Okay, so what do you think will need to happen for that mark to move just one centimeter to the right?

More specifically, using the example of Connie:

> *Barry:* If I am getting this right, you said that you are struggling with the divorce, specifically about why it happened and your part

in it, so you are looking to explore this and gain some insight into what perhaps was your contribution. You marked the *Interpersonally* Scale the lowest *(Barry picks up the ORS)*. Does that mark represent this struggle and your longing for some clarity?

Connie: Yes.

Barry: So, if we are able to explore this situation and reach some insights that resonate with you, do you think that it would move that mark to the right?

Connie: Yes, that is what I am hoping for and that's what I think will help me. I know I wasn't perfect in the relationship and I want to understand my part. I already know his part!

The ORS, by design, is a general outcome instrument and provides no specific content other than the broad domains. It offers a bare skeleton to which clients must add the flesh and blood of their experiences, into which they breathe life with their perceptions. At the moment in which clients connect the marks on the ORS with the situations that are distressing, and to what they would like to accomplish, the ORS becomes a meaningful measure of their progress and a potent clinical tool.

With Larry, although he scored over the cutoff with a score of 28.9, his *Individually* and *Interpersonally* scales were lower than others—6.1 and 6.8, respectively. Larry's problems with the courts and his PO were connected to the *Individually* scale. Larry and I discussed how we might move this mark over a bit and address the PO's concerns about his drinking. After a lively conversation, we concluded that looking at his drinking in detail might be a good start, given that the PO would be pleased that we were addressing it.

There is nothing heavy-handed or cast in stone about this. Client goals can change, and sometimes rapidly. The space between the client's marks and the far right represents the zone of potential treatment gains and topics of discussion—what they want to work on that may move their mark up, even a little. So if the client's desires change, don't worry but continue to connect the work to that space on the ORS open for improvement. For example, with Larry, his mark on the *Individually* scale first represented his distress about the DUI and the courts, with improvement coming from getting the PO off his back and securing driving-to-work privileges. In Session 4, the open space on the *Individually* scale evolved to represent the benefits accrued from a reduction in his drinking.

Finally, connecting the client's experience to the ORS has other benefits. It can help you and the client stay on track by providing a way to focus the session back on the lowest rated scale when the conversation goes astray. The

ORS helps prioritize topics as well as thematically tie different elements of the discussion together. Simply pick up the ORS and redirect to the issue at hand as well as what can be done in session and beyond, to move the mark to the right.

> **Bottom Line:** *It is important that the client understand that the marks on the scales should be connected to and reflect those issues that are the grist for the therapeutic mill. From the get-go, ensure that the measure is relevant to both the client's experience and the work that will ensue in therapy. If that connection isn't made, then the ORS becomes an emotional thermometer reading of weekly moods in response to the inevitable ups and downs of life. And then it is worthless.*

Given that the first ORS provides the comparison point for all future work with the client, it is essential to get a good rating. This means striving to get the most accurate rating of the client's experience possible, a sincere appraisal of his or her life. Encourage a frank discussion of the issues involved, express your desire to be helpful, and get the idea across that therapy works best when the ORS is an accurate reflection. In general, any score 35 or above is not a good rating, certainly one that should alert you to question whether it matches the client's description of his or her life. Even people who consider themselves doing very well in life do not tend to rate this high.

People score above 35 on a first session ORS for two main reasons: Either they don't understand the ORS, or they are disgruntled and are blowing it off. Neither is difficult to overcome. For example, I was doing a consult for an agency that was already using PCOMS, so I incorrectly assumed that the client understood the ORS. I administered the measure and the client scored a 38.1. I was surprised, given that I was purportedly doing a consult because the therapist and client felt stuck. But I said that things must be going really well, and the client just looked at me in a confused way and launched into a horror story of what she had to go through to get to the appointment. She had to get up 4 hours earlier than usual and had experienced two panic attacks. In fact, she said her life was riddled with panic, making every day an ongoing battle. I simply picked up the ORS and asked, "Where do I see the rather extreme struggles that you are describing on the ORS?" To which she answered, "Is that what that's for?" She redid the ORS and scored a 12.9. Clients have to understand the ORS, and it has to have meaning arising from their specific life circumstances. Clients who rate the ORS over 35 and then after a few minutes start telling you how badly their lives are going do not understand the measure. All you have to do is ask about it; perhaps the easiest way is to simply inquire where the distress that the client is describing can be found on the ORS.

How about folks who just blow off the ORS because they are angry about being in your office or who are disgruntled for some other reason? For example, I saw Darrell, a referral from the DUI court, who jerked the ORS from my hand and completed it in about a nanosecond. He just took the pencil and drew a line down the right side of the page. I dutifully measured the marks and totaled them to a score of 38.8. I commented on how well he was doing, especially considering his recent arrest. (He had opened the conversation by angrily telling me that he was forced to be there by the courts because of a DUI.) When I asked him how the referring PO would rate him, he told me he did not give a flying f--k about what his PO thought.

Even with this inauspicious start, after a while of talking about things, Darrell lightened up with me when he figured out that I wasn't there to nail him about his drinking. He told me through tears that his girlfriend had kicked him out and he was really sad about that—she meant a lot to him. Darrell also told me that he had been sleeping in his truck and was also concerned about losing his job. After commiserating, I asked him to help me understand how his life could be so hard while his ORS looked like he just won the lotto and spent a week in Hawaii with Angelina Jolie. He laughed and told me that he was pissed off in the beginning and rated the ORS without thinking much about it—that he had just blown it off. I asked Darrell if he would do it again because it would help us keep track of our work together and make sure he was getting where he wanted to go. And he did. His score was 18.3 with a 3.4 on the *Interpersonally* scale. The impact of Darrell's drinking on his relationship with his partner became the focus of our work. And when he was sober for 3 months, he invited his ex-partner to join him in therapy. Sometimes you have to work at that first ORS—to secure a good rating that reflects what is going on in the client's life. It is worth the effort.

But please take clients at face value unless you have evidence from *them*—not referral sources or family members—to the contrary. Err on the side of believing that there is a good reason for the client to rate it as he or she did.

> **Bottom Line:** *Getting a good rating on the ORS that reflects the client's described experience and reasons for service is critical to PCOMS. It's up to you to make that happen. Transparency is the rule. Just ask clients for help if their scores don't make sense to you. It usually makes sense to them. If not, ask the client to redo the ORS. And if it makes sense to the client but doesn't to you, take it at face value.*

Step Four: Introducing and Discussing the SRS

The best thing about the SRS is that it helps you build a strong alliance. It encourages you to not leave the alliance to chance and ignore the innumerable studies demonstrating the relationship between a strong alliance and positive outcome. Chapter 1 established that therapists who are better at forming strong alliances with more clients are the ones who are the most effective. The SRS is the only psychometrically reliable and valid instrument on the planet designed to be a session-by-session real-time alliance measure. This is important because clients drop out of therapy for two primary reasons: One is that therapy is not helping (hence the importance of monitoring outcome), and the other is alliance problems—they are not engaged or turned on by the process. The most direct way to improve your effectiveness is simply to keep people engaged in therapy. Traditionally, clients give their evaluation of the alliance with their feet—they walk out and don't come back.

The SRS, like the ORS, is best presented in a relaxed way that is seamlessly integrated into your typical way of working. And like the ORS, it designed to be a light-touch, checking-in process that exemplifies the culture of client privilege and feedback, opening space for the client's voice about the alliance. It is given at the end of the meeting but with enough time left to discuss the client's responses. Here are some example introductions to the SRS:

> This form, the Session Rating Scale, looks at how it went for you today, with the idea being that I really want to know whether you think we are on the right track, that we are talking about the right stuff, and whether my style and approach are a good fit for you—so I could do something about it if it wasn't working out for you. When clients and therapists talk about these things, it tends to make the outcome come out better.

> Let's take a minute and have you fill out the other form that asks your opinion about our work together, the Session Rating Scale. It's kind of like taking the temperature of our session today. Was it too hot or too cold? Do I need to adjust the thermostat to make you feel more comfortable? The ultimate purpose of using these forms is to make every possible effort to make our work together beneficial for you and go the way you want it to go. If something is amiss, you would be doing me the best favor if you let me know, because then I can do something about it. Would you mind doing this for me?

Those are just examples, and you have to translate the introduction into your natural way of communicating with clients. One thing that I learned over the years is that I have gotten a lot more response from clients when I have deemphasized that the SRS is about their "feelings" about the "relationship," because it is hard for folks, in general, to talk about these things. So if you want people to run out of your office shrieking, say something like, "The SRS enables you to share your innermost feelings about our relationship." Instead I have found that introductions that use a metaphor like temperature and don't mention relationship at all, or call the SRS a rating of the session itself instead of me or the relationship, yield better discussions. The SRS itself is a bit of an externalization of the alliance. It is a lot easier to mark the scales lower than to talk about it. That's the whole idea. People will indicate a concern on the SRS when they never would have brought it up otherwise. But you have you use your clinical skills here. Getting feedback on the SRS is a nuanced interpersonal process that requires you to finesse a response from clients by making them feel comfortable about offering you feedback.

A valid concern often arises regarding the high scores clients typically report on the SRS. Therapists worry that clients do not rate the SRS honestly because they don't want to hurt the therapist's feelings or because they are filling it out in the presence of the therapist. Or, in other words, clients will inflate their scores because of social desirability and/or demand characteristics. It makes sense that some would have this concern, given that the suggested cutoff is 36 out of 40 and most clients do tend to score the SRS very high.

So although these concerns are reasonable, they come from misunderstandings of both the SRS and alliance measurement in general. First, and to reiterate, there is no bad news on the SRS. It is not a measure of competence or ultimate ability to form good alliances. It is a gift from the client, actually, that allows therapists the opportunity to both alter the service and be a better therapist with that client. And, of course, unless the therapist really wants negative feedback, he or she is very unlikely to get it. So if you are striving for feedback and not putting any value on positive scores—in fact quite the opposite—then social desirability and demand characteristics don't make much logical sense. In that case, the desire to please, to be socially appropriate, would lead to a demand for lower scores, not inflated ones.

Second, all alliance measures tend to be scored high by clients. This is not just a phenomenon of the SRS but runs across alliance scales in general. So what does that mean? It could say that clients score alliance measures so high because of social desirability or demand characteristics. But clients score alliance measures high regardless of whether the therapist is present or not (Pesale & Hilsenroth, 2009). Project leader and University of Kentucky professor Jeff Reese and colleagues just confirmed this with the SRS as well (Reese et al., 2013). Clients were randomly assigned to one of three alliance feedback conditions: SRS completed in the presence of the therapist and the results discussed immediately; SRS completed alone and results discussed next session; or SRS completed alone and results not available to the therapist. No significant differences in SRS scores across the feedback conditions were found. Additionally, the analysis showed that SRS scores were not correlated with a measure of social desirability. These results indicate that alliance scores were not inflated by the presence of a therapist or by knowing that the SRS scores would be observed by the therapist.

So what do the high scores mean? My preferred interpretation is that it is just plain hard for human beings to give critical interpersonal feedback.

It's hard enough in our closest relationships! But perhaps even harder to give negative feedback to someone trying to help us, especially given the disparity in power between therapist and client, combined with any socioeconomic, ethnic, or racial differences. When was the last time you told your physician, "Listen, you're making a big mistake with me"? So we should recognize the difficulty of the task and give clients a break. It's all good. High scores are good, low scores are even better.

And it means this whole process of securing feedback comes back to—us! This includes being comfortable in our own skin when we ask for feedback, to really want it, to respond gracefully and do our best to accommodate our work to the feedback, and, finally, having an authentic desire to coax the client into a frank discussion about their preferences regarding our work with them.

The cutoff of 36 may be a bit of overkill, given that more recent data indicate that the average first-session SRS scores range from 33.5 to 33.9 and increase from there. But the importance of the alliance warrants erring on the side of caution. Moreover, exploration of the alliance in and of itself helps build the alliance. So if a client scores less than a total of 36, or less than 9 cm on any dimension on the SRS, there is a *potential* problem that should be discussed, as well as an opportunity to enhance your relationship. Given these parameters, you can do a very quick visual check and then integrate the results into the conversation.

This is not complicated or heavy-handed. There are only two choices. Either the SRS is 36 or above or not. And your actions are equally simple: Either you thank the client for the feedback and invite him or her to share any future concerns—letting him or her know it's the best favor he or she could do for you; or you thank the client for the feedback and explore why the ratings are somewhat lower, so that you can try to fit what he or she is asking for. A high rating is a good thing, but it can be difficult to interpret unless you unfold it a bit more. A lower rating is cause for celebration and can yield information that makes the difference between success and failure.

But don't stress about it. Remain open and keep encouraging the client to let you know if there's anything else you can do. But don't think for a minute that you will get critical feedback from everyone. Some clients will never do it.

Keep in mind that this is not like having work done at your car dealer and being told about the forthcoming customer survey: "Make sure you mark all the questions 'excellent' or 'extremely satisfied' or they will take it as a bad rating." Just remember that you *want* a "negative" rating, you want the client to be comfortable enough to tell you if something is wrong. So don't be the therapist depicted in Figure 2.4!

Good initial alliances that stay good portend a positive outcome, but those that start off lower and improve over time are an even more robust

Figure 2.4. How not to administer the Session Rating Scale. From "When I'm Good, I'm Very Good, But When I'm Bad I'm Better: A New Mantra for Psychotherapists," by B. Duncan and S. D. Miller, 2008, *Psychotherapy in Australia*, Nov., p. 65. Cartoon by John Wright. Copyright by John Wright. Reprinted with permission of John Wright.

predictor (Anker et al., 2010). The SRS provides a structure to systematically address the alliance, gives you a chance to fix any problems, and demonstrates that you do more than give lip service to forming good relationships. Your appreciation of any negative feedback is a powerful alliance builder.

> *Thanking and inviting:* Let me just take a second here to look at this SRS—it's kind of like a thermometer that takes the temperature of our meeting here today. Wow, great, looks like we are on the same page, that we are talking about what you think is important and you believe today's meeting was right for you. Please let me know if I get off track, because letting me know would be the biggest favor you could do for me.

Here is how it went with Connie:

Barry: Looks like we were on the right track.

Connie: This helped me a lot today. This is just what I needed.

Barry: Was there anything in particular that I should make sure I do next time that you liked about today.

Connie: I liked your guiding questions and the way you led the session.

Barry: Thanks, that's very helpful.

So the idea here is simply to say thanks and continue to invite any feedback to improve the service. Getting at what the client liked about the session can also be useful. Anything that helps a conversation about the alliance is good. For example, Connie said that she liked my guiding questions. She was very anxious at the beginning of the session and was having trouble getting started. When silence is not helping the client reflect but instead creating more tension, I tend to structure things more until things relax a bit. And that's what I did with Connie, and she liked it. As you gain experience with using the SRS, you will figure out more ways to make conversations about the alliance in a way that increases client engagement and partnership in the process.

How about when it falls below 36 or any individual scale is below 9? The only difference in your response is that you thank and explore, instead of thank and invite. Don't be expecting specific feedback or grand revelations, although they do happen from time to time. Usually the feedback is vague and general. Remember, it is hard, for nearly all of us, to give interpersonal feedback, especially critical feedback; any feedback, though, is communicating something. Just try to get at what it is. "Is there anything else I could have done differently, something I should have done more of or less of, some question or topic I should have asked but didn't?" Another useful question is, "Do you have any advice for me for next time, anything that would make it a little better?"

Thanking and exploring: Let me quickly look at this other form here that lets me know how you think we are doing. Okay, seems like it could have gone better. Thanks very much for your honesty and for giving me a chance to address what I can do differently. Was there something else I should have asked you about or should have done to make this meeting work better for you? What was missing here?

Sometimes clients say that not enough time has passed for them to know or that the score is the best they can give, and offer no explanation. Consider Harold. I thought the session went pretty well, and after administering the SRS I saw that two of the scales were below 9 cm and that the total score was 33.6.

Barry: Thanks for doing that, Harold. Looks like it could have gone better for you today. That's why this thing is great. It allows us to talk about stuff that sometimes is hard to talk about. I really appreciate you letting me know things could be better, because that allows me the chance to do better. What could I have done differently?

Harold: Well, it wasn't really bad or anything. Might just take some time.

Barry: Okay, great. Was there something else I should have asked or another topic I missed?

Harold: No, it's just that I think it will take a while for me to trust that this is going to do any good. I don't know much about this therapy stuff. I pretty much have just been seeing the psychiatrist and taking the medications.

Barry: Okay, that makes sense. So the marks on the "approach" and "something missing" aspects were a bit lower than the others. So, part of this is a time thing—so, if we are on the right track, your scores will likely go up?

Harold: Yes, I think so. After we talk a bit more about what I can do about my damn ruminations.

Barry: Gotcha. That makes perfect sense. When we get rolling more on some specific strategies, like you said you were looking for, that should increase your trust in this process?

Harold: Yes, I think so.

Barry: So we'll get on that next time for sure and we'll keep an eye on things to make sure your trust is building.

Harold: Sounds good.

When time seems to be an issue, set the expectation that the SRS score will increase as time goes on, as you are able to address anything specific the client has noted. It doesn't go this way all the time. Sometimes you just get a shrug or "I don't know." No worries. If you have a hunch about what may have led to the lower rating, now is the time to mention it and check it out with the client. Just keep the lines of communication open and continue to invite. I have had clients who say that nobody's perfect and that's the best I can do. Or they will rate me low but never let me know why, or rate me high all the way through. It's all okay. Continue to leave space for feedback, continue to want it, and many clients will take advantage of it. Even if they don't, your attention to the alliance will help secure a strong one. Clients appreciate our efforts here, especially when we do our best to accommodate their feedback. This is one of the rare areas in life where we even get points for trying.

> **Bottom Line:** *Talking about the relationship is hard; building a culture of feedback takes a concerted effort. Don't expect too much, but recognize that your authentic attention to the alliance via the SRS builds a strong partnership that will keep the client engaged through therapy's ups and downs.*

CONCLUSION

> Improving personal and organizational performance without constant feedback is like trying to pin the tail on the donkey when we're blindfolded. Only through knowing where we are, can we change where we are going.
>
> —Jim Clemmer, *Don't Wait to See the Blood*

This chapter detailed what it takes to start becoming a better therapist, the practice of PCOMS. First, there is the simple process of introducing, administering, and scoring the ORS and SRS, which involves (a) building a culture of feedback, (b) understanding that there is no bad news on the measures and viewing feedback as a gift that can only improve outcomes, (c) fitting the introduction into your own language and style, ensuring that clients understand that the ORS is designed to keep their perspective front and center and will be collaboratively used to monitor their benefit, and (d) scoring the measures. Second, there is the more clinically nuanced aspect of integrating the ORS and SRS into practice: (a) discussing the client's score in relation to the clinical cutoff and allowing the client to make sense of it, (b) connecting the client's described experience of the reason for service to his or her marks on the different scales, (c) ensuring that the client's rating represents his or her described experience (i.e., that you have a good rating on the ORS), and (d) discussing the client's score on the SRS, thanking him or her for the feedback and either inviting the sharing of any future concerns or exploring any concerns that were noted.

With the feedback culture established and the first session under your belt, the business of evidence-based practice, one client at a time begins, with the client's view of progress and the alliance really influencing what happens and making you a better therapist in the process. This is our topic for the next chapter.

CLIENTS ARE THE BEST TEACHERS: THEIR STORIES DOCUMENT OUR DEVELOPMENT

> A good action is never lost; it is a treasure laid up and guarded for the doer's need.
>
> —Edwin Markham

A gas furnace explosion when Maria was 6 years old killed both her father and sister. Her mother collapsed emotionally after the accident and spent most of her days in bed. Maria had essentially grown up without a parent and, partly as a result of that, had been repeatedly sexually abused by an uncle.

By the time I saw her, Maria was 35 and had been in therapy for most of her adult life. She held a highly responsible but unsatisfying job in a biotechnology company. Maria had tried to kill herself five times, leading to five psychiatric stays. She called her latest therapist eight or nine times a day, leaving agonized messages with the answering service, demanding to be called back. The literature on "borderlines" frequently admonishes therapists not to respond to their "manipulative" attempts to extort attention, and not to reward their "infantile neediness." So Maria's demands were rarely, if ever, met by her therapists, whose failure to respond provoked her into escalating levels of distress and self-harming. She was diagnosed borderline and was on Prozac when her discouraged, resentful, and burned-out therapist referred her, with a sense of relief, to me and an investigation I was involved in called the "impossible case project" (Duncan, Hubble, & Miller, 1997).

After consultation with my colleagues, I decided to encourage Maria's calls and nurture rather than limit our relationship. I worked hard to court Maria's favor during our first three sessions, and it wasn't easy. She sat in my office tight-lipped, twisting a handkerchief in her hands. She told me from the first session that she wanted her phone calls returned, because she only called when she was in really bad shape.

I returned her calls when I had spare time during the workday and again in the evenings after my last client, talking each time for about 15 minutes. Perhaps because I reliably called her back, she rarely called more than once or twice a day. Once, when in distress, she left a message for me after hours without leaving her number. When the service called me, I went back to my office to get her number and called her. In our sessions, she seemed to get softer and softer.

Then, after our sixth session, I went on a backpacking trip with my son, Jesse, entrusting my colleagues to cover for me. After setting up camp the first night, I felt inexplicably worried about Maria. This was before cell phones. So I hiked 4 miles back to my truck in the darkness and drove to a pay phone in a nearby town to see how she was getting along. She was okay.

That call proved to be a turning point. Afterward, Maria became proactive in therapy and outside it. She started going to church, got involved in a singles group, and signed up for additional technical training that would allow her to change jobs. Her thoughts of suicide stopped and she discontinued the antidepressant. In sessions, we talked less about how lousy she felt and more about how she could change her life. Over the next 6 months, she left her unrewarding job, where everyone knew her as a psychiatric casualty, and joined a medical missionary project in Asia.

Six months later, she wrote to let me know that things were going pretty well for her in northern Thailand.

> I picture myself in your office, just telling you stuff and you listening. Every time I called you, you called me back. It didn't always help, but you were there. And I realized that is just what a little girl would want from her daddy, what I had been missing all my life and wanting so badly. Finally, when I was 35 years old, someone gave it to me. I sure am glad I got to know what it feels like to have someone care about me in that way. It was a beautiful gift you gave me. You also made me realize how much God loves me. When you called me that weekend you went backpacking, I thought to myself, 'If a human can do that for me, then I believe what the Bible says about us all the time.' So thanks for loving me—because that's what you did.

Maria taught me to honor the client's view of the alliance—she knew that she needed a certain sort of contact to heal, and I gave it to her. That was not all I did, but it was the affectionate container for our conversations that included discussions of what she wanted to change and how she could make it happen. Maria also taught me the power to be found in simple acts of human caring. Of course, I had no idea of the connection of my actions to her desires for a loving father in her life. Within the limits of what I can ethically and personally manage, I have learned to provide as much human caring as possible.

3

HOW BEING BAD CAN
MAKE YOU BETTER

However beautiful the strategy, you should occasionally look at the
results.

—Sir Winston Churchill

Don't tell anyone, but therapists are not successful with all their clients.
You say this isn't front-page news. Then why don't we say out loud that, for
most of us, about 50% of our clients don't benefit? Why isn't there a more
systematic recognition of this fact? Clients don't get better, so the story goes,
because they are resistant, too sick, traumatized, or whatever else the latest
explanations are for a lack of change. Or (another perennial excuse), the
therapist is not masterful enough, lacks experience, or hasn't learned the
latest and greatest. Shoot the client, or shoot the therapist. Take your pick. I
pick neither. Instead, I choose to follow the wisdom of that sage psychotherapist, Mae West, who said, "When I'm good, I'm very good; but when I'm bad,
I'm better." Didn't you know that Mae West was a psychotherapist?

Mae West's famous quip, at first pass, hardly seems like words for therapists to live by but, as it turns out, they are. By identifying clients who are not
responding to your usual fare, when, in other words, outcome is bad, you have
the chance to make it better in two ways: First, by changing something about

http://dx.doi.org/10.1037/14392-003
On Becoming a Better Therapist, Second Edition: Evidence-Based Practice One Client at a Time, by B. L. Duncan
Copyright © 2014 by the American Psychological Association. All rights reserved.

the therapy that turns things around and, second, if things don't turn around, by moving clients to different providers or venues of service that better suit the possibility for change. Being bad, or when clients are not progressing, offers you the opportunity to do your very best work, to be even better with both that client and with everyone who follows.

This chapter details the use of the Partners for Change Outcome Management System (PCOMS) in the second session and beyond, both when there is change and when there isn't. Becoming a better therapist requires you to identify clients who are not benefiting, keeping them engaged while you collaboratively brainstorm what can be done differently, and then, if the lack of change persists despite your best efforts, releasing them to other options.

TRACKING OUTCOMES WITH PCOMS

Advice is judged by results, not by intentions.
—Marcus Tullius Cicero

At the second and subsequent sessions, PCOMS provides the evidence upon which you base your practice. You and the client monitor the amount and rate of change on the Outcome Rating Scale (ORS) that has occurred since the prior visit as well as since intake. The longer therapy continues without measurable change, the greater the likelihood of dropout and/or poor outcome. In short, the scores are used to engage the client in a discussion about progress, and more importantly, what should be done differently if there isn't any.

There are only two possibilities: Either the client is improving or not; the ORS score is increasing or it's not. A way to understand the amount of change that are you are hoping for is via a statistical metric known as the *reliable change index* (RCI). The RCI indicates change that is greater than chance, error, or maturation of the client. The RCI on the ORS is 6. The RCI is just a benchmark that provides an easy way to know if you are on the right track. Change that both exceeds the RCI and crosses the clinical cutoff (25 on the ORS) is considered *clinically significant* (Jacobson & Truax, 1991). Reliable change is sometimes called *improved*, and clinically significant change is at times referred to as *recovered*.

There are a few options available to track outcome with your clients. You can note the client's intake score in your progress note and compare the current session ORS with the previous one you have in the client file, or you can plot the scores on paper-and-pencil graphs or with Excel so you can see change or lack thereof over time. Another option is the web-based PCOMS systems, which graph and compare the client's progress with the expected

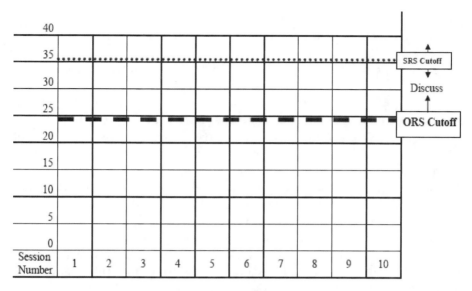

Figure 3.1. The ORS/SRS Graph. ORS = Outcome Rating Scale; SRS = Session Rating Scale. *Note:* Download a free working copy at https://heartandsoulof change.com

treatment response (ETR) of clients with the same intake score (the mean trajectory based on over 400,000 administrations of the ORS). The first two options are free (Figure 3.1 depicts the graph that is part of the free download at https://heartandsoulofchange.com); the web-based options are not. They are described in Chapter 5.

There is definitely a value added to plotting the scores or displaying the computer-generated graphs. Graphs provide a visual component to the feedback process that many clients find helpful. In one glance, just as the client's initial ORS score tells you how the client is viewing his or her life, a graph tells the story of the client's progress in therapy. It offers an additional way to focus on the client's benefit and what may need to happen if there isn't any. Graphing, as will be discussed in Chapter 4, seems indispensable when working with a couple or family, helping to manage multiple viewpoints about change while offering a method to discuss what the similarities and differences mean.

Many clients will complete the ORS in the waiting room, and some will even plot their scores on the graphs and greet you discussing the implications. Using a scale that is simple to score and interpret invites clients into the process of monitoring.

Recall the quote from Orlinsky, Rønnestad, and Willutzki (2004) in Chapter 1 that boils down more than 1,000 studies about the process of psychotherapy into one word: *participation*. Anything that increases client participation is likely to have a beneficial impact on outcome.

When Things Are Changing: When You're Good, You're Very Good

When ORS scores increase—in Ms. West's words, when you're good—a crucial step to being very good is to empower the change by helping clients see any gains as a consequence of their own efforts, perhaps even as a part of a newly emerging identity. This requires an exploration of clients' perception of the relationship between their own efforts and the occurrence of change (Duncan, Solovey, & Rusk, 1992); it is also helpful to encourage clients to reflect about the meaning of the change in the context their unfolding life story. At the least, it is important that clients come to view the change as resulting from something they did and can repeat in the future.

Even if clients resolutely attribute change to luck, fate, your expertise, or a medication, they can still be asked to consider in detail: (a) how they took advantage of what was offered by others, (b) what they did to use the changes to their benefit, (c) what they will do in the future to ensure their gains remain in place, and (d) how the changes reflect new chapters in their lives. The point here is that it is helpful for clients to see that, although other factors were involved, the change was a result of some inner or outer action that they precipitated.

Helping clients take credit for steps in the right direction casts them in their rightful roles as the main characters in their stories of change, the heroes or heroines of their own life journeys. You shine a spotlight on any accomplishments and request that the client take a bow for his or her creativity, courage, and good ideas. Basking in the limelight of success keeps the positive performances coming. Recall the retiree, Harold,[1] from the last chapter: Harold made rapid improvements and by the fifth session had made significant gains, scoring a 23.4.

> Barry: *(holding the graph)* Harold, looks like things are definitely looking up. Your score is up 9 points over when you came in—a reliable change, which simply means that it is greater than chance and a change that is likely to stand the test of time.
>
> Harold: Things are definitely better.

---

[1] The client vignettes illustrating the use of PCOMS are accurate depictions of what is possible with adding systematic client feedback to clinical practice. All clients, however, will not respond similarly, nor will all psychotherapies end so cleanly. In addition, some clients will not be interested in the measures or in discussing them. Moreover, PCOMS is not a panacea for all the complexity inherent to working with people in distress but rather simply identifies who is and who is not benefiting. The rest is up to you. That said, the examples are representative of most clients' responses to PCOMS when it is delivered in a collaborative way by an authentic therapist trying to be helpful.

Barry:	Why do you think that is?
Harold:	Well, a lot of reasons really. For one, I have really cut my load— I gave up my role as president of the homeowners' association and we are looking to sell our house and get into a condo. The house is a big pain—always something to do or going wrong.
Barry:	Sounds like you are making some decisions to really make your life more manageable.
Harold:	Definitely. And I am working hard not to make a mountain out of a molehill! I'm using the cognitive strategies we discussed and I really like the "task focusing" when I start to feel panicky about anything.
Barry:	Okay, you have taken action to lighten your load, and you have developed coping skills that enable you to show the anxiety who's boss!

Another way to focus on the client's efforts is to make "before-and-after" distinctions. The idea is to encourage client reflection and to distinguish between the way things were *before* the change and how things are now, *after* the change. This invites clients to explore the significance of their actions and tell a different story about their lives—one of triumph, enlightenment, and tenacity. The change itself is a landmark on the landscape of the client's life—something that he or she can always point to as the place in the journey where a different path was taken. At its best, fleshing out all the nuances of success creates a newfound identity of wisdom and competence gained from the school of hard knocks.

Here is how it went with Harold.

Harold:	Yeah, I guess I did finally step up here and do something about the stuff that was getting me down. I didn't think that ever in a million years I would have even considered leaving the homeowners' association or selling the house.
Barry:	You did really step up—that's a good way to say it. You weren't going to take this thing lying down anymore. Sounds like a bit of a new you has emerged.
Harold:	I think so. After all, I am retired and I need to start acting like it. I worked hard as an engineer for many years, always a stickler for details, making sure that every *i* was dotted and every *t* crossed—and driving myself nuts when they weren't. But I guess that isn't necessarily the best way to approach everyday life.
Barry:	Okay, I think I am getting this, but can you say a little more about what is different about you?

Harold: Sure. I was so organized and so concerned about how every-thing was going to play out that I didn't spend much time actu-ally living my life. Now I am doing that. I find myself really liking a slower pace and being more in the present, like we talked about.

Barry: Any example come to mind that illustrates the new you?

Harold: I built my daughter a birdhouse over the weekend and what I would have done is obsessed about doing it so much that I wouldn't have noticed myself even doing the work of it. I'd be so into thinking how the next step should be done that I wouldn't have appreciated the fun in doing the current step I was working on. It sounds kind of clichéd, but I like being in the moment and the joy that exists there. Not like I am going all Zen or anything!

This is an exciting and gratifying process to behold—a new client iden-tity constructed or a new chapter added. When it happens, you can stick a fork in them—because they're done. Harold and I continued to empower the changes and discuss possible setbacks until Harold reached a plateau, or where his ORS scores stayed at the same level for a couple of sessions. We discussed spacing out the sessions or ending therapy, and which option Harold felt more comfortable with. Benefit represented on the ORS never means that it is time to throw the client out but rather is a catalyst to discuss stepping down services, spacing them out, or terminating them altogether. Everything is transparent and negotiable. Harold wanted to space out his sessions but continue to come to therapy. He said he didn't feel confident enough yet to stop. I asked him how long he would need to maintain his gains before he would feel confident to stop seeing me. Harold thought that 3 months would do it. He was right. We scheduled the next session in 2 weeks, then 3 weeks the next two times, and then scheduled the next ses-sion 1 month out. Harold terminated at that session, feeling ready to go at it alone and comfortable to call me if he wanted.

When clients reach a plateau or what may be the maximum benefit they will derive from therapy, it is time to start planning for continued recovery outside of therapy. As illustrated with Harold, this could mean just reducing the frequency of meetings and continuing to monitor the client's goals. For others, it could mean referral to self-help groups, peer supports, or other com-munity resources. Although the overwhelming majority of clients are ready to move on once their distress has been reduced enough for them to see a clearing, a few will want to stay on. Consequently, it is also useful to include a culture of recovery in your work. This simply means conveying the attitude that there is a beginning and an end to therapy and that recovery is a lifelong journey that continues outside of therapy.

If clients are not stepped down after they have reached maximum benefit, the graph can start to look like a saw with ORS scores rising and falling with the everyday vicissitudes of life—the ORS becomes an emotional thermometer and therapy becomes an ongoing commentary on life events. When the ORS represents life in general instead of connecting the client's perception of his or her life to the purpose of the service, problems can ensue. Clients can walk away feeling less empowered to handle life's ups and downs, believing themselves to be reliant on the therapy. Ongoing service in the absence of continued benefit can have other negative effects as well—more on that later.

On the flip side, the client may stop therapy before he or she reaches maximum benefit. In this scenario, the client's change is steep (according to the graph) and he or she discontinues before the plateau occurs. Although this scenario or what is called *underutilization* is not as big a problem as *overutilization* (continuing without benefit or after maximum benefit has been achieved), it is cause for conversation with the client. Many clients are ready to bolt once they experience some relief from the problem. This is fine and perfectly understandable. However, they can experience more change if they hang out for a little while longer, for one or two more sessions. In our Norway Feedback Trial, we found that the most effective therapists had a few more sessions, about one to two more than less effective therapists on average. Other research also supports that clients tend to benefit by additional sessions (e.g., Howard, Kopta, Krause, & Orlinsky, 1986). So it makes sense to say something like this after you have empowered the change and attributed it to the client's efforts:

> Great. So glad things are moving in the right direction. A lot of people are ready to pull up stakes and move on once they have made some gains, and that is perfectly okay. But it also may make some sense to come back a time or two just to further consolidate the gains and form a plan for the future. Your call, totally. What do you think?

> **Bottom Line:** *The ORS is at its best when the client sees it as a reflection of his or her life viewed through the lens of what psychotherapy can offer. When things are better, you can capitalize on the noted change by empowering the client to take ownership of the change and his or her contribution to it, sometimes culminating in a newfound identity of mastery over the presenting concerns. When scores plateau, it doesn't mean catapulting the client out of therapy; rather, it's time to discuss stepping down services or termination.*

When Things Are Not Changing—Checkpoint Conversations (When You're Bad, You're Better)

A more important discussion occurs when ORS scores are not increasing. The ORS gives clients a voice in all decisions that affect their care, including whether continuing in therapy with the current provider is in their best interest. ORS scores are never an indication of therapist ineffectiveness, absolute or otherwise, but rather an expression of the benefit the client is reporting from the services provided—for this pairing of client and therapist. When the ORS is not demonstrating change, it allows both interested parties to reflect about the implications of continuing a process that is yielding little or no benefit. The intent is to support practices that are working and challenge those that don't appear to be helpful. The conversation with clients who are not benefiting begins with talking about whether something different should be done to identifying what can be done differently, and progresses to doing something different, and ultimately to referral if change does not happen.

> Okay, so things haven't changed since the last time we talked. How do you make sense of that? Should we be doing something different here, or should we continue on course steady as we go? If we are going to stay on the same course, how long should we go before getting worried? When will we know when to say "when"?

Later sessions gain increasing significance and warrant additional action—what we have called *checkpoint conversations* and *last-chance discussions* (Duncan & Sparks, 2002). In a typical outpatient setting, checkpoint conversations are usually conducted between the third and sixth meetings, and last-chance discussions are initiated between the sixth and ninth sessions. This simply means that by the third to sixth encounter most clients who benefit from services usually show it on the ORS, and if change is not noted by then, the client is at a risk for a negative outcome. Ditto for the sixth to ninth session, except that, then, everything just mentioned has an exclamation mark. Different settings—such as inpatient or residential, case management, and other services that tend to be longer-term—will have different checkpoint and last-chance numbers.

Determining these highlighted points of conversation requires only that you collect data. The calculations are simple, and directions follow later in the chapter. Establishing these two points helps evaluate whether a client needs a referral or other changes based on a typical successful client in your specific setting. The same thing can be accomplished much more precisely by the web-based systems that calculate the expected treatment response or trajectory of change based on the database of ORS administrations. It is safe to say, however, that the three-to-six- and six-to-nine-session benchmarks are pretty accurate for most outpatient psychotherapy settings because, even if clients are in therapy for longer periods of time, they have likely *begun* to change by these benchmarks (e.g., see Baldwin, Berkeljon, Atkins, Olsen, and Nielsen, 2009). Keep in mind that the two identified points of action are a call for conversation and not for rote referral, termination, or anything else.

If change has not occurred by the checkpoint conversation or, in other words, "when you're bad," this is your opportunity to be even better. The first-line approach is to focus on the alliance. Simply go through the Session Rating Scale (SRS) item by item. Alliance problems are a significant contributor to a lack of progress. Sometimes it is useful to say something like, "It doesn't seem like we are getting anywhere. Let me go over the items on this SRS to make sure you are getting exactly what you are looking for from me and our time together." Going through the SRS and eliciting client responses in detail can help you and the client get a better sense of what may not be working.

A common alliance problem emerges when the clients' goals don't fit with our sense of what they need. This may be especially true if clients come to us with certain emotionally charged diagnoses or presenting problems. Consider 23-year-old Carly, who was about to be evicted from her apartment and hospitalized—her landlord was threatening to call the police because of health violations that would likely result in a hospital admission.

Carly was referred to me at this time of crisis, and I was in full-press hospitalization-prevention mode. Her mom, Angie, a nurse, called me and gave me the rundown of her diagnosis (schizophrenia) and all the gory details about her last hospitalization being precipitated by a refusal to take medication and an emergency admission after drinking bleach. Angie was clear in her perspective that my job was to convince Carly to take her medication. With that hanging over my head, and with my own missionary zeal to keep Carly out of the hospital, we met for the first session.

Carly conceded that her apartment was a health hazard and her landlord could call the police at any moment and that her mom was freaked out about her medication, but she didn't much want to talk about any of that. Nor did she want to talk about the voices she heard. Instead, she expressed a desire to go to school. I admit, as much as I know about the importance of the alliance and working on client goals, I was quietly dismissive of this desire. After all, it seemed that the pending eviction and hospitalization were far more pressing. So therapy with Carly floundered. After starting out quite engaged, she settled into a more passive stance and answered questions as briefly as possible. Carly was at risk for dropout or a negative outcome— perhaps the hospitalization that I was desperate to prevent.

Although she usually reported that everything was going swimmingly, at the third session, a discrepancy began to emerge on the goals scale of the SRS. Although she gave a 9 or above on the rest of the scales, she only gave a 7.6 to the goals scale. During the checkpoint conversation, at the end of the fourth session, I reviewed her responses on the SRS in hopes of addressing problems that have been missed or gone unacknowledged. When I queried about her rating of the goals, Carly repeated her desire to go to school in nearly a whisper.

I looked at the SRS and off came the blinders! When I finally asked Carly about her goal, she related a story about always wanting to be a chemist. She sparkled when she spoke of her first chemistry set she received for Christmas when she was 10 years old. Carly excelled in school in the sciences and often won the yearly science fair awards. Noticing that it was the most I'd ever heard her talk, I began asking Carly more about her love of chemistry and what she wanted to do with it. I also put the brakes on efforts to get her to clean her apartment. I did ask the landlord for some more time after I obtained Carly's permission to do so.

I turned my attention to what I should have done from the get-go—what it would take to get Carly in school. We explored several local options, as well as online possibilities. In the context of these discussions, Carly brought up her meds, which led to an exploration of her propensity to cut them off cold turkey and how counterproductive that was. I offered to work with her and the prescribing doctor to wean her off one medication at a time, which she accepted. Carly started an online course.

Carly's SRS score improved on the goal scale and her ORS score increased dramatically. After a while, she started attending a community college and, ultimately, after I stopped seeing her, she finished her degree at a nearby university. She cleaned her apartment as well, in anticipation of a classmate's visit for work on a class project. It wasn't all smooth sailing; there were a few storms to weather, and I saw her periodically over a long period of time. But her involvement with school successfully resolved many of the concerns her landlord and mom had. And addressing her desire to reduce her medications increased her adherence to the one she continued to take. Walking the path cut by client goals often reveals alternative routes to improvement that would have never been discovered otherwise. And your appreciation for and flexible accommodation of any negative feedback are powerful alliance builders—they really made the difference for Carly and me.

Back to the ORS: A lack of progress at this stage may simply indicate that you need to try something different[2]—nothing specific may come of your conversation with the client about the alliance. Don't worry about that. Just making the effort to discuss the alliance can yield dividends. Doing something different can take as many forms as there are clients: inviting others from the client's support system, using a team or another professional, a different conceptualization of the problem or another psychotherapy approach,

---

[2]Doing something different when current solutions are not working is a very simple but elegant idea from the interactional approach of the Mental Research Institute (MRI; Watzlawick, Weakland, & Fisch, 1974). The MRI posited that problems arise from the continual application of ineffective solutions. A client who is not responding to a clinician's usual solutions identified by PCOMS allows the application of this simple idea to therapy. Identifying clients at risk and then doing something different, exemplifying the notion of "if at first you don't succeed, try something else."

or referring to another therapist, religious advisor, peer services, or self-help group—whatever seems to be of value to the client. Here the main goal is to identify and discuss what the options may be. Of course, if any option in particular really resonates with the client, that strategy or idea is then implemented, and progress is monitored via the ORS.

Consider Matt, a 20-something software wizard, who because of a recent promotion was frequently on the road troubleshooting customer problems. He loved his job. Even so, traveling had become an ordeal. Matt had a personal problem that made flying unpleasant—an inability to urinate in public restrooms, especially on planes. At the outset, it caused only mild discomfort and was solved by monitoring his fluid intake and repeated visits to his bathroom before leaving home. In time, though, the problem began to cause intense apprehension before each trip, excruciating feelings of pressure in his bladder while on the plane, and sometimes hair-raising panic attacks. One time his inability to "go" on a long trip to the West Coast resulted in a retention episode and a trip to the ER for a catheter—a demeaning and demoralizing experience that only increased the episodes of panic in anticipation of travel. Hopeless and demoralized, the young man considered changing jobs. As a last resort, he decided to seek psychotherapy.

Matt and I seemed to hit it off, and the SRS confirmed that we had a good start. He was particularly glad that he could finally talk about his difficulty, an embarrassing problem that often has other connotations about one's masculinity. Matt didn't have any particular ideas, definitely communicated some urgency for resolution, and looked to me for guidance, so I suggested some possibilities. In short order, he was helped to implement relaxation and "self-talk" cognitive–behavioral strategies, which he diligently practiced in session. As agreed, he employed them preceding his next trip and while on board the plane. The results were far from encouraging. The problem intensified and his sense of shame along with it. More alarming, his mood became decidedly hopeless.

Matt was at significant risk for a negative outcome: either dropping out or persisting in therapy without benefit. At the third session, when the ORS reflected no change, I went over the SRS and we settled on the item "The therapist's approach is a good fit for me." Matt hesitated, so I asked him, "Matt, in your heart of hearts, do you think the strategies we are using to address this situation are going to make a difference for you?" He quietly said no. It motivated us to brainstorm a range of possibilities for the remainder of the session. During this exchange, Matt expressed in no uncertain terms how much his problem was interfering with his work. The possibility that he'd have to endure any extended separation from his own bathroom had become almost unthinkable. He became quite animated, even angry, in conspicuous contrast to the passive resignation that had characterized previous sessions.

When one of us said the words "pissed off," we both broke into raucous laughter. A possibility was discovered.

Later in the visit, I suggested that there were a lot of ways to tackle this problem, that changing how one thinks during the problem is a way, but another is changing what one feels. I wondered aloud whether instead of responding with hopelessness when the predicament occurred, Matt could work himself up into righteous anger about how the problem was sabotaging his life. Matt liked that idea and added, since he was a retro rock-and-roll buff, that he could also sing Tom Petty's "Won't Back Down" during his tirades at the toilet. From then on, he permitted himself, when standing before the urinal, to become thoroughly incensed, "pissed off," and somewhat amused. His problem soon resolved.

Of course, this kind of collaborative, creative process could have happened with any therapist working with Matt. The difference is that the use of the ORS spotlighted the lack of early change. Impossible to dismiss, it brought the risk of a negative outcome front and center. Without the findings from the ORS, I would likely have continued with the same strategies for several more sessions, hoping that these reasonable methods would eventually take hold. As it was, the evidence obtained through the measure pushed me, and Matt, to explore different options.

Finally (and this is especially helpful when things seem to be mired down at the checkpoint session and your usual approach is not getting results), it is worth exploring the client's sensibilities about what needs to happen— or what I have called the "client's theory of change" (Duncan et al., 1992; Duncan & Miller, 2000), an idea that has served me well. Chapter 1 emphasized, in the section on model/technique factors, the importance of both the client's and therapist's belief in whatever approach is chosen. An approach that rings true with the client will likely increase the expectation for change as well as participation. The client's theory of change unfolds from a conversation structured by your curiosity about the client's ideas, attitudes, and speculations about change, starting somewhat like this:

> Many times people have a pretty good hunch about not only what is causing a problem but also what will resolve it. Do you have a theory of how change is going to happen here? Or perhaps something that has worked for you in the past? Or even something that you think might be helpful that you heard about from family, friends, or the media?

Consider Ken, a 35-year-old construction supervisor who was convinced that he was going crazy because panic attacks were becoming ever more intrusive. I thought we connected well, and Ken indicated so on the SRS. Ken told me that he didn't have a clue what the panic episodes were about or what to do about them. The only thing that he was doing that was working was drinking, and he didn't see that as a good way to cope. Ken looked to me for some suggestions, something he could do to manage the anxiety. Trying to address his request as well as his perspective about my role, I called up my training in cognitive–behavioral therapy and strategic therapy. We tried a combination of relaxation training, challenging the beliefs that led to the panic, and some strategic monitoring (symptom prescription). But nothing happened, and none of these approaches seemed to resonate with Ken.

So, in the fourth meeting, I went over the SRS but lingered on the "approach" scale and asked Ken about his ideas about how he could tackle the panic attacks. Ken said that maybe he could try and understand what they were about, an idea his wife believed to be important. Ken shared that in tough times he always talked to his dad, but his dad had passed away some 6 months before. He noted that he felt alone in his struggles, although he knew that really wasn't true because his wife was supportive and he had some good friends. As I'm sure you would have done, I asked him if he believed there to be a connection between his father's death, his feeling of aloneness, and the panic. Ken replied with tears, and a quiet yes.

A different kind of discussion ensued, drawing on my existential training, of not only Ken's confrontation of his own mortality but also the incredible dread that accompanies the realization of our essential aloneness in the world. A new theory of change evolved, one that seemed to make a lot of sense within the four big existential givens: death, freedom, isolation, and meaninglessness. I bounced these ideas off Ken, and it made a difference. Ken found these conversations useful, his ORS scores increased, and his panic attacks subsided. This story, of course, says nothing about the absolute value of cognitive–behavioral therapy, strategic, or existentially informed therapy—all therapy approaches provide useful ideas to pursue. Rather, Ken's therapy illustrates that exploring the client's ideas about change, perspectives that resonate with the client, and you, can enable different, more fruitful directions to emerge. This is an important issue to your development as a therapist, and I'll pick it up again in Chapter 5. And, again, the conversation was stimulated by the open recognition of a lack of benefit identified by the ORS.

Potholes

Sometimes a client's scores will drop precipitously. In this case, the first order of business is getting the client's explanation of what has happened. Is the drop related to the reason for therapy—a deterioration in an ongoing issue—or is it the *pothole phenomenon*, where some recent event is holding sway over the client's rating? If it's a deterioration, then this signals the necessity to have a heart-to-heart about what needs to happen differently to quickly turn things around. Refer to the prior discussion about the lack of change, although a drop in the ORS does increase the urgency.

But a pothole effect warrants different action. The pothole metaphor goes like this: The client hit a pothole on the way to the session and got a flat tire. It was raining cats and dogs, and the client's nice clothes were soaked and soiled. Then the client was in such a hurry that police radar caught him or her, and so on. You get the idea. The pothole effect is where the events of the day, rather than how the week has gone related to the reasons for service, overly influence the client's response on the ORS. If the client reports it is a pothole, then ask him or her to redo the ORS looking at the week in general and related to the reasons for therapy. If the event or events seem to trump the original reasons for therapy, then, of course, go with it. Just reconnect the issues at hand to the open spaces on the ORS, as discussed in the previous chapter. Be cautious about turning everyday life events, the ups and downs of being a human being, into therapy issues.

For example, I was seeing Keesha, a strong-willed 15-year-old, about academic problems as well as her rather enthusiastic shouting matches with her stepmother. Things were going well, and we had already discussed spacing things out. So I was surprised one day to see a very upset Keesha, and even more so when I totaled her ORS score to a 12.2. When I asked her what was up, Keesha told a very troubling story of double betrayal. She had walked out of fifth-period class for a restroom break and discovered her best friend and boyfriend kissing. After commiserating with Keesha and discussing what she intended to do, I asked her if that "double whammy" was what accounted for her low score on the ORS. When she said yes, I asked her to redo the ORS relative to how it has gone since I saw her last regarding the two reasons she entered therapy: her grades and her relationship with her stepmom. So I dealt with the situation but refocused the therapy, and the ORS, to the task at hand.

When Things Are Not Changing—Last-Chance Discussion (When You're Bad, You're Better)

If you and the client have implemented different possibilities and the client is still without benefit, it is time for the last-chance discussion. As the name implies, there is some urgency for something different because most clients who benefit have already achieved change by this point, and there is significant risk for a negative conclusion. A metaphor I like is that of the therapist and client driving into a desert and running on empty, when a sign appears that says "last chance for gas." The metaphor depicts the necessity of stopping and discussing the implications of continuing without the client achieving the desired change. At the very least, supervision or a cotherapist should be considered. And that, too, can turn things around. There is no last chance for the client, just for this particular therapist–client pairing.

Again, this is not a subtle dig at long-term work with clients. A longer course of sessions spaced out over longer periods of time can make great clinical sense at times (as it did with Carly). Some clients do take longer, no doubt. However, continuing to see clients in the absence of benefit is another story altogether, a matter discussed below.

Here are several questions to reflect about in last-chance circumstances. The longer the therapy goes without change, the quicker the last option—failing successfully—should be exercised.

- What does the client say about the lack of change? Remember that you are in this thing together.
- Is the client engaged in purposive work to address the problems at hand? In other words, what about the alliance and the SRS? In both the client's and your heart of hearts, do you think this therapy with you is going to make a difference?
- What have you done differently so far? What of the identified options have you already employed?
- What can be done differently now? We all have limits. Have you exhausted your repertoire?
- What other resources can be rallied, both from your support system and the client's? How can you bring in fresh blood—new ideas and directions?
- Is it time to fail successfully?

Sherry had pretty much been through the mill when I saw her, in therapy for much of her 31 years. She had been diagnosed borderline and had a history of trauma and abuse. Sherry thought she had pretty much dealt with all that and was moving her life forward—she now lived independently and had started school. Her initial ORS was 22.4, and Sherry was looking to address her self-described binge eating and obesity. Given that she reported some success with Overeaters Anonymous (OA) and journaling, drawing upon solution-focused ideas, I worked with her to expand what was working while hoping to diminish what wasn't. Things were worse for her at night, and that was when the cravings came to call.

Sherry's initial SRS was only a 31.2. When I explored further, she explained that I didn't really know her and it would take time. True to form, I suggested that the SRS could track that for us, and the score should go up as I got to know her better. Sherry agreed. But it didn't go up much. At the checkpoint conversation, there was no change on the ORS, so I went over the SRS. But no new information was gleaned. Sherry thought we should continue with the strategies we were doing—taking what worked for her during the day and employing those methods at night in conjunction with her OA group. Over the next three sessions, we worked to fine-tune her strategies. Since being around people and relational support were critical, we discussed more concrete ways to involve people at night, such as online chats and e-mail, phone calls and texts, and evening OA meetings.

At the sixth session, however, there was still no change, and the SRS had improved only to 32.8. It was definitely time for something different. We discussed the questions listed above and frankly addressed the possibility of a referral, but Sherry said she wanted to try a consult first. So we did. I arranged for a consult with one of my colleagues while I watched via a camera feed to a monitor. Having someone else interview your clients is a wonderful eye-opening experience, revealing how easy it is to get into conversational ruts with clients. That's why "new blood" can be so helpful. It wasn't 10 minutes into the session with my colleague that Sherry reported that her eating problems were likely related to her protecting herself from getting into a relationship, adding parenthetically that she was a lesbian.

I asked Sherry if she wanted me to refer her to my colleague or perhaps a therapist who specialized in working with gay/lesbian issues. But she declined. Sherry added that she knew I was gay-friendly from the referral source, but she hadn't thought her sexuality was relevant to what we were working on. The new focus made a difference. We discussed Sherry's loneliness and its relationship to her eating problems, and we mapped out a plan to involve her in situations more apt to yield potential romantic partners. Having these potential encounters gave her more to look forward to and increased her involvement in OA and exercise activities. The ORS scores increased over the cutoff, as did the SRS scores.

As noted with Sherry, the last-chance discussion is the time when a referral and other available resources should be discussed. If you have created a feedback culture from the beginning, then this conversation will not be a surprise. Rarely is there justification for continuing to work with clients who have not achieved change in a period typical for the majority of clients seen by a particular practitioner or setting. But rarely is not never. These situations are highly idiosyncratic and should be negotiated on an individual basis. The ORS helps keep us honest and addresses the lack of change transparently. These are conversations that I never had before I started using the ORS and SRS.

Why should we seriously consider moving the client on at this point? Recall how much of the variability of outcomes is attributed to the therapist and the nature and quality of the alliance between the client and the therapist. If we hold people in therapy with us, we could actually *be* the problem, because they might be better served with someone else. Although talking about a lack of progress often allows you to snatch victory from the jaws of defeat, it is still impossible for all of your clients to benefit. There is, however, a way that you can be useful even with clients who are not responding at this point. Where in the past I might have felt like a failure when I wasn't effective with a client, I now view such times as opportunities to stop being an impediment to the client's change process. When I'm bad, I'm better. Now the work is successful both when the client achieves change and when, in the absence of change, I get out of the way.

Failing Successfully: When I'm Bad, I'm Better

As illustrated with Carly, Matt, Ken, and Sherry, it's often possible to change course and make the therapy experience far more productive for clients. But what happens when you have implemented new or different strategies and the therapy is still failing to produce benefit? What if you have exhausted all you know to do? This can be singularly confusing if the therapeutic alliance is strong—after all, referring someone whom you don't like or doesn't like you is likely a relief, but when you genuinely connect with the person, letting go can be more difficult. It may be hard to believe that stopping a great relationship is the right thing to do, and I have had my own doubts about it. In my career, there have been many memorable clients who taught me invaluable lessons about the work that I love. One of the greatest lessons I learned, though, did not occur until I had over 24 years of experience—and it made me a fan of Mae West.

Eighteen-year-old Alina sought help because she felt completely devastated. In her estimation, she'd lost everything she'd worked her whole life to achieve. After captaining her high school volleyball team, commanding the first position on the debating team, and being named valedictorian, she'd won a full scholarship to Yale. She was the pride of her Guatemalan community—proof of the many benefits that her parents had envisioned would come with living in the United States.

Her unqualified success unraveled during her first semester away from home and the insulated environment in which she'd excelled. She began hearing voices. After a visit to the university counseling center, Alina was admitted to a psychiatric unit and dosed with antipsychotics. Despondent, she threw herself down a stairwell, prompting her parents to bring her home. Alina returned home in utter confusion, still hearing voices, and with her self-image badly eroded. Besides seeing herself as a failure and major disappointment to her family, she believed she'd let down everyone else in her tight-knit community.

I was the 20th therapist that the family had called, and the first who agreed to see Alina without medication, a precondition she imposed. From the start, it looked as though we hit it off famously. Her investigation on the Internet had revealed my consumer-driven philosophy and my leanings away from pharmaceutical solutions as first-line interventions, both of which scored high marks with Alina. For my part, I admired her humility and intelligence. I was especially taken by her spunk in standing up to psychiatric discourse and asserting her preferences about treatment. I couldn't wait to be useful to Alina and get her back on track. When I administered the ORS, Alina scored a 4, the lowest score I had ever seen.

We discussed at length her experience of demoralization—how the episodes of hearing voices and confusion robbed her of her dreams, and how her years of hard work had yielded nothing. I did what I usually found to be helpful: I listened, commiserated, validated, and worked hard to mobilize Alina's resilience to begin anew.

But nothing happened. By the third session, she remained unchanged despite my best efforts. The therapy was going nowhere fast—a score of 4 was a rude reminder of just how badly therapy was progressing. At this checkpoint session, I went over the SRS with her and, unlike many, Alina was specific about what was missing and revealed that she wanted me to be more active; so I was. She wanted ideas about what to do about the voices, so I provided them—thought stopping, guided imagery, content analysis. But no change ensued, and she was increasingly at risk for a negative outcome. Alina told me she had read about hypnosis on the Internet and thought that might help. I was around in the 1980s, when you couldn't escape hypnosis training, so I approached Alina from a couple of different hypnotic angles—offering both embedded suggestions and stories intended to build her immunity to the voices. She responded with deep trances and gave high ratings on the SRS. But—and this is a very big but—the ORS remained a paltry 4.

At the last-chance discussion, we discussed what we had done and what was left to do. One thing we hadn't done was to involve her family, which Alina always had put the kibosh on. I brought it up again because it was all that seemed left to do; I had definitely exhausted my repertoire. I knew we needed fresh blood. After Alina again refused family involvement, we discussed the possibility of a referral but settled instead on a consultation with a team of therapists (led by Jacqueline Sparks). Generally, I observe consults with another therapist conducting the session via the monitor, but Alina wanted me to be in the room. As is often the case when you bring new people in the mix, the conversation with Jacqueline introduced considerations that I hadn't thought of and one seemed especially important because it really brought Alina to life.

Our sessions had been characterized by long silences and rather cryptic conversations, but when Alina started talking about the sequence of events after she arrived at Yale, that all changed. Alina told the story of her first semester and how she realized that she was "a 10-year-old trapped in an 18-year-old body," that all the other women were going out with men and she was this frightened child. She called herself "socially retarded" and surprisingly expressed anger and frustration with her parents and community for sheltering her so much. Her reluctance to involve her family finally made sense. Jacqueline and the team commented on the "family differentiation" issue, and an agreement was reached that it seemed important to pursue.

After Alina rated the encounter very high on the SRS and the session ended, I commented on how well the session went and how much more animated Alina seemed. I asked if it made more sense for her to pick up on the ideas with Jacqueline. Alina responded, "No way. You and I can go from here." Since we had some fresh ideas to pursue, I agreed. And we did for a couple sessions. No progress, though—her ORS score remained firmly fixed at a 4.

Now what? We were at the ninth session, well beyond the number of visits clients typically require for the start of change in my practice. After collecting data for several years (more about that later), I knew that 75% of the clients who benefited from their work with me would show it by the third session. Ninety-eight percent who profited would do so by the sixth. Considering these results, was it right to continue seeing Alina? Was it ethical?

Despite our mutual admiration society, it wasn't right to continue. A good relationship in the absence of benefit is a good definition of dependence. I shared my concern that her dream would be in jeopardy if she continued seeing me. This session was videorecorded, and if you were to watch the video, you would be likely struck, as many are, by the decided lack of fun that both Alina and I had during this discussion. We look like two depressed peas in a pod—so much so that people sometimes ask if I am intentionally mirroring Alina for joining purposes. Not even close: In the video I am simply bummed out, like Alina, about her lack of change and the ending of our relationship—breaking up is hard to do. And, frankly, I was nervous. In fact, watching this video is embarrassing. I said "you know" 17 times in the snippets that follow (edited out, thank goodness). But I knew I needed to do it nevertheless. We look like two folks who have just lost their best friend—there are long silences punctuated by deep sighs.

Barry: Wow, still no real change.

Alina: (shakes head)

(long pause)

Barry: Okay, all right (looking at the graph). Well, now, let's see, we need to talk about this because this really concerns me, when I'm seeing people as long as we've been seeing each other and nothing is really happening as a result of it. So, we need to discuss what maybe some options are about that. We've tried a lot of different kinds of things and we've talked about a lot of things, and it doesn't have to say anything bad about either one of us, either you or me, either one, just that, somehow, it's not quite the right fit (*sigh*).

Alina: (*head down, very quiet*) Mm hmm.

Barry: Frankly, Alina, I don't know what to do. You have any thoughts about that?

Alina: (*not looking up*) I don't know if it's not the right fit, I think it's maybe me.

Barry: Well, generally speaking, that's not the way it goes; it's more that either my particular approach or style, although you may like me and all that and I appreciate that, but that somehow it's not the right mix for something good to happen for you.

Alina: (*still head hung*) Mm hmm.

(*long pause*)

Barry: One thing that we could do is, you could see someone else, you could see Jackie or someone else here or outside of here if you'd like. Or, I'm just throwing this out for us to talk about. You know, I really like you and I like talking to you, but I also want to see things improve in your life and I kind of want to be a part of getting you to where you can have some improvement in your life, not being an obstacle to that. So that's one thing, that's one reason why I do these things with people; so we're not getting anywhere and we need to kind of problem solve that and figure out what we need to do next about that. Because, and again I don't look at it as anything that I'm doing bad or wrong or you're doing bad or wrong, I mean that doesn't even really come into it. It's really that, you know, we are forming this partnership to try to make a difference in your life, right?

Alina: Yeah.

Barry: And although we definitely like each other, we're not making much of a difference in your life. So, sometimes, new blood can help that. So, what do you think of that?

Alina: I don't know, I guess you're right.

(*long pause*)

Barry: (*picking up the graph*) One of the reasons we do these measures is that they're predictive of eventual outcome; so if clients don't have some experience of some change fairly early on in the process, it's predictive of no change in the long-term process.

Alina: Mm hmm.

Barry: So that's why it concerns me for there not to be any movement. If you change to someone else, it opens up the whole new window again. Does that make sense?

Alina: (*head still hung*) Yeah.

Barry: That's kind of the idea behind this whole process. Do you think you want to give it a shot with Jackie? Does that seem a reasonable thing for you to try?

Alina: Yeah, I could. (*looking up*) I still don't mind working with you.

Barry: Well, I like working with you, but we're just not getting anywhere.

Alina: Mm hmm. (*long pause*)

Barry: So would you be willing to give it a shot, to talking to Jackie a couple of times and see if that can get anything positive going?

Alina: Yeah, okay.

You're right. I was relentless. But I needed to step aside and allow another opportunity for Alina with another therapist. By the fourth session with the new therapist, Alina had an ORS score of 19.3 and enrolled to take a class at a local university. Moreover, she continued those changes and reenrolled at Yale the following year with her scholarship intact! When I wrote a required recommendation letter for the reinstatement of her scholarship, I administered the ORS to Alina and she scored a 28.9. By getting out of her way and allowing her and me to "fail successfully," Alina was given another opportunity to get her life back on track—and she did. Alina and Jacqueline, for unknown reasons, just had the right chemistry for change. Alina ultimately graduated from Yale.

This client turned out to be a watershed for me. I believed in heeding the results of the measures, especially how it placed clients at center stage and pushed me to do something different when clients didn't benefit. Nevertheless, I struggled with letting go of those clients who didn't benefit, in whose lives I had become personally invested. Alina awakened me to the perils of such situations and showed a true value-added dimension to PCOMS—namely, the ability to fail successfully. As many therapists encounter over their careers, for me this young woman represented a client whom I was tempted to see for as long as she wanted. I cared deeply about her and believed that, in time, I'd surely find a way to help her.

But such is the thinking that leads to "chronic clients." Therapists— no matter how competent, trained, or experienced—can't be effective with everyone they meet. PCOMS makes it easier to determine when clients aren't improving and arrive at more objective decisions about what to do about it. Although some clients want to continue in the absence of change, far more do not, when offered a graceful way to exit.

When I have reached this point with clients, I reiterate my commitment to help them achieve the outcome they desire, whether with me or someone else, or on their own. I stress that this encounter says nothing about them personally or their potential for change. If the client chooses, I continue to meet with her or him in a supportive fashion until other arrangements are made, or even remain involved as a consultant. But rarely do I continue to work with clients whose scores on the ORS show little or no improvement by the sixth or seventh visit, unless we have charted a definitively different course.

Sometimes the folklore of clinical practice, just as the idea that ripping off bandages rapidly is the best approach, includes the notion that clients need only maintenance or sustenance work, or that a positive relationship is enough to provide for a client in tough circumstances. I probably could have justified this stance with Alina. While these ideas may make sense at times, we are not, generally speaking, doing clients any favors by thinking that our services are what is holding them together—what I call "finger in the dike" services. Instead of holding them together, we could very well be holding them up, perhaps keeping them from recovery by miring them in services that are not promoting growth. The idea that the client is damaged goods and will not follow a recovery path—that they need us to survive—is surely implicit in the concept of maintenance work.

Therapy, then, can become a place for clients to hang out and talk, receive support, and combat loneliness. Therapy can do these things at times, but it should also create the possibility for clients to attain these benefits in the community—not from a professional. Without an aspiration toward helping clients achieve more independence in the community, therapy can be a disservice to clients—creating dependency and fostering a client identity of helplessness and pathology. Of course, I don't mean that keeping clients who are not benefiting is always harmful but, rather, that each situation needs to be transparently negotiated. And we must at least challenge ourselves to consider the implications.

The thing to guard against here is the tendency to explain client non-response to services through theoretical filters and clinical folklore. Doing that puts us right back where we started, where the field has traditionally been: attributing the lack of change to the client. On the contrary, client nonresponse simply means something else should be done.

The client is final arbiter of what the ORS scores mean, but we must at least ask the hard question: Are we helping or hindering? The scores are catalysts for conversations with clients of a kind that had rarely happened before, at least for me. PCOMS is a way to support what is working and challenge what is not, providing more than just another theory to guide practice, as well as the antidote to the often poisonous pontifications about why clients are not responding to therapy, at which many members of our profession have become so adept.

CALCULATING YOUR CHECKPOINT
AND LAST-CHANCE SESSIONS

Realists do not fear the results of their study.

—Fyodor Dostoyevsky

Not all settings or therapists are alike. Your checkpoint and last-chance sessions may be different, so it makes sense to gather your own data. A relatively simple method for tracking change based on the work of Ken Howard (Howard, Moras, Brill, Martinovich, & Lutz, 1996) enables you to determine the probability of success for a specific client by a given session at a particular time. The steps are:

1. Collect ORS data on all clients for at least 6 months.
2. Separate the successful from the unsuccessful outcomes, noting the session at which each met or exceeded 6 points. An alternative that also incorporates clients who take longer to achieve reliable change is to note the session at which clients who achieve reliable change *begin* the change.
3. Chart the results on a graph with the number of sessions increasing along the bottom (*x*-axis) and the percent of successful clients along the side (*y*-axis).

An inspection of my practice depicted in Figure 3.2 shows that the majority of successful clients changed by the third session, and the overwhelming majority achieved a reliable change by the sixth meeting. So for clients in my practice, the checkpoint conversation should likely occur in the third session and the last-chance discussion by the sixth meeting. All of the clients who achieved a reliable change had done so by the seventh session. The advantage to this calculation method is it allows you to quickly determine if progress is happening in a manner typical for successful outcomes *without* having to make any statistical calculations.

Those calculations are more than sufficient for generating a dialogue with clients about the value of therapy. However, if you are looking for something a bit more precise, or you want to calculate the expected treatment response by intake score, the method described doesn't cut it. A significant limitation is the reliance on the RCI to separate successful and unsuccessful

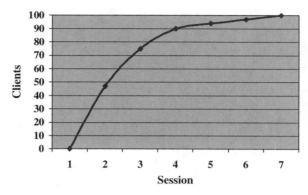

Figure 3.2. Change curve of successful clients in my practice.

cases. The problem is that the RCI is an average, arrived at by aggregating clients of varying levels of severity. As a result, it is likely to underestimate the amount of change necessary to be considered reliable for some (those in the severe range), while overestimating the amount for others (those in the mild range or over the cutoff). A more precise method, discussed in Chapter 2, is to predict the score over the course of services (the expected treatment response) based on the score at intake.

CONCLUSION

There is peace in the garden. Peace and results.
—Ruth Stout, *The Ruth Stout No-Work Garden Book*

This chapter charted the ins and outs of tailoring psychotherapy based on PCOMS: (a) plotting the ORS scores on a graph, (b) comparing the current ORS score with the last and since intake, and (c) looking at the progression of change or lack thereof. In this case, there are only two options: Either there is change, or there isn't. If there is change, work with clients to take responsibility for the change and empower their ability to continue progress. Facilitate discussions to tease out before-and-after distinctions. Begin to space out sessions and discuss termination when the client reaches a plateau. If there is no change, discuss what needs to happen next. If no change persists, the discussions increase in urgency, represented by the checkpoint conversation and the last-chance discussion, both intended to brainstorm options and entertain the possibility of referring the client elsewhere. If no change still persists, it is time to fail successfully, or gracefully move the client on to another provider or venue of service and exercise your ability to help clients in a different but equally important way.

The basic principle is straightforward: Our daily clinical actions can be informed by reliable, valid feedback about the factors that drive change in therapy. These factors include our clients' engagement, their view of the therapeutic alliance, and—the gold standard—the client's report of real progress. Truly, monitoring the outcome and the fit of our services helps us know that when we're good, we're very good, but when we're bad, we can be even better.

CLIENTS ARE THE BEST TEACHERS: THEIR STORIES DOCUMENT OUR DEVELOPMENT

It is easier to discover a deficiency in individuals, in states, and in Providence, than to see their real import and value.

—G. W. F. Hegel

Molly was part of a project that I mentioned in the last chapter, in which my colleagues and I studied clients who were "multiple treatment failures" and which resulted in the book *Psychotherapy With "Impossible" Cases* (Duncan, Hubble, & Miller, 1997). We learned that success could occur in the most difficult circumstances when the person's own ideas were recruited and implemented. We also discovered, predictably, that alliance problems accounted for most of the treatment "failures" that found their way to our investigation. Molly is my favorite story from that project. I was so impressed with her that ever since I have used her to teach thousands of therapists, via video in my trainings, the value of recruiting client strengths and ideas, and especially the central importance of the alliance.

Molly's parents were divorced after a contentious separation. Nine-year-old Molly was sleeping in her mom's (Kim's) bed and having trouble adjusting to a new apartment, school, and friends. At a mental health clinic, Molly was identified as coming from a "dysfunctional family." Diagnosed as having separation anxiety disorder, she was referred for weekly social skills group therapy. After a few weeks, Kim reported that Molly was also experiencing nightmares. The group therapist responded by also seeing Molly individually. The therapist encouraged Molly to remove herself from her parent's problems. He invited Molly's dad into therapy, but he never showed. After 6 months of concurrent group and individual treatment, things were worse: Molly was having more frequent nightmares and was beginning to struggle at school. Kim requested a different therapist, a female this time.

The new therapist suspected sexual abuse and played games with Molly looking for sexual themes, to no avail. Three more months passed and things continued to get worse—Molly's grades took a nosedive. Kim next requested a therapist outside the clinic. Instead, a psychiatric evaluation ensued that reconfirmed the diagnosis of separation anxiety disorder (and added that Kim had borderline tendencies, a diagnosis often reserved for those who complain about services). An antidepressant was prescribed to relieve Molly's separation anxiety. More time passed and no change occurred. Molly, in twice-weekly treatment for nearly a year and now on medication, had become, at the age of 10, an "impossible" case.

The main goal of the "Impossible Case" project was to investigate how impossibility developed—how clients came to suffer the so-called bloated file syndrome (staying in therapy for extended periods of time without benefit). The project deconstructed all the ways that impossibility had run its course with Molly: First, what I call the Killer Ds (*dysfunctional* family and separation anxiety *disorder*) were in full force—her therapists understood her behavior through those perceptual filters and ultimately discounted Molly and her strengths. Second, the therapists followed their own ideas about change, rather than asking for Molly's, despite the lack of positive treatment response. Molly's first therapist, following a family therapy tradition, believed that Molly had been "triangulated," and the second, without any evidence to suggest that Molly was a victim of sexual abuse, set a course to explore for it. Finally, the crucial container for any change process, the alliance, was given short shrift. Molly was not an active participant; she was not a partner in her own change endeavor.

Kim, dedicated to her daughter's welfare, discontinued the medication and demanded an outside referral. That brought Molly to our project. In my first meeting with Molly, I asked her what she believed would be helpful for resolving the "nightmares and sleeping in her own room" problem. To this, Molly expressed astonishment that someone finally wanted her opinion. She then suggested she could barricade herself in her bed with pillows and stuffed animals. The barricade would "ward off" the nightmares and her fears. In the second session, she reported that her plan was working. The excerpts below reflect Molly's observations about what was not helpful in her treatment experiences.

> Molly: So what I'm saying to all therapists is we have the answers, we just need someone to help us bring them to the front of our head. . . . It's like they're locked in an attic or something, like somebody locked them in a closet and nailed them down . . .
>
> Barry: So the things the therapists told you to do didn't help?
>
> Molly: It didn't help. I didn't want to do them. They weren't my ideas, and they didn't seem right.

***

> Molly: I feel a lot better now that I came up with the solution to sleep in my own room, and I did it and I'm proud of myself. And I couldn't be proud of myself if you told me, "How about if you barricade yourself in with pillows, maybe that'll work?" I wouldn't feel like I've done it. So basically, what I'm saying is, you don't get as much joy out of doing something when somebody told you to do it.

Molly was obviously wise beyond her years—when provided the opportunity, Molly revealed her inventiveness, derived her own solution, and in that process, enhanced her self-esteem.

But the real lessons of Molly's course on how to do therapy are about the therapeutic alliance:

> Molly: All my other therapists haven't asked me what I wanted to work on. They asked me questions and I didn't really want to answer these questions because, shouldn't I be telling you what I think about this? (*Barry laughs.*) I mean you are not here to tell me my life or anything. (*Both Molly and Barry laugh.*) You're a therapist—you're supposed to sit there and listen to me talk! But if they are saying, well, your mom tells me that your dad is doing such and such a thing or more stuff. It's like, since when did I start having problems with that?

Molly made it clear she felt discounted and ignored. What she perceived as important was not solicited. Her goals were not given priority, and her collaboration not encouraged. The alliance literature would accurately predict her negative outcome.

Recall that this is the same child who was placed in a social skills group, diagnosed with separation anxiety disorder, treated with medication, and seen for a year! If a gem like Molly can be missed working with therapists with all good intentions, we must take special caution to ensure that we build strong alliances and are mindful of clients' existing abilities. Returning to Molly one final time, note how she nails the pitfalls of not including the client as a valued partner:

> Molly: And therapists are basically telling you what they want you to do. . . . And it is like that they think they are some almighty power or something. (*Both laugh.*)
>
> Barry: That drives me nuts when they think they are the almighty Word.
>
> Molly: Like they are God. (*Looks up, extends arms, and sings as though in a choir.*)

Barry:	(*Both laugh.*) Oh, that is music to my ears, Molly. You know, we think a lot alike.
Molly:	It's like, hang on, I am also somebody. And you laugh at what I mean to be funny; and back at my old therapy, whenever I said something, she just busted up. It's like, hey, I have an opinion, too!
Barry:	She did not take you seriously . . .
Molly:	No! And she even said, 'I love working with kids and I work really well with kids.' (*Leans forward and looks very serious.*) Every kid that she sees, goes for, like, years . . .

Molly is a caution, no doubt, and has been a powerful teaching tool to illustrate alliance pitfalls to avoid.

When I first submitted *Psychotherapy With "Impossible" Cases* to a publisher, an initial reviewer of the book called my alliance-focused approach "naïve" and "overly simplistic." He panned it so hard that the original publisher turned it down and I had to go to another. He was "embarrassed" by my "complete induction into my clients' views," offended by my "joining with clients as if they were unquestionably telling the absolute truth," and critical because I "fell in love with my clients." I plead guilty as charged on all three counts. I see these "criticisms" as the real crux of the work.

4

GETTING BETTER WITH COUPLES, FAMILIES, AND YOUTH

We are continually faced by great opportunities brilliantly disguised as insoluble problems.

—Mark Twain

Using the Partners for Change Outcome Management System (PCOMS; Duncan, 2012) with just two in the room—you and the client—seems eminently doable. Your attention is on one person, the conversation is between the two of you, you have only one measure to start the session and one to close, and there is generally little distraction. But surely the system breaks down when you are talking about two or more clients? Especially if that "or more" happens to be a family of five with a toddler, an extremely active 5-year-old, and a sullen teen? And what about the couple who leave you feeling like a referee at a wrestling match? In short, it might seem that PCOMS with couples and families just *has* to be unworkable: too much time, too much orchestration, too much paper, and, plain and simple, too much effort.

Not so fast. The Child Outcome Rating Scale (CORS; Duncan, Miller, & Sparks, 2003a) and Child Session Rating Scale (CSRS; Duncan, Miller, &

Jacqueline Sparks contributed substantially to this chapter.

http://dx.doi.org/10.1037/14392-004

Sparks, 2003b) were, in fact, designed specifically to allow the use of PCOMS with families. It seemed unfair that youth and their caregivers could not take advantage of the known benefits of a feedback system, especially given that therapeutic services to families are offered in such a broad spectrum of settings. And couple therapy, of course, is widely practiced with a well-researched array of approaches. Clients in these modalities, not just those in the tidier individual client–therapist dyads, need to have a voice in their services and their benefit monitored. So how can even brief instruments be used where the number of persons and the complexity of interactions significantly multiply the demands on the therapist from the outset?

Fortunately, evidence, both empirical and experiential, is accumulating to the effect that PCOMS is not only doable with couples and families but is also effective. After a brief look at the lessons taught by the research evidence of PCOMS with couples and youth, as well as other invaluable tips gleaned from the studies of couples arising from the Norway Feedback Trial, this chapter covers the how-to with youth, couples, and families. It addresses frequently voiced questions to allay any logistical and feasibility concerns you may have regarding the use of PCOMS with more than two in the room and to let you see that a seemingly insoluble problem is merely a disguise for a great opportunity to do better work.

NORWAY FEEDBACK TRIAL AND ITS OFFSPRING

Nothing you do for children is ever wasted.
—Garrison Keillor, *Leaving Home*

In 2009, "Using Client Feedback to Improve Couples Therapy Outcomes: A Randomized Clinical Trial in a Naturalistic Setting" was published in the *Journal of Consulting and Clinical Psychology* (Anker, Duncan, & Sparks, 2009). It is worthwhile to focus on what this study was about because it is the prototype for future couple and family feedback trials and is, so to speak, the mother of four offspring studies. The largest trial to date, the Norway Feedback Trial enrolled 205 heterosexual Euro-Scandinavian couples seeking relationship counseling. The couples were randomly assigned to one of two groups: feedback (PCOMS) or treatment as usual (TAU). Therapists served as their own controls, working equally with both groups. And the therapists in the study were not "true believers" and had never used client feedback in their work. So we tried our best to make the study a true and fair test of the effects of feedback.

Recall from Chapter 1 that PCOMS couples had nearly 4 times the rate of clinically significant change and over twice the percentage of couples in which both individuals achieved reliable and/or clinically significant change. Moreover, when data were collected from the couples 6 months later, those in the feedback group were still doing much better, with nearly 3 times the percentage of couples in which both partners attained reliable and/or clinically significant change. In terms of "real-world" differences, feedback couples were 46% less likely to be separated or divorced at 6 months posttreatment. In short, this was news to write home about. If someone told you that by having your couples answer four brief questions at the beginning and end of each session, you would quadruple their chances of having a successful outcome short-term and double them long-term, would you say, "Nah, too much trouble"?

The mass of data collected from the Norway Feedback Trial (thanks to the meticulous work of Project colleague Morten Anker) became a gold mine for other analyses that have added to our understanding of what makes couple therapy tick. We (Anker, Owen, Duncan, & Sparks, 2010) started with the alliance, examining data from 250 couples because I was burning to answer the question I asked in Chapter 1: whether the alliance is predictive of outcome in and of itself, or whether the strong link found between the alliance and outcome is simply a by-product of the therapy's effectiveness. In other words, do strong alliances really produce better outcomes, or do improving clients produce stronger alliances? It is a classic chicken/egg question. And it is often used to dismiss the importance of the alliance, in that some say that the alliance literature is *only* correlational. As it turns out, this is like saying the data about cigarette smoking and lung cancer are also *only* correlational.

When we examined alliance scores, we found that, in fact, the alliance predicted outcome over and above early change. And we looked at a far more stringent criterion than simple early change because we considered change that exceeded the reliable change index. So these were individuals who changed a lot, and the alliance still predicted outcomes over and above even that. This means that a good alliance is not simply something that happens because people improve in therapy but rather is something that actually helps people change. We also found that first-session alliance scores were not significant predictors of outcome and that alliances that started over the mean and increased (called the *high linear cluster*) were associated with significantly more couples achieving reliable or clinically significant change: 77.1% of couples in the high linear cluster both changed, as compared with 45.5% of couples who started below the mean and whose scores didn't increase over the course of therapy. These results suggest, first, the need for ongoing alliance monitoring and, second, that the relative starting place of the alliance may not be as important as whether it improves over the course of treatment.

Consistent with our wanting to learn directly from clients, in the 6-month follow-up portion of our investigation we included a short questionnaire

(Anker, Sparks, Duncan, Owen, & Stapnes, 2011) about what couples liked and didn't like about their therapy. The responses fell along two dimensions that will be familiar if you know about Bordin's (1979) classic definition of the alliance, namely, relationship and tasks. Favorable comments fell more along the relationship side of the equation. Interestingly, couples also valued therapists who could remain neutral. But when it came to tasks, there were more negative comments. Respondents complained that they wished the therapist had given more advice and had structured things more to provide a safe place for highly charged discussions. Negotiating tasks and matching client expectations is an important alliance endeavor, one that requires "stepping up" when clients are asking for more guidance and structure.

An additional, and somewhat surprising, finding was that many clients wished that their therapist had been more proactive in arranging appointments, checking in between sessions, and being flexible in scheduling. Who thought this had anything to do with the price of tea in China? Apparently, according to these clients, it does. Looking back at Bordin (1979), there it is: "Collaboration between patient and therapist involves an agreed-upon contract, which takes into account some very concrete exchanges" (p. 254)—something to keep in mind when you think therapy only includes the space between "how has the week gone" and "we have to end now." Clients in the feedback group had significantly fewer negative comments in this area than those in the nonfeedback group.

That clients come into couple therapy for different reasons and wanting different outcomes was empirically reinforced by the third Norway Feedback Trial offspring (Owen, Duncan, Anker, & Sparks, 2012). It might not be a big surprise that this study found that when both members of the couple wanted to improve the relationship, the majority of them did, and only about 8% were separated or divorced 6 months posttherapy. When one member of a couple wanted to improve the relationship and his or her partner wanted clarification about continuing the relationship, 45% separated at 6 months posttherapy. Finally, when both in the couple were seeking clarification, 56% had separated at follow-up. These results suggest that initial feedback about the goals for couple therapy is critical to ensure that the therapist is on target with strategies that are a good fit for their reasons for seeking counseling.

Couples clinicians play multiple roles in both strengthening and helping dissolve partnerships in constructive ways. This study supports this assertion. Regardless of whether one or both individuals desired an outcome of clarification about continuing the relationship, higher distress during this tumultuous time was apparent and reflected by Outcome Rating Scale (ORS) scores. Couples in all three categories of goals realized significant reductions in distress pre-to-post, surpassing the reliable change index on the ORS. Therapy appeared to be helpful regardless of goal, although those with the goal of improving the relationship fared better. In other words, therapy was shown to be helpful even with couples on the verge of divorce. Couple work is tricky, and PCOMS can diminish the guesswork and help the therapist devise approaches that are in sync with client goals.

One other study spawned by the Norway Feedback Trial, mentioned in Chapter 1, just entered the published domain. Owen, Duncan, Reese, Anker, and Sparks (in press) asked the million-dollar question: What makes some therapists more effective than others (in this case, more effective in couple therapy)? Therapist effects accounted for 8% of the variance. Recall that what didn't make a difference was the therapist's gender or specific professional discipline. However, those who had more experience working with couples did significantly better, accounting for 25% of the variance attributable to therapists. Even more important was the therapist average alliance score, accounting for 50% of that variance. So if you are a couple therapist, there are two clear pathways to become better: alliance building and time in the trenches with couples. Chapter 5 will show you how you can be sure that you are learning from your experience.

PCOMS WITH YOUTH AND FAMILIES

The Norway Feedback Trial revealed that PCOMS is not just for individuals; it also shows real promise for expanded treatment systems. Studies that test feedback with children and families have lagged behind, perhaps because collecting and analyzing data from multiple clients is more complicated. Nevertheless, one published cohort investigation is charting the course. As reviewed in Chapter 1, Cooper, Stewart, Sparks, and Bunting (2013) evaluated outcomes for 288 youth ages 7 to 11 receiving counseling informed by PCOMS in their schools in Northern Ireland. The youth were referred by teachers or parents/caregivers because of social, emotional, or behavioral difficulties. At the completion of treatment, 88.7% (child's rating) showed improvement and 77.6% of caregivers reported reliable change. In addition, the authors compared their effect sizes (ES) for the Strengths and Difficulties Questionnaire (SDQ) scores against those from primary school–based counseling in the U.K. in which PCOMS was not used. They found an approximate twofold advantage in effect on the caretaker-completed SDQ when PCOMS was used (.99 vs. .47 and .58), and a small advantage in effect on the teacher-completed SDQ (.55 vs. .39 and .44). Although this was not a family feedback trial and was focused on children in the schools, it regularly included caretakers in the therapeutic process and demonstrated a feedback effect for both youth on the CORS and caretakers (and teachers) on the SDQ.

> **Bottom Line:** *The findings on PCOMS with couples and youth demonstrate its potential to improve overall effectiveness across age ranges and modalities. Below are some take-home lessons from PCOMS couple and youth studies:*

- Use PCOMS with couples, families, and youth. You significantly enhance your chance of a positive outcome by doing so.
- When looking at your data and outcomes, consider whether both members of a couple or a parent–child dyad have benefited. Morten Anker also suggests that it is informative in considering couple outcomes to separate couples into the three goal categories discussed above (see Figure 4.1).
- Monitor the alliance throughout therapy. Ascending scores are a good sign; don't be discouraged if the first session is a bit low, but rejoice when it improves.
- Use the Session Rating Scale (SRS) to determine if your approach is matching the goals for each member of a couple

THE COUPLE FIRST SESSION RELATIONAL GOAL SCALE

Name:... Date:.............

Please indicate your own personal goal for couple therapy. Please do this independently of your partner.

1. My goal is: (check only one)

    ☐   Improve the relationship

    ☐   Clarify whether the relationship should continue

    ☐   End the relationship in the best possible way

    ☐   Other

2. Do you think your partner is in agreement with your goal?

    ☐   Yes

    ☐   No

Figure 4.1. The Couple First Session Relational Goal Scale (available for use). Copyright 2007 by Psychologist Morten Anker, PhD. Reprinted with permission.

or family. If members of the couple or family have different goals, negotiate a goal and an approach all can agree on. Even if goals are different for a couple and one wants out or clarification while the other doesn't, couple therapy can be helpful (recall that all three groups achieved significant reductions of distress).

- Use the SRS to determine if your approach is a good fit for the couple or family at hand. Expand your repertoire to provide more structured and directive approaches to those who want that.
- Use the SRS to expand your relational repertoire and work on your alliance skills in complex interpersonal situations. Remember that your alliance abilities count for half (at least) of any differences between you and your colleagues.
- Increase your couple caseload hours over time to enhance your effectiveness with this modality, but in such a way that you are learning the lessons that couples teach (see Chapter 5).
- Attend to clients' needs both during the session and between sessions, keeping in touch and being flexible about meeting times and scheduling.

NUTS AND BOLTS OF PCOMS WITH COUPLES AND FAMILIES

The value of an idea lies in the using of it.

—Thomas Edison

In truth, couples and family work is not for the faint of heart—not for those with little tolerance for noise, commotion, complexity, and the need to think on your feet. Think of it as sometimes like a three-ring circus—there is so much going on, you don't know what to attend to first: the high-wire act, the trained lions, or the clowns. Take this, and add on even a brief, feasible system like PCOMS, and it seems a formidable task. Fortunately, however, rather than adding complexity, PCOMS is an anchor, providing an orienting point to begin a session and a ready-made means for summarizing at the end.

When using PCOMS with couples and families it is good to adopt the Girl/Boy Scout motto: Be Prepared! The last thing you want is to escort family members into the office or meet them in their home and not have all the tools of the trade ready to go. Make sure you know how many people you will be seeing, their ages, and their likely developmental/intellectual level. This way you can collect the appropriate measures to be used, the correct number of clipboards (if there are not enough writing surfaces), and enough writing implements. Here's a refresher: Teenagers (ages 13–17) will use the ORS and children (ages 6–12), the CORS (see Figure 4.2). Have available the Young Child Outcome Rating Scale (YCORS; see Figure 4.3) for those under age 6 and provide crayons. The point is, don't leave anyone capable of writing or scribbling out of the process. This communicates that everyone matters and you are interested in everyone's views, however they express it. To reduce the amount of paper, it is helpful to have the ORS/CORS on one side and the SRS/CSRS on the other.

Here is an example of not being prepared, and yet another illustration of the fact that you can't do it as badly as I have. In my defense, it was after my last client on a Friday afternoon and I was already in that space in my head that had me home, sitting on my patio, watching the birds, and enjoying my favorite beverage. You know the feeling. My notes were done, my stuff put away, and my laptop packed, and I was headed out the door when my cell phone rang. It was a school counselor, who said, "Barry, you gotta see this kid. She cut her arms and is going to wind up in the hospital!" I thought, "Nooooooo! Anything but that—don't you understand I am already at home on my patio sipping a cold, malted, brown-colored soft drink?"

But the school counselor was a friend and a referral source—and I am a sucker for a prevention-of-hospitalization story—so I said I would see the kid and the mom. The video shows me talking to a very disgruntled Erica about the ORS while looking for one to give her. I look in one folder, then another, hemming and hawing along the way, looking at many forms ("I know it's in here somewhere") while trying to maintain some professional decorum. Finally, in the third folder, I find the ORS and administer it, and then I can't find my centimeter ruler. Finally, I give up and just estimate the numbers. Audiences think it is quite a hoot. But, you know what, Erica didn't mind and the session went terrifically, and this delightful, precocious kid didn't go to the hospital. But better to be prepared!

Although there are validated guidelines, clinical judgment comes into play regarding the appropriate instrument for any given child or adolescent. For example, some 12-year-olds may find the CORS "babyish," insulting their real (or presumed) level of maturity. This was the case for Erica. When I met her in the waiting room, she seemed to be 12 going on 27 when her mom, Nancy, asked me to see her daughter first. But use whatever they think works best for them; it doesn't hurt to just ask and let them choose if you're not sure. On the other hand, a teen may have some developmental challenges and more readily take to the CORS.

In the case of a family entering services because of a problem related to a child or adolescent, the parent or caregiver scores only the CORS (for a child) or ORS (for an adolescent), based on his or her perception of how the child or adolescent is doing. Asking the parent or caregiver to score his or her own ORS sends the message that we are interested in their functioning,

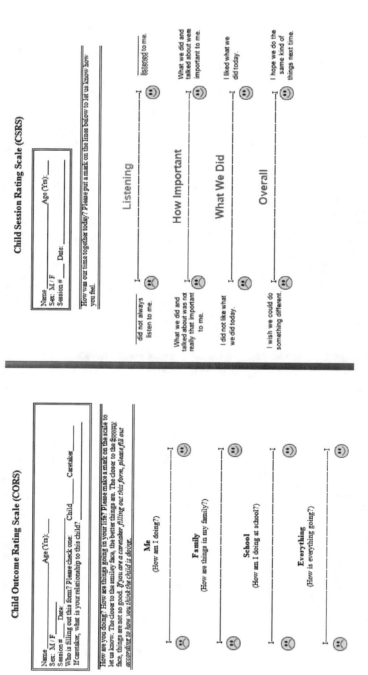

Figure 4.2. The Child Outcome Rating Scale and Child Session Rating Scale. Copyright 2003 by B. L. Duncan, S. D. Miller, and J. A. Sparks. Reprinted with permission. For examination only. Download free working copies at https://heartandsoulofchange.com.

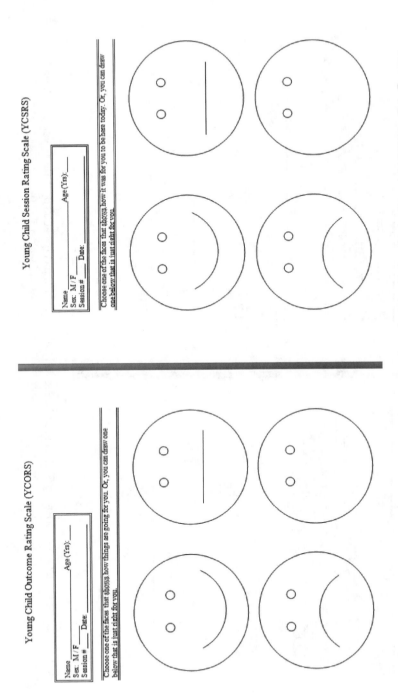

Young Child Outcome Rating Scale (YCORS)

Name _____ Age (Yrs): ___
Sex: M / F
Session # ___ Date:

Choose one of the faces that shows how things are going for you. Or, you can draw one below that is just right for you.

Young Child Session Rating Scale (YCSRS)

Name _____ Age (Yrs): ___
Sex: M / F
Session # ___ Date:

Choose one of the faces that shows how it was for you to be here today. Or, you can draw one below that is just right for you.

Figure 4.3. The Young Child Outcome Rating Scale and Young Child Session Rating Scale. Copyright 2003 by B. L. Duncan, S. D. Miller, A. Huggins, and J. Sparks. Reprinted with permission. For examination only. Download free working copies at https://heartandsoulofchange.com.

even though that is not the reason for service. That message could risk the alliance because parents or caregivers may believe that the therapist, rather than being aligned with their view of the problem, instead has a covert belief that they themselves are the problem. The primary point is to ensure that the therapist accepts the reason for seeking help and communicates that as clearly as possible through both verbal and nonverbal means to clients.

Parental and caregiver scores of a child who is presented as the reason for service provide crucial perspectives of how therapy is going. From the CORS validation study, we know that parent/caregiver scores are correlated with children's and adolescents' scores. In other words, when youth record a change, caregivers typically report similar amounts and directions of change, and vice versa. In some circumstances, it is also useful to get others who are significantly involved with a child, or so-called collateral raters, to score their views using the CORS/ORS. For example, a teacher instrumental in referring a child for counseling or a probation officer assigned by a court to monitor a youth charged with a delinquency offense is a good candidate to bring into the process. People who play pivotal roles in the child's life can become witnesses to and advocates for positive change. Periodic meetings with these individuals, the youth, and family can facilitate support for the efforts of a child or adolescent and collaboratively contribute to goal setting and strategies for problem resolution.

Once the initial how-to is mastered, the instruments provide a welcome port in a storm. The same may be true for the children and families who come to expect the familiar ritual of starting and ending with the measures. The trick is to get practiced and comfortable enough so that PCOMS is not an awkward, half-done activity that detracts from the flow of conversation, but one that facilitates a meaningful discussion.

Introducing and Scoring the ORS/CORS With Couples and Families

You have selected the instruments, everything is ready, and you are face-to-face with either a reasonably focused, calm couple or family, or one that is filling up the space with energy and noise. You simply need to go through the steps of the introduction as you would with any individual client, ensuring that everyone in the room knows the major points that the ORS brings to the show (i.e., it is a way to ensure they get what they are looking for and that their voice stays central) and understands how to complete it.

Introducing the ORS to families requires tailoring your talk to the age, understanding capability, and level of attention of multiple family or couple members. Even with just two clients, one may be more attentive and one more disengaged or skeptical. The key is to size up as quickly as possible whether a blanket explanation will suffice or more individualized descriptions are required. For example, in the case of a 7-year-old who immediately goes for the matchbox cars in the corner of the room, you will need to go to him, get down to his level, shake his hand, introduce yourself, and show him what you want him to do, letting him know that you really want to get a sense of how he thinks things are going for him. From then on, it will be important to include him in this manner, no matter what part of the room he migrates to. In the best of all scenarios, a parent or caregiver will assume the role of therapist helper—asking the child to join him or her, explaining what is needed with the instrument, and helping him to fill it out, while still respecting his unique voice and point of view.

Okay, you are primed to use the measures with a family you are seeing for the first time. You are visiting them in their home and, when you are invited into the small living room, you are surrounded by cacophony—the TV at least 5 decibels higher than your comfort zone, a 4-year-old chasing a very large and friendly dog who greeted you with exuberance and a thorough (and uncomfortable) sniffing, two older siblings, ages 6 and 8, arguing (screaming might be a better descriptor) about who gets to sit in the armchair, and a harried mother trying to finish her phone conversation as she nonverbally directs traffic to get everyone clustered around the coffee table for the meeting. Panicked, you can't possibly see how pulling out x number of sheets of paper, explaining the measures, and providing the rationale can fly under the circumstances. So, you abandon your best intentions.

In so doing, you have squandered an opportunity. Here's a secret. Families that some would pejoratively label "chaotic" appreciate your help with focus and structure. Children and teens, being naturally curious, want to see what this activity is all about and generally will jump right in. Lo and behold, to your wonderment, the room quiets, if only briefly, as all are immersed in their first counseling task. Future meetings get started almost automatically, with even very active children coming to expect the structure provided by the opening assessment of how they are doing.

And that's exactly what happened with the above-mentioned family when I did an in-home consult. The family quickly gathered around the coffee table, curiosity piqued by my explanation of the forms, and joined in the family activity—even the 4-year-old (the Young Child measures are not scored). As is often the case, I was able to solicit help from one of the children to graph the scores with me. Essentially, PCOMS, from the very beginning, provides a critical demarcation of the therapy process. It communicates to the family, "This is a special time," and helped carve out a focused space in the midst of the family's everyday life in which important matters related to everyone's well-being could be discussed. Rather than escalating chaos, it brings order, giving a consistent, predictable structure when most needed. Most of all, it engages everyone early on and helps maintain that engagement over time. At the same time, you are giving hope that you are not intimidated by who they are and, therefore, just might be someone who will be helpful to them.

Sometimes children or their parents are confused about how to use the *School* line on the CORS if it is summertime and the child is not in school. The *School* scale parallels the corresponding *Socially* item on the ORS. It is the child's or caregiver's perceptions of the child's peer friendships and social-based activities or responsibilities, his or her social world. So during the summer it might be, for example, summer camp, music lessons, sports, scouts, spiritual groups, summer job—all of which pertain to social functioning and maintain the parallel "item integrity" between the ORS and CORS.

If school academic or behavioral concerns are the purpose of service but you are working with the child during the summer, the child can look back and rate the last week of school as a starting point. Then the scale can be used to represent the work done to address those concerns over the summer. If school is not the reason for service, the scale can reflect current social relationships in general, during or outside of the school year. If any social domain is the impetus for service, the child rates the scale accordingly. The important point is that the child's/caregiver's concerns need to be represented in a way that therapy can address, so that progress is reflected on the CORS.

The instruments are filled out, and now you have all these forms to score. It seems daunting, but fitting it into your natural rhythm of beginning a session will put everyone at ease. Let everyone know that you will take a few moments and then you will check out the results with them. By simply letting people know this, you can relax, and the time does not seem as awkward. As you gain experience, you can multitask while you add the scores. You can enlist a graphing helper and give the family the task of assigning colors to each member. You can explain how the measures work (e.g., four 10-cm lines totaling 40 cm) and make brief comments about each, the lowest and highest score or where you see agreement or disagreement among the clients.

Discussing Clients' Scores, the Clinical Cutoff, and Connecting the Marks to the Reasons for Service

Now that you have completed the scoring, the clients need to understand what their scores mean and have a shared understanding of how the scores reflect their reasons for seeking therapy. It helps to lay all the forms out on an open surface (e.g., coffee table, kitchen table, or floor) where everyone can take a look. This is a powerful gesture communicating that the work is collaborative, the therapist will not be the private keeper of special information, and everyone's point of view will be known and valued. It is not unusual for children to flock around a set of scores with a natural curiosity for who scored what. Partners are often similarly curious about their partner's scores and will readily make comments about similarities or differences with their own. The ORS allows everything to be literally on the table right from the beginning—the agreements and disagreements that everyone except the therapist, until now, knows about.

The clinical cutoff facilitates a shared understanding of the measures and is often a step toward connecting the scores to the reason for seeking or receiving services. Keep in mind that the cutoff is different depending on age. Twenty-five is the cutoff for adults, meaning that, on average, persons seeking clinical services will fall below that and those not typically seeking counseling will score above. Although adolescents use the ORS, their cutoff is slightly higher, 28. Children's cutoff on the CORS is higher still, 32. The cutoff for parents'/caregivers' scoring the CORS and the ORS for an adolescent is 28. Briefly let each person know, in everyday language that is understandable to them, whether they are above or below the cutoff. As with individuals, for those showing below-cutoff scores, you can assure them that they made a good decision to come in. For those scoring above the cutoff, you can simply validate their score by saying that it looks like things are going pretty well, which often leads to the next logical question: What are the reasons for meeting at this time?

Erica scored a 35 (I didn't have a ruler, but later, when I scored it, the actual total was 34.3) on the ORS. This may surprise you; she had cut her arms in response to a romantic breakup, yet she saw herself as doing very well. You might think that she is hiding or misrepresenting her distress. I would dissuade you from either interpretation and take the score at face value. Erica *did* see herself as doing well in all areas of her life—she was popular, independent, and a good student—and viewed the cutting as an isolated incident requiring only some convincing of her mother that she was okay so that her boy privileges could be reinstated. In other words, her description of her life matched her ORS score. Erica's mom, Nancy, confirmed that Erica was doing well and also considered the cutting incident, although troublesome, as part of an overall picture of a well-adjusted teenager. Nancy scored Erica on the ORS as a 32 (actually a 31.6). Here is how the clinical cutoff conversation went with 12-year-old Erica:

Barry: Okay. Great. Things look like they are going very well for you. The way this works is that each of the lines is 10-cm long and they total to 40 points. You scored 35 out of 40. People usually think their lives are going really, really well when they score that. Is that true for you?

Erica: Well, yes, things are very good, but I did cut my arm because of this one boy.

Barry: Okay, so things are going well for you overall, but this cutting thing happened recently and that's why you find yourself here. Do you want to tell me about it?

Erica: I like this boy named Jake and I can tell him anything. I can tell him more than my friends who are girls. And he understands it. But I found out he liked me and when I was falling for him I didn't really show it, but now that I am falling for him, like now, he doesn't like me that much. So, that's why I cut my arm.

The ORS gave me a rapid understanding of how Erica saw this situation and her therapy. She wasn't looking for any psychological exploration of her reasons for the cutting (she in fact learned of cutting as a coping mechanism from *Teen People Magazine*). When clients score over the cutoff, as Erica's example illustrates, it doesn't mean they are lying (even if they are mandated); it just means that they are not experiencing much distress in their lives (and if they are mandated, they are certainly experiencing less distress than the person who wants them in therapy). The only distress that Erica was experiencing resulted from the fact that her mother had grounded her, and it was reflected in her slightly lower score on the *Interpersonally* scale.

With any client, and perhaps especially with kids who score over the cutoff, caution is warranted about any approach that focuses on matters other than the issues at hand. Why? Think about it. What do we therapists often do with folks who *think* they are doing well? We put on our Wicked Witch costume, suddenly turning green, growing warts and a humongous nose, and we stir the cauldron. Laughing devilishly as we mix the steaming brew with large strokes, we shriek, "Oh, you think things are going okay, do you? We'll see about that, my pretty!" That is what the school counselor was worried about with Erica, but it was not what I did. Dealing with the cutting, putting it into perspective, and moving this family on with their lives were central to the work.

The next vehicle for connecting the ORS and CORS to the reasons for service relates to the specific domains. Simply seeing which domain or domains are scored lower allows you to hone in on the most distressed dimension. You can comment on this area and ask if the score on that domain represents the reason for seeking or being referred for counseling. Or you can allow the conversation to reveal the reason for service and then make the connection to the lowest domain. Once that is established, there is a shared understanding regarding which domain is the focal point for tracking change. For example, typically couples will come in with the interpersonal domain scoring lower than others. It is not hard to confirm that this is what they want to address through counseling. It also lets you know in a heartbeat who is more distressed about the relationship and who likely set up the appointment—and perhaps who was dragged in by the partner.

Of note, children or adolescents who score above the cutoff will often still provide a clue to what is troubling them by placing one mark slightly lower than others, as Erica did. Don't be deterred by the high score, but mention that he or she might want to talk about school, or family, or whichever scale is lowest. Finally, the domain scores offer a glimpse of what is going well in a person's life. It is worthwhile to briefly mention this when reviewing the ORS/CORS scores, or, at least, make a mental note to inquire more about these areas at some point later in the interview.

As the session unfolded with Erica, it became clear that the removal of her privileges, especially her phone privileges with boys, was her primary concern. Her rating of how she was doing *Interpersonally* was slightly lower than the rest of her ratings. So I simply asked if her grounding and subsequent conflict with her mother accounted for the lower mark. Erica responded affirmatively, and I asked her what we needed to do to move it up a centimeter. She replied that we needed to convince her mom that she was okay.

> **Bottom Line:** *Allow the ORS to put the dynamics of the situation, family, and therapy on the table and ready for action.*

When People Agree on the ORS

Couples and families either agree about their views of the level and areas of distress or they don't. The key when folks agree is to comment on it as a strength, highlight the commonality, and use it as a stepping stone to establish mutual goals. The following is an excerpt from a consult I did with a foster parent, Sophie, and an adolescent, Lisbeth, who were referred because Lisbeth had not attended school for nearly a year and a half.

Barry: (*talking to Sophie because Lisbeth has her hood up and is looking away*) When I work with people I like to use this very brief form about how you all see things going in your lives and how you see Lisbeth doing. This is also a way for adolescents to have a voice about how things are going in therapy.

Sophie: She does take advantage of that.

Barry: That's good! That's a good way of making sure things go well. So that's what this form is for. It's also so we can track whether or not you are getting anywhere with the services, whether this therapy is helping. That's the whole idea.

Sophie: It took her a year to get used to her therapist . . . she didn't say anything . . . isn't that right, Lisbeth? (*Lisbeth says nothing.*)

Barry: I am sorry, I didn't even ask you if I could call you Sophie. Is it okay if I call you that?

Sophie:	Sure.
Barry:	And please call me Barry. (*still talking to Sophie*) Would you be willing to do this brief form for me?
Sophie:	Yes
Barry:	This is you looking at her seeing how she is doing (*Sophie reads instructions.*). Lisbeth, would you do this for me? It gives a snapshot of how you think things are going in your life. (*Lisbeth, hood still down, dramatically grabs the clipboard out of Barry's hand.*) Thanks a lot!

(*Both fill out the forms, and hand Barry the ORS.*)

Barry:	Thanks! (*as Barry scores the measures*) So the way this works is, it is four 10-cm lines for a total score of 40, and what I do then is take this centimeter ruler and measure your marks.
Lisbeth:	We don't need an explanation. We can read it!
Barry:	Okay. You already know about this?
Lisbeth:	I don't care for it, buddy.
Barry:	(*still adding the numbers*) I appreciate that you did it given that you don't care for it. I hope that you will find it helpful. (*Lisbeth slumps in chair with hood over her face; Sophie intently watches everything Barry does with the measures.*) You scored a 12.6, Lisbeth, which is very low and indicative of someone who is having a real hard time and is maybe kinda hurting. Is that right?
Lisbeth:	Maybe, but I don't care about a social life or school and I don't care about family.
Barry:	Okay, so it fits but you don't much care about it. (*Lisbeth doesn't respond.*) The cutoff is 28 on the this ORS form so people who score under that tend to be people looking for something different in their life.
Lisbeth:	I am just fine where I am.
Barry:	Okay, you know, Sophie, you scored a 12.7 looking at Lisbeth, which is almost exactly what she scored. So you guys are on the same page about how things are going.
Lisbeth:	I make it very clear!
Barry:	That's great! I think when teens and caregivers are on the same page about how things are going, it helps a heck of a lot. You are starting with a shared understanding of things. And you are both identifying the areas of most distress on the *Socially* scale.

And is that reflecting the whole not-attending-school issue? That's what they told me was the reason for this consult.

Sophie: Yes.

Barry: Great. Because, you know, a lot of times, adolescents and care-givers see things quite differently . . . and you two are definitely on the same frequency here.

Lisbeth: Oh, piss off!

This rather feisty beginning took a little over 3 minutes, but that was enough time to comment on what each person's score meant, their similarity to one another and how that was a great place to start, and posit the connection of the lowest score to the reason for service. We will pick up with this family in Chapter 6, as part of a discussion of the alliance.

When People Don't Agree on the ORS

Erica and Nancy agreed about Erica doing well, and Sophie and Lisbeth agreed about Lisbeth not doing well, but what about everyone else? Repeat (or sing) after me: "Don't worry, be happy." Couples and families seek counseling because . . . they can't agree! It is true that, in the midst of disagreeing about everything from who takes out the garbage to who's responsible for the last argument, there can be a collective agreement about the degree of distress and the general domain of that distress. However, it is also true that disagreements often include how clients see the problem that led to counseling. Why is this not a cause for despair but a reason to be happy? For starters, different scores are concrete and visible, allowing therapists to inquire early on about everyone's unique perceptions and beliefs. The sooner this is done, the quicker goals for each person can be identified and efforts made to link these into a common strategy and mutually desired endpoint. Alternatively, discrepant scores may persist, and therapists can successfully validate those differences and still work toward a positive outcome (recall the couple study in which even couples with discrepant goals benefited from therapy). Different scores are to be expected and simply represent the reality and complexity of working therapeutically with more than two in the room.

Disagreements between clients in their scores on the ORS really speak to the dynamics present anyway. It just puts those differences front and center in the first minutes of the session. Consider Nathan, a 15-year-old recently suspended from school for "violent outbursts" against teachers, and his grandmother, Margaret. Nathan had recently come to live with Margaret after being removed from his mother's home because of her active addiction and violations of probation. Nathan went from inner city Detroit to rural Montana, quite a culture shock for everyone involved.

Barry: *(Margaret and Nathan complete the ORS and hand it to Barry.)* Thanks. Okay, I'm going to add this up and tell you what it means and you can let me know if it makes sense and fits how you see things. This is four 10-cm lines and I just total it up after I measure your marks with this centimeter ruler . . . Nathan, you scored a 33.2, and that basically says that life is going pretty well for you. The cutoff on this ORS for adolescents is 28, and when people score over that it generally says that things are going well, that they are scoring more like folks who are not talking to people like me. Does that fit?

Nathan: Yes. *(Margaret looks at Nathan with an exaggerated smirk.)*

Barry: But it looks like the *Socially* or school area *(Barry had explained that this scale captured Nathan's life at school)* is the one that you marked the lowest.

Nathan: Right, I get in trouble at school.

Barry: Okay, we'll get to that in a minute. And Margaret, your look at Nathan says that things are pretty rough right now, you scored a 9.9 in looking at how Nathan is doing . . . that there are significant problems.

Margaret: Yes, I definitely think that there are, especially at school. He is suspended now. And he is not too easy to live with at home either.

Barry: Looks like you made a good decision to be in counseling. Okay, oh, and you also have rated the *Socially* scale the lowest, so you two are on the same page about that, although your total scores are different. Margaret, is that what you are referring to, the school suspension and problems there in your mark here? *(Barry lifts up her ORS and Margaret nods.)* So you have different views about what is going on here, on the one hand, but both of you see the biggest concern in the same place. But that's good that we know that from the beginning. Let's see if we can make sense of that and move things forward. I think, Nathan, in one way, our job is to bring your grandma's view of you more in line with your view of yourself, and bring both of your marks to the right a bit more

	on that *Socially* scale. That might be one way of thinking of what we are up to here. Does that make sense?
Nathan and Margaret:	Yes.
Barry:	So you both marked the *Socially* scale the lowest. Who wants to start with that? Or feel free to start wherever you want.

Different scores, then, are not a big deal and only serve to bring everything out in the open. This can be very helpful with couples as well as kids and caretakers. Couples often come in for different reasons and have very different motivations for therapy. The ORS gives you an instant read on things like who is in the most distress about the relationship and who perhaps was coerced into therapy. Not surprisingly, the one wanting to work on or save the relationship is often the one demonstrating more distress on the ORS. Also not surprising is that the one who is dragged to therapy or the one who is there to clarify whether the relationship will continue are often over the cutoff. The discussion of distress via ORS scores shines a light on these important issues, allowing their open discussion and subsequent planning for how therapy can meet both individuals' needs. And, as illustrated in our study about couple goals for therapy, such information allows therapy to help couples who are separating as well as those who stay together. Using the measures helps to identify a host of dynamics very early in the process as well as where therapy progress will be registered on the ORS.

Getting a Good Rating: One That Accurately Reflects the Client's Experience

It is important to remember that the younger the child, the higher the scores are likely to be; the cutoff for ages 6 to 12 on the CORS is 32. High scores, therefore, are to be expected on the CORS, and a score of 31 is communicating that the child is in some distress. Children can even score higher and may be expressing discomfort by a 9 on any given scale. It is important, therefore, to look for variation in domain scores with high youth scores; any deviation between one domain and others is a flag. For example, an 8-year-old has a total score of 35, but the *Family* scale accounts for the entire 5-point differential. Clearly this child is conveying information. It would be wise to ask about why the *Family* scale is down a bit and not the same as the others, recognizing, however, that it could simply reflect a recent tiff with a parent or sibling. Children who score this way may, however, want you to pay attention but not know how to say it outright. The forms give them a voice that is quieter, and perhaps safer, than to say "Something's wrong," or "I need some help."

But what about the child who flatlines the form from the beginning at 10's and continues that at each session? A few things are helpful to keep in mind for this scenario. Children are likely receiving services not because they asked for them but because someone else, generally a parent or teacher, thought it was a good idea. They are, in essence, mandated clients, so at the start keep in mind that it is entirely possible that they are simply not distressed about the situation that led them to services—someone else is. So, don't assume that their high scores are not accurate.

However, you should also make sure that children understand the measure and how it will be used. But know right from the beginning that not all kids are going to get it. The measure was validated on 6-to-12-year-olds but that doesn't mean that all 6-, 7-, and 8-year-olds are going to understand the CORS. Some never get it no matter what you do. Children of this age can be very here-and-now oriented. In this case, carrying topics and themes from session to session just doesn't work, and the measure winds up describing how the child is feeling at the moment or how the car ride to the office was experienced. But many do get it, and the older the child, the more likely it is that he or she will understand the connections that are made between the discussions in session, the reasons for service, and what happens between sessions. Of course, this is your role: to make all those connections manifest at multiple levels of understanding. But if they don't, it's all good. Keep using the CORS with your young clients so that they have a voice in the process, but don't use their scores in your database. You will almost always have another rater with a child, so it's not a problem when children don't understand it.

When a child you believe understands it still scores very high (above 36), acknowledge the marks as true: "It looks like things are going pretty good," followed by, "Will you let me know if anything changes?" Later, the child might mention some areas of her life that are far from a 10, or a parent/caregiver might describe events that seem at odds with her scores. At this juncture, you can take out the form and, in a sincere and curious way, say, "Mara, help me out here. Your mom seems worried that you are not making new friends since you moved and you told me that you hate school. How does that fit with this line here [pointing to the "10" on the School scale] that says everything is okay with school and your friends?" Give her some time and ask, "Do you want to do a different mark [offering her the pencil and the form]?" If she says no, so be it—it is absolutely ill-advised to debate a client, ever. By trusting her voice, you make it more likely that, if she is not completely letting you in, she will at some point in the future. If you know the child's score to be invalid, that it is not matching the client's description of his or her life, then don't record it in your database and use the parent's or caregiver's ratings.

Introducing and Discussing the SRS

You have spent the allotted time delving into your clients' dilemmas, struggles, hopes, and dreams, the kind of special connection unmatched in any other professional sphere and the privilege enjoyed by all of us doing this work. It is now time for some very important feedback: How did your clients experience the session, your attention to them, your ability to grasp their situation, your helpfulness in offering insight, suggestions, or new perspectives? Without a read on the alliance, therapy can easily derail. Moreover, simply requesting this type of feedback is likely to strengthen the alliance, especially if the feedback is negative and the therapist responds to and addresses the concerns. However, in couple or family work, the alliance is a multi-voiced variable and alliance formation is consequently more complicated. For example, scores on the SRS will indicate if both members of a couple like how the therapy is going, or if you have become another bone of contention in their relationship. SRS ratings will also let you know if you have pulled off one of the more remarkable feats for anyone working with families—being liked by parents/caregivers *and* an identified child or adolescent. If the answer is "not so much," no need to despair; this is good to know and helps you recalibrate, preferably before they leave the office or you leave their home or other place of service.

Again, make sure you are prepared and have the forms readily available for the appropriate ages. As with the ORS, the adult SRS is used for adolescents. The CSRS (see Figure 4.2) is suitable for ages 6 to 12. There is even a YCSRS (Figure 4.3) with four large faces that children under age 6 can color, to feel included with the rest of the family. Then be sure to leave enough time to explain the instrument and respond briefly to the feedback.

The explanation for couples and families is the same as for an individual client, with the caveat that you attend to the age and developmental level of youth in a family—literally get down to his or her level if necessary to make sure he or she understands. Beyond that, the key points to communicate are the same: You want to know how they think things went, and their feedback can help you make sure they are getting what they want from counseling and adjust things if they are not.

Finally, offer any assistance needed for clients to fill out the measure. Sometimes children, or even members of a couple, mistake the first line "I felt heard, understood, and respected" ("_____ listened to me" on the CSRS) to mean their sense of being heard, understood, and respected (listened to) by a parent, sibling, or partner during the meeting. This needs to be clarified; the item refers to the therapist's hearing, understanding, and respecting the client.

Sometimes, even with further explanation, the tension between members may carry over to ratings on the SRS. Your tone at this juncture is critical.

Clients can easily pick up on nervousness or hesitancy. Most clients are polite, and if they feel a certain comment might offend the therapist, may decide to keep it to themselves. However, when the therapist is genuinely relaxed and communicates—both verbally and nonverbally—a true desire for feedback, clients are more likely to provide it. For some clients, there may be family or cultural influences that create more hesitancy. For example, younger clients may feel it is not okay to tell an adult they didn't like something he or she did. Or, in some cultures, it may be considered disrespectful to speak negatively to a woman or someone considered an elder. If this is the case, the therapist can explain that providing feedback will not be perceived as negative but as positive, strange as that may seem. You can then reiterate your desire to hear what they think so that the best outcome can be secured.

When responding to SRS feedback, let's go back to what we learned before we could tie our shoes. When someone does you a favor, what do you say? That's right: *Thank you*. Any and all feedback ought to be accepted with gratitude—gratitude for their time, honesty, and helpful information. The therapist's demeanor during this process ought to be genuine, open, and non-defensive. Remember, a few "dings" on the scale is a bonus, given low to high is golden. Beyond saying "thank you," the therapist inquires about what was missing or how to move up any mark that even slightly dips below a nine, or what went well that the clients want you to continue. That is all there is to it—a light-touch, checking-in process of genuine curiosity about how to make things go as well as possible.

Second Session and Beyond

If all goes well, your clients will return, or invite you back to their home, for another meeting. For this session and all subsequent ones, the task is the same as with an individual: Are things better or not? At the risk of sounding repetitive, things are not quite so clear-cut when you are working with more than one client. While it may be that you get fairly consistent agreement among members of a couple or family regarding the two possible change scenarios, it may be more likely that you will encounter different views. For example, a spouse may be seeing things improve because his wife has returned to live in the home, but her view of the situation indicates deterioration. Or a mother may report improvement because the agreed-upon strategies reduced the conflict with her adolescent, but the daughter rates things lower because she feels controlled. Welcome to couple/family work. This is of course the crux of it, the challenge: to create a therapeutic context where everyone, different views and all, benefits from the experience of counseling. Perhaps the best way to judge success is when both persons in a couple benefit and when caregivers and kids benefit. Recall from the Norway trial that the percentage of couples *both* of whom achieved change was over twice as high with feedback as it was with TAU.

Regardless of the congruence or discrepancy between client scores, the task of the therapist from session to session is the same as for an individual: Identify client perceptions of progress and the alliance and respond appropriately. To keep track of several individuals, it is helpful or even essential to graph scores from week to week on a single sheet of paper. Different members of a family or couple can be represented by different-colored lines. Taken as a whole, the graph captures a picture of the change process. A picture is worth a thousand words, and clients are intrigued with seeing their progress superimposed graphically with other family members or their partner. The graph often has particular appeal for youth, who can readily interpret what the lines mean and how they reflect their own and their caregivers' views.

ORS/CORS scores serve as megaphones for client change. This is especially true when the quick and rich exchanges between multiple clients and a counselor make conversations in therapy even more difficult to follow. When change shows up as higher scores on the ORS or CORS, and improvement over several weeks is clearly delineated by a graph, it begs to be explored. It is interesting to see how a simple jump of even a few points on the ORS can spur conversation about how small changes can be carried forward to address the problems at hand. For those readers who are versed in solution-focused therapy (e.g., Berg, 1994), these ideas will not be new. However, the systematic collection of progress data via the ORS/CORS energizes and concretizes the concepts, making them even more accessible as powerful tools for change.

As with individuals, when change is not forthcoming, or things are worsening, it is time to have a conversation about doing something different and follow the guidelines set forth in Chapter 3. The presence of more than one client in the room offers the unique advantage of having just that many more opinions to draw on to figure out what is preventing progress and how to get things moving forward. Instead of bemoaning the complexity of working with many clients at a time, celebrate that you now have a chance to harness the collective energy and wisdom of an entire couple or family.

CONCLUSION

Chaos is a friend of mine.

—Bob Dylan

In couple work, PCOMS has a growing track record for improving outcomes, as evidenced by the Norway study and its later replication (see Reese, Toland, Slone, & Norsworthy, 2010). In addition, a large cohort study found robust efficacy for use of client feedback with troubled youth (Cooper et al., 2013) as well as caretakers. Family trials are the next step, but clearly the adaptability of PCOMS across ages and modalities appears promising.

Incorporating PCOMS to guide the work with more than two in the room, while admittedly presenting some extra challenges, ultimately facilitates engagement and lessens rather than increases the complexity of the work. For all our angst about what do you do when . . . (fill in the horror story du jour for couple/family work here), PCOMS offers an elegant and practical way to harness the innate energy of multiple clients. Rather than just creating more paper, the measures help organize meetings, give focus to therapeutic conversations, and provide guideposts as therapy proceeds.

CLIENTS ARE THE BEST TEACHERS: THEIR STORIES DOCUMENT OUR DEVELOPMENT

I always tell the truth. Even when I lie.

—Tony Montana (*Scarface*)

Nora was a delightful 7-year-old who suddenly started soiling herself when she was at school. The problem had persisted through pediatrician visits and an EAP counseling service that ultimately made the referral to me. In the first session, I saw Nora and her mom, Kathleen, together for a while, but Nora didn't say much and Kathleen indicated that she wanted to talk to me privately. So I escorted Nora to the waiting room and showed her the toys, books, and TV. Then Kathleen expressed her concerns as well as her belief that the encopresis was related to the death of Nora's biological father, who was recently killed in a car accident. Although Nora never knew her father, Kathleen believed the death was largely responsible for Nora's soiling problem. As I tried to wrap my head around that, Kathleen spent most of the session talking about how Nora had been abandoned by her father as well as all the things that had been tried to help Nora with the problem.

I learned a lot, but unfortunately it didn't leave much time for Nora. After commiserating with Nora about the toughness of her problem and how embarrassing it was, I asked her what she thought it was about and what she should do about it. Nora couldn't wait to tell me about this very mean third-period math teacher she had, Mr. Miller, who wouldn't let her go to bathroom. Nora said that she repeatedly raised her hand to be excused but that he ignored her and that was why she soiled her pants. I was appropriately indignant and told Nora that this just wasn't right.

Unfortunately, it was time to end the session, and other clients had already arrived. So I told Nora that we would get into this more in the next session and figure out what to do about it.

The next week I asked Kathleen's permission to start out with Nora to both explore Kathleen's hypothesis regarding the biological father but also to hear the full story about mean Mr. Miller. We played a couple of games together while we talked, but not much came out of the discussion about her biological father. But Nora came to life when I mentioned Mr. Miller. Nora hated this guy. With unbridled energy, she described situation after situation in which he always gave her a hard time and not others. Mr. Miller particularly favored boys, and it was Nora who got in trouble whenever boys would pick on her. She described one incident in detail in which a boy next to her pulled her hair three times before she punched him, whereupon Mr. Miller stood her in a corner and wrote her name on the board. Regarding the soiling problem, Nora explained, she just couldn't get to the restroom in time. Mr. Miller, Nora said, allowed the kids to go to the restroom by rows, and that was the way it was done, regardless of Nora's need to go quicker. Nora asked and was ignored; she waved her arms and was overlooked; and she stood up to no avail. As Nora told me about this heartless teacher, she became more animated, demonstrating each of her failed attempts to get his attention, with all the attending frustration.

I couldn't believe what a jerk this Mr. Miller was. I asked Nora what she thought could be done to set this guy straight, and I offered to call him (after I talked with Kathleen) to see if I could get to the bottom of this. But Nora had a different idea. She thought it better to have her mother write Mr. Miller a note. She even knew what she wanted the note to say. It was important that it properly put him in his place, essentially scolding him and telling him that he had better let Nora go to the bathroom. This sounded like a good plan, especially given that this solution was Nora's and she was participating in a meaningful way in our work together. I invited Kathleen to join our discussion, and Nora and I presented the note idea to her mom. Although Kathleen looked confused and a bit out of sorts, we composed the note right there. I continually checked out what we were writing with Nora to ensure that the note captured her sentiments. Nora was very happy with the note and put it in her purse to take to school to give to Mr. Miller. She skipped happily to the waiting room. The note must have really put that guy on notice because Nora never soiled her pants again.

But that's not the whole story. After Nora and I shared her plan with her mother, Kathleen asked once again to speak to me alone. She told me that Nora's math class was actually her fifth period and that her teacher was a woman—in fact, Nora had no male teachers, and, finally, there was no Mr. Miller at all in the school! Kathleen was at a loss about what to do about this and was worried that Nora's lie reflected deeper psychological issues. I reassured her that children have rich fantasy lives and that I wondered if this was a way that Nora has devised to solve her soiling problem.

I suggested that we implement the plan anyway to see what would happen and that we could immediately regroup if there was no movement, so to speak. So this impassioned, compelling story of the malicious Mr. Miller, with all its attending nuance and detail, was a lie, a big fat fabrication. But it worked. Nora defeated the poop problem. Perhaps it was Nora's way of "externalizing the problem" or saving face with an embarrassing situation, or maybe Kathleen was right and it was Nora's way of working through issues about her biological father and his death. Who knows? Follow-up revealed that the problem had vanished and that Nora had stopped talking about mean Mr. Miller.

Although one can speculate many reasons why Nora suddenly took control of her soiling problem, the fact remains that the lie served a purpose and was somehow therapeutic. Nora helped me to continue my reflection about lies and the truth in psychotherapy. Most lies are decidedly not malicious in nature, and it may be that clients have very good reasons for lying, and maybe, sometimes, the client is telling the truth, even when it is a lie.

5

USING PCOMS TO ACCELERATE YOUR DEVELOPMENT

Taking charge of your own learning is a part of taking charge of your life, which is the sine qua non in becoming an integrated person.
—Warren G. Bennis, *On Becoming a Leader*

Becoming a better therapist requires you to be proactive about two things: getting feedback from your clients and attending to your growth as a therapist. The previous four chapters detailed how to do the former. Now it is time to turn to your development, a critical factor that affects your ability to do good work, as well as your staying power as a viable force for change in clients' lives. As the Venn diagram in Chapter 1 (Figure 1.2) illustrates, you definitely matter in the therapy effectiveness equation.

As noted in Chapter 1, the field has not provided much help with regard to our professional growth. Sure, we are often exhorted to take care of ourselves and our relationships, as well as to continue our professional development, but not much guidance is offered about how to be proactive about becoming a better therapist. We are left to join the field's obsession with model and technique as the primary method of development and to hope that the platitudes about experience making us better will hold true.

http://dx.doi.org/10.1037/14392-005
On Becoming a Better Therapist, Second Edition: Evidence-Based Practice One Client at a Time, by B. L. Duncan

But now there is a better way. A massive, 20-year, multinational study of 11,000 therapists conducted by researchers David Orlinsky of the University of Chicago and Michael Helge Rønnestad of the University of Oslo not only provides a clear path to understanding therapist development but also captures the heart of our aspirations and perhaps the soul of our professional identity. For their book, *How Psychotherapists Develop: A Study of Therapeutic Work and Professional Growth* (2005), they collected and analyzed detailed reports from nearly 5,000 psychotherapists about the way they experienced their work and professional development. Since then, 6,000 more therapists have participated in the study as a collaborative project with members of the Society for Psychotherapy Research. In combination with the Partners for Change Outcome Management System (PCOMS), their study provides a framework for accelerating your growth. This chapter explores the implications of that massive study, integrates the findings with PCOMS, and details how you can take charge of your development and increase the percentage of your clients who achieve meaningful change.

TAKING YOUR DEVELOPMENT SERIOUSLY

When a man [sic] does not know what harbor he is making for, no wind is the right wind.

—Lucius Annaeus Seneca

One of the many fascinating aspects of the Orlinsky and Rønnestad (2005) investigation of therapist development is the consistency of response across therapist training, nationality, gender, and theoretical orientation. The study portrays psychotherapy as a unified field, despite what our warring professional organizations and theories often tell us. The specific findings reaffirm some characteristics that therapists already know about themselves and includes new, illuminating details.

As noted in Chapter 1, therapists stay in the profession not because of material rewards but because—above all—they value connecting deeply with clients and helping them to improve. Orlinsky and Rønnestad (2005) termed both what therapists seek in their professional careers and the satisfaction they receive from the work they do *healing involvement*. This concept describes therapists' reported experiences of being personally engaged, communicating a high level of empathy, feeling effective, and being able to deal constructively with difficulties. PCOMS provides a means to increase healing involvement and is a perfect fit with its definition: PCOMS ensures that justice is done to the relationship, effectiveness is a known commodity, and problems with either the alliance or outcome are handled in a way that enhances client experiences.

Healing involvement is the pinnacle of therapist development and represents us at our best—those times when we're attuned to our clients and the path required for positive change becomes clearly visible; those times when we can almost feel the "texture" of our therapeutic connection and know that something powerful is happening. But what causes this, and more important, how can we make it happen more often?

According to Orlinsky and Rønnestad (2005), healing involvement emerges from therapists' sense of *cumulative career development* (hereafter *career development*), as they improve their clinical skills, increase mastery, gradually surpass limitations, and gain a positive sense of their clinical growth over the course of their careers. As therapists accrue the hard-earned lessons offered by different settings, modalities, orientations, and populations, they want to come out on the positive end of any reappraisal of their experience. We apparently *need* to feel that we are improving with experience, that we are better than we were before.

But an even more powerful factor promoting healing involvement is what the authors called therapists' *sense of currently experienced growth* (hereafter *current growth*)—the feeling that we're learning from our day-to-day clinical work, deepening and enhancing our understanding and abilities. Orlinsky and Rønnestad (2005) suggested that this enlivening experience of current growth is fundamental to maintaining our positive work morale and clinical passion, central to our very survival as therapists. According to their study, the path to current growth is clear. It's intimately connected to therapists' experiences with clients and what they learn from them, and not to workshops and books trumpeting the latest and greatest advances in our field. Almost 97% of the therapists studied reported that learning from clients was a significant influence on their sense of development, with 84% rating the influence as "high." Apparently, therapists genuinely believe that clients are the best teachers.

But the finding that most impressed Orlinsky and Rønnestad (2005) was therapists' inextinguishable passion to get better at what they do. Some 86% of the therapists in the study reported they were "highly motivated" to pursue professional development. It appears that no matter how long they've been in the business, therapists still want to learn more and get better. To the question "Why is our growth so important to us?" Orlinsky and Rønnestad posited a close link between healing involvement and current growth. The ongoing sense that we're learning and developing in our day-to-day work gives a sense of engagement, optimism, and openness to the daily grind of seeing clients. It fosters continual professional reflection, which, in turn, motivates us to seek out training, supervision, personal therapy, or whatever it takes to be able to feel that the developmental process is continuing. Borrowing a term from Jerome Frank, having a sense of current growth "remoralizes" us, repairing the abrasions and stressors of the work and minimizing the danger of falling into a routine and becoming disillusioned. Orlinsky said:

> [It] is the balm that keeps our psychological skin permeable. Many believe that constantly hearing problems makes one emotionally callused and causes one to develop a "thick skin." But not therapists. We need "thin skin"—open, sensitive, and responsive—to connect with clients. (Duncan, 2011b, p. 41)

Current growth, then, is our greatest ally for sending the grim reaper of burnout packing: We *need* to feel we're growing, to fend off disenchantment.

Achieving a sense of healing involvement, the Mecca of therapist development, then, requires a continual evaluation of where we are compared with where we've been (career development), looking for evidence of our mastery. And we must keep examining our clinical experiences, mining our sessions for the golden moments that replenish us (current growth). The Orlinsky and Rønnestad (2005) study contains important information about who we are and what we have to do to remain a vital force in our clients' lives. It shows that our professional growth is a necessary part of our identity, as is our need to harvest the experiences that restore and enlighten us.

But let's do a reality check here: What is the evidence of our mastery or our professional growth? How do we know that we are learning from experience? Consider psychologist Paul Clement, who collected outcome data over his 26-year private practice (Clement, 1994). Impressively, he reported that 75% of his clients were rated as improved at the end of treatment. Keep in mind, however, that this effectiveness rate did not take into account a 19% dropout rate, and it was Clement, not the clients, who rated improvement. More relevant to our discussion is the fact that Clement assumed that he had improved over time—but the cold, hard reality was that, after he looked at his effectiveness over time, he discovered that he was no more effective after 26 years of practice than he'd been as a new graduate. The belief that experience alone will ultimately lead to better outcomes or professional growth is just as deceiving as the belief in the Holy Grail. There is only one way to know if we are learning from experience, and that is to track outcome.

Routine collection of client feedback allows you to monitor your outcomes and plot your career development, so you know about your effectiveness and, especially, so you can implement and evaluate strategies designed to improve your outcomes.

Career Development and Tracking Outcomes

Given the spreading institutional and funder pressures for accountability (see Chapter 8), combined with the call for outcome management by professional organizations, the collection of client-based outcome data to guide practice will likely become routine in the near future. For example, the American Psychological Association (APA) Commission on Accreditation (2011) suggested that students and interns "be provided with supervised experience in collecting quantitative outcome data on the psychological services they provide" (C-24). APA also created a new outcome measurement database to encourage practitioners to select outcome measures for practice (see http://practiceoutcomes.apa.org).

For outcome management to continue to grow, its inclusion in training programs is important. Ionita (2013), in a survey of Canadian psychologists, identified a lack of training as the biggest barrier that prevented clinicians from implementing outcome measures. Hatfield and Ogles (2004) found that those clinicians who assessed outcome had received substantial training; early training has a significant effect on practitioners' attitudes and behavior. Many programs across the country have implemented PCOMS and more are doing so every day. Two members of the Heart and Soul of Change Project (my organization; see https://heartandsoulofchange.com) have published articles about the benefits of implementing PCOMS in graduate training: Jacqueline Sparks (Sparks, Kisler, Adams, & Blumen, 2010) at the Family Therapy Program at the University of Rhode Island, and Jeff Reese (Reese, Usher, et al., 2009) in the Department of Educational, School, and Counseling Psychology at the University of Kentucky. Students are taught to use PCOMS to enhance therapist flexibility, evaluate outcome, and improve overall effectiveness. Additionally, many programs are using web-based software (see below) that allows automated data entry and real-time warnings to therapists when client ratings of either the alliance or outcome fall outside of established norms. It also permits data to be stored and analyzed, providing a base for supervision as well as faculty and student research. Most important, student therapists and clients receive immediate feedback about therapy progress, enhancing student learning, client engagement, and ultimate outcomes. Some of the other programs (including contact person), exemplifying the major disciplines, are the Graduate Psychology Programs at Our Lady of the Lake University (Joan Biever); the School of Social Work, University of New England (Danielle Wozniak); and the School of Humanities and Communication, College of Counseling, Columbia International University (Harvey Payne).

Consider the benefits for these budding clinicians and for you when you decide to monitor your outcomes over the course of your career. You will actually know how you are doing, without conjecture, in direct contrast to the way things have been to this point. You will not be in the dark about your effectiveness and suffer the same fate as Clement above or the clinicians in the Dew and Riemer (2003) and Walfish, McAlister, O'Donnell, and Lambert (2012) studies, reported in Chapter 1, who only had their fantasies to understand their effectiveness. Take the guesswork out of the equation. Becoming a better therapist is a proactive process. When you know how effective you are, you can plan, implement, and evaluate strategies to improve your outcomes. In short, tracking your career development permits you to learn from your experience, not repeat it.

And there is good reason to believe that it will help you get better. Another finding in the Norway Feedback Trial is germane to the purpose of this chapter. First, recall that nine of 10 therapists benefited from PCOMS. The effect of feedback, however, varied significantly among therapists. The less effective therapists (those with the worst outcomes without PCOMS) benefited *more* from feedback than the most effective therapists. Feedback, therefore, seems to act as a leveler among therapists, raising the effectiveness of lower or average therapists to that of their more successful colleagues. In fact, one therapist in the low-effectiveness group without PCOMS became the therapist with the *best* results with feedback. We return to the lessons learned by this Norwegian therapist later in the chapter. For now, this finding provides a hopeful implication: Regardless of where you start in terms of your effectiveness, you, too, can be among the most successful therapists.

Charting Your Career Development

Getting an accurate look at your development isn't complicated or expensive. You can start by simply entering your Outcome Rating Scale (ORS) data into an Excel file and tracking outcomes over time with calculations available in Excel: average intake and final session scores, number of sessions, dropout rates (more on this later), average change score (the difference between average intake and final session scores), and, ultimately, the percentage of your clients who reach reliable and/or clinically significant change (RCSC; see Chapter 3), and your effect size (ES). These easy-to-calculate performance indicators provide a detailed look at your development over time. You may also include client demographic information if you are interested in finding out which clients benefit the most and least from your services.

Average change provides a ready snapshot of how things are going. If your average change is 6 points or thereabouts, that's great. It means that on average your clients achieve reliable change from their encounters with you. The percentage of your clients that achieve RCSC provides a quick and easily understood metric of your effectiveness. This is a good way to track your development over time. ES is another way to understand change that sounds a lot more technical and complicated than it really is. A simple pre–post ES is just the average difference between the first and last session ORS scores divided by the first session standard deviation (SD) of the ORS (Excel will calculate the SD of your clients at session 1 and the ES, or you can use 8 as the *SD*). The usual reported ES of psychotherapy is 0.8 and the usual reported control group ES is 0.2 (accounting for the often heard comment that the therapy is four times more effective than no therapy). If you are anywhere in the neighborhood of .8, then you are in the all good range. Excel is a great way to start and will even plot ORS scores on a graph so that you can discuss progress in therapy with your clients. I tracked my outcomes with clients for many years with Excel before a software program was available.

There are easier ways to track your outcomes and career development, but they do involve some cost. First, if you work in an agency, you likely use some variety of electronic health record (EHR). These programs often have open data fields as well as graphing and data analysis functions. You could consult with your IT department or the EHR company to see if you can enter ORS scores, graph them, and aggregate the data to give you your average change, percentage reaching reliable change, and effect sizes. This could involve programming costs. Of course, such a system would not administer the measures or include the algorithms discussed in Chapter 2.

Then there are the web-based systems of tracking outcomes. But first let me say that there is a conflict of interest here. I have a financial relationship with the products I am about to discuss. Please keep this in mind as you evaluate whether either of the two systems is for you. Also know that there are other electronic outcome-tracking systems available using other measures (see Castonguay, Barkham, Lutz, and McAleavey, 2013, or Lambert, 2010, for a review). The first system is BetterOutcomesNow.com. I am a partner in this business that provides a web-based application of PCOMS. And I also license another company, MyOutcomes.com, which translates PCOMS to a web-based application. Here I receive a royalty based on sales. Both systems use the recently developed algorithms, administer the measures, compare the client's progress to the expected treatment response (ETR) based on the intake score, graph the scores, and aggregate the data at individual and agency levels. MyOutcomes.com also provides feedback messages and suggestions, written specifically to clients, geared toward informing clients of their progress.

More relevant to tracking outcomes and your career development, both systems enable a wide range of data collection and statistical reporting possibilities for individual practitioners and organizations. Both offer the ability to mine your data according to many parameters of time and performance. The single bit of information that is likely to be the easiest to understand and use is the percentage of your clients who reach the target. That is simply the percentage of clients who reached or exceeded the average change trajectory, or ETR, for clients entering services with the same intake score. The target score is the maximum score on the ETR line.

BetterOutcomesNow.com also calculates the percentage of your clients who attain reliable or clinically significant change. Tracking percentage of target and RCSC (either or both) provides an ongoing commentary about how effective you are. I encourage you to evaluate both systems as well as other options to find the best match for your particular needs and budget.

A brief word about dropouts: *Dropout* is a rather pejorative description. It places the onus on the client and essentially blames him or her for not attending some unspecified number of sessions. Client benefit seems a far better way to look at clients who have not returned for service. What we are trying to avoid is the client who discontinues service in an unplanned way, without experiencing reliable change or the ETR target. If it's planned, then we have referred the client on to greener pastures; or, in terms of healing involvement, we have dealt constructively with an encountered difficulty. If it is unplanned but the client reached target benefit or reliable change, then that is okay, too.

Of course, this doesn't include those clients who attend only one session. Some of these clients may have gotten what they were looking for, but some did not. The intake ORS score is telling. If the client was above the cutoff and didn't return, it is likely that he or she received all the services required; however, if the client scored under the cutoff, it may be that he or she didn't receive services that were satisfactory. A phone call or e-mail to these clients may prove helpful in understanding why they did not return, as well as obtaining information about how to categorize it for your records. It also offers an opportunity, if the client didn't get what he or she wanted, to invite the client in for another try with you or someone else.

Now you are ready to take charge of your career development. Simply track your effectiveness over time in any way that makes sense to you, either time increments (e.g., by quarter or annually) or by number of closed cases (e.g., 30 most recent closed cases vs. previous 30 closed cases). For confidence in the results, 30 is probably the minimum number. Also plot your unplanned terminations that did not reach reliable change or ETR targets. Tracking your outcomes in this manner allows you to consider your development and to strategically implement ideas, practices, and models, as well as to build skills to improve your effectiveness. You will readily see whether your efforts are paying off, and if your chosen methods need to be tweaked or changed outright.

Consider one example that illustrates what can happen when you monitor outcomes and take a proactive stance about your career development. Certified Trainer Morten Anker has been collecting outcome data since 2005. In 2006, 50% of his couple clients reached ETR and in 2013, 62.3% attained the ETR target. When asked how the improvement occurred, he suggested a combination of factors, some general and some specific. Generally, he thought that being more focused on his development and reflecting more about what could done differently with at-risk clients was a major contributor, as well as simply knowing that he was monitoring outcomes, pushed him to stretch himself. Specifically, and largely based on the recognition of clients who were not benefiting, he sought out training in two areas: a more proactive search for and application of couple strengths to address their relational concerns and the ability to intervene and provide empathy with couple affective experiences with those clients who were more emotionally oriented.

And the result: Not only measureable improvements in effectiveness but also a new take on his work. Anker has reported that he feels more confident in bringing different ideas and working styles into action, thereby accommodating more couples. He concluded by saying, "It's a strange mixture of being confident, uncertain, and humble. . . . Believing in my own skills and that somehow, in this foggy, uncertain ground something useful and good for clients will come of it" (M. G. Anker, 2013, personal communication).

At some point in time, your growth in effectiveness will slow down and eventually you will plateau. That is perfectly okay. And don't get freaked out if you are not as effective as you thought or think you should be. Be realistic. For example, Okiishi et al. (2006) looked at the effectiveness of 71 therapists who saw at least 30 clients for a total of 6,499 clients. Using the Outcome Questionnaire 45.2 (OQ) system as the outcome measure, the authors contrasted the top and bottom 10%, the most and least effective therapists. The clients of the top 10% changed nearly 3 times more than the bottom 10%. More germane to what you should expect, the top 10% most effective therapists achieved a reliable and clinically significant change rate of 43.9%, while the bottom 10% attained a 28.0% rate. So don't beat yourself up if you are less than 50% reaching target or RCSC. Most of us are. Keep in mind that you are including all your clients (except one-session clients) and not just completers, as most studies do. Also recall that you are now dealing constructively (failing successfully) with those clients who are not reaching target.

> **Bottom Line:** *Charting your career development and implementing strategies to improve your effectiveness puts you in charge of your growth as a therapist. Making your career development a central consideration will likely increase your sense of healing involvement, accelerate your growth, and benefit your clients. Whatever your effectiveness is, don't stress.*

CURRENT GROWTH

It's not what you look at that matters; it's what you see.
—Henry David Thoreau

According to the Orlinsky and Rønnestad study (2005), the most powerful influence on your development is your perception of your *current growth*, your here-and-now sense of ongoing improvement in your understanding and ability to do this work. Recall that therapist experiences of current growth are mainly influenced by the quality of their clinical work with clients. Learning from clients was consistently endorsed as the most influential factor impacting current growth, with the exception that supervision won by a nose for novices. But your involvement is required; you have to keep your head and heart in the game despite all the reasons—like unrealistic productivity requirements; mountainous, meaningless paperwork; and gut-wrenching client circumstances—that conspire to have us give up on ourselves and accept monotony and negative outcomes. This is where client feedback can really help us.

Tracking your outcomes gives you a big-picture view of your career development and a microscopic view of your current growth. Looking at who is and isn't benefiting offers opportunities for learning what is working and what is not; you also can glean much from how you turn things around for the clients who are not benefiting, and how you manage "failing successfully." Your reflections and discussions with colleagues and supervisors, as well as with clients, will permit you to squeeze all the learning out of each situation. There is much there to be had, and attending to feedback can help you make the most of it.

Clients provide the opportunity for constant learning about the human condition, different cultures and worldviews, and the myriad ways in which people transcend adversity and cope with the unthinkable. But, although we learn a great deal almost by osmosis from our clients, tracking outcomes takes the notion that "the client is the best teacher" to a different, higher, and more immediately practical level. Tracking outcomes with clients not only focuses us more precisely on the here-and-now of sessions, it takes us beyond mere intuition and subjective impressions to quantifiable feedback about how the client is doing. We get unambiguous data about whether clients are benefiting and whether our services are a good fit for them. From their reactions and reflections, we receive information that we can use in figuring out the next step to take in therapy. This in vivo training promotes the expansion of our theoretical and technical repertoire. In short, tracking outcomes enables your clients—especially those who aren't responding well to your therapeutic business-as-usual—to teach you how to work better. In fact, clients who *aren't* benefiting offer us the most opportunity for learning by helping us, actually demanding, that we step outside of our comfort zones.

Start by collecting the graphs of all of your current clients. Separate the graphs into two piles: clients who are benefiting and clients who are not. Consider the following, with regard to the clients who are benefiting:

- What is working with these clients?
- What is client feedback telling you about progress and the alliance?
- How are you interacting with these clients in ways that are stimulating, catalyzing, or crystallizing change?

- What are these benefiting clients telling you that they like about your work with them?
- What are they telling you about what works?

Also consider the clients who are not benefiting:

- What is working in the conversations about the lack of progress?
- What is client feedback telling you about progress and the alliance?
- How are you interacting with these clients in ways that open discussion of other options, including referral?
- What are these not-benefiting clients telling you that they like about how you are handling these tough talks?
- What are they telling you about what works in these discussions?
- What have you done differently with these not-benefiting clients? How have you stepped out of your comfort zone and done something you have never done?

The idea here is to consider the lessons that clients are teaching us in their feedback via the ORS and the Session Rating Scale (SRS) and to more proactively reflect about these lessons and their importance to our development. Recall the anonymous Norwegian therapist who became the best therapist in the group after using feedback. Here are her reflections about her current growth after adding PCOMS to her work:

Feedback helped me be more straightforward, more courageous. I inquired more directly about what we could do together. I conveyed more of a sense of security, knowing that clients would set me straight. Clients taught me how to handle it when I was not useful. I never had this information before, so I didn't have this opportunity.

***

Clients and I reflected more on their changes and on the sessions. We got more concrete regarding change, how it started, and what else would be helpful. PCOMS helped me to be more to the point and focused.

***

ORS feedback pinpointed that we have a common responsibility. I seemed to carry too much of the load before. Shared responsibility engages clients more.

***

PCOMS helped me take risks and invite negative feedback. So, I asked for it, showed I could handle it, validated it, and then incorporated it in the work. That is what it's all about, real collaboration.

***

It made things visible, more tangible. I used the graphs. Clients had to reflect more, and it even challenged them. The graphs brought more clarity—I could refer to the graph and say, "What did you do here at this point where things were better?"

***

All in all, PCOMS made me feel more secure and I was more in tune with what was happening. I am now more collaborative and allow things to emerge rather than following a set way to work. I definitely dared more, and did new things. Clients were always there to bring me back in. I would say, "If you hadn't told me that, this therapy wouldn't work." It always seemed vague before, without the feedback.

The therapist noted several things that feedback brought to her work and what she had learned from her experiences with clients: the value of clarity and focus, of shared responsibility, purpose, and true collaboration—and, important, a sense of security and the courage to take risks, allowing uncertainty to be part of the work (more on that in Chapter 7). Her development seemed to be accelerated by her attention to how feedback enhanced her work—her sense of current growth.

Learning from your experiences applies not only to PCOMS but also to your work in general; any differences can be important markers that can accelerate your development. Just as Chapter 3 detailed the process with clients, you can empower yourself by noting your changes, putting a magnifying glass on them, and understanding how you were able to pull them off. Recognize that these improvements depict a new chapter in your development as a therapist. Perhaps you did something for the first time with a client, or a light went off and you now understand something in a different way. Maybe, because of a client presentation or request, you applied an explanation and solution that you previously had only denigrated. Or perhaps you noticed that you were bit more keen, engaged, and interactive when the conversation moved in unplanned ways. When you articulate what is different about your work, you make it more real and are more likely to continue it in the future, so it is important to clearly detail what you are learning as you go along. Take the time to tease out your new insights and methods as you examine your current clients. Ask yourself these questions or any others that help you make sense of your current growth:

How is it different from what I would have done before?
What are the before-and-after distinctions?
How am I going to continue with the strides I have taken?
How was I able to be different this time?

Was it planned or just emerged? Is this a new pattern for me? What does this change say about my development as a therapist? What does it say about my identity as a therapist?

Routine collection of client feedback provides similar benefits for both therapists and clients. Using the measures helps you and the client clarify goals, close out distractions, and find out for sure how things are going. PCOMS sets apart a period of time in each session and allows you to test your assumptions and adjust to client preference, allowing you to master new tools and learn new ideas. Perhaps, also, acquiring client feedback and experiencing your current growth may encourage you to enjoy your craftsmanship for its own sake. When you are enjoying the work of psychotherapy for its own sake, I believe it is likely that your clients are benefiting. This may be what the art of therapy is about. And, as the Norwegian therapist who went from nearly worst to first aptly illustrates, securing PCOMS places you in an accelerated course of development, bringing your current growth to light in ways that can help you write new chapters in your story about being a counselor.

> **Bottom Line:** *Orlinsky and Rønnestad (2005) asserted:*
> *We strongly recommend that practitioners of all professions, career levels, and theoretical orientations give careful and serious attention to their current work morale as reflected in their ongoing sense of development as psychotherapists. (p. 196)*

THEORETICAL BREADTH

Believe those who are seeking the truth; doubt those who find it.
—André Gide

Orlinsky and Rønnestad (2005) also identified *theoretical breadth* as an important influence on healing involvement, although less so than career development or current growth. They suggested that understanding clients from a variety of conceptual contexts enhances therapist flexibility in responding to the challenges of clinical work. Indeed, therapists at every career level who combined several theoretical orientations tended to have greater amounts of career development. Integrative–eclectic practitioners were the "most growing" therapists—a good reason to take the plunge in many conceptual pools.

This makes sense. Possessing a range of understandings of client problems as well as possible methods to address them allows therapists to experience healing involvement more often with more clients—a suggestion in line with what the eclecticism/integration movement has been telling us all along (e.g., Norcross & Goldfried, 2005; Stricker & Gold, 2006). PCOMS can help here. Tailoring your approach based on client feedback will lead you to more theoretical breadth as you expand your repertoire to serve more clients. PCOMS enhances your ability to be tuned to client preferences and encourages your flexibility to try out new ideas in search of what resonates with clients— opening you to a range of theoretical explanations and attending methods.

Therapist allegiance to any particular theoretical content involves a trade-off that enables and restricts options. Theoretical loyalty provides a clear direction but is inherently limiting; cookie-cutter therapy is much easier and safer to do, but will be useful for only a portion of the people you see. This realization is the raison d'être of psychotherapy integration/eclecticism, which continues to dominate how therapists understand and conduct clinical work (Lambert, 2013). Stricker and Gold (2006) suggested that, counter to manualized therapy, which might perhaps be described as "theoretical loyalty on steroids," integration/eclecticism is synonymous with psychotherapeutic creativity and originality. In short, therapists' preference for more eclectic integrative practices speaks to their desire to foster what works with the client in the office now.

Allegiance to any theoretical dogma can also be unwittingly oppressive. Theories are not neutral; they were created by someone, and that someone (or some persons) did not channel truth but operated within his or her own social location—meaning gender, race, ethnicity, social class, sexuality, and historical time—with all the biases that go with it. By valuing theoretical flexibility, we are less likely to try to force a model on someone whose life experiences and view of reality may be quite different from our own.

One by-product of this increased theoretical breadth is in helping us let go of the idea of Truth with a capital T, so that we respect and utilize the unique worldview, culture, and preferences of each client. This means that you have to grapple with the "truth" value that you may have ascribed to your favored theories. You may have to challenge yourself when you think theories represent how people *really* are and what people *have* to do to realize benefit or make changes.

We probably can hold, at most, only two or three systems of therapy in our heads at one time. However, we can access far more frames or explanations of the difficulties that clients bring to therapy. But to do that, we have to open ourselves to Jerome Frank's observation that the important stuff that models offer is not their inherent truth across clients but, rather, a rationale for the client's problem and a ritual to solve it (Frank, 1973). Knowing that all models can be boiled down to an explanation and remedy makes them far easier to get a handle on and try out—not the arduous 2 years of intensive supervision to understand or implement that is often portrayed. But you might want to keep that to yourself.

In their provocative chapter about model and technique in *The Heart and Soul of Change*, Anderson, Lunnen, and Ogles (2010) concluded:

> Clearly, the "truth" of any model and associated strategies is not critical to success. Rather, each merely offers an opportunity for engagement of the client and therapist in a process that promises to be helpful. . . . The implications for treatment are clear. Clinicians not only need to be aware of the many meaningful cultural myths available, but [also to be] open to altering techniques, style, and approach in order to achieve a better fit with the client. (pp. 146, 148)

So how does one broaden theoretical horizons or remain open to "the many meaningful cultural myths available?" First, pay attention to those theories that just plain make sense to you: the ones that fit your own views of human nature, problems, and solutions. Expand what you already know. For example, the interactional approach particularly rang true for me (thanks to an early mentor, Scott Fraser). That affinity led me to embrace the myths and rituals of other similar approaches over the years—like Eriksonian, solution focused, language-based, and narrative therapies—which, although different from one another, generally come out of the same camp. Another early mentor, Steve McConnell, an existential psychotherapist, introduced me to the humanistic perspectives that opened me up to the likes of Rogers, Bugental, and Yalom. Finally, my stress management experience during my internship under the supervision of Fred Ernst and Joe Rock allowed me to see the benefits of behavioral and cognitive–behavioral ways of working. With each new understanding, I became more flexible in my approach, could consider more options, and had more things to bring to the table for discussion with clients. It also allowed what Rønnestad and Skovholt (2013) called *continual professional reflection*, a more seasoned way to embrace the lessons of clinical experience. Perhaps most important, I, like many modern eclectic therapists, became aware that all approaches have validity—they are but metaphorical accounts of how people can change in therapy—and became open to the advantages of many theoretical perspectives.

PCOMS can assist us to broaden our theoretical horizons. Lack of change on the ORS sounds the alarm and stimulates a reconsideration of any approach we are using and stretches us to add new ideas to our repertoire. The *Approach* scale on the SRS encourages a frank discussion with the client about the fit of our methods and the impetus to find ways that resonate more with the client and encourage his or her participation. Navigating the waters outside our safe therapy harbors allows new discoveries for us and our clients.

Another way to expand your theoretical repertoire is to listen to your client's ideas and throw your self-consciousness to the side—let the client's theory be your theory with that client. Tailoring your approach to your client's ideas provides opportunities for expanding your theoretical breadth. This may not be so easy to do if a client's ideas rub you the wrong way. For example, at one time I was biased against any historical expedition into clients' lives. I didn't like the archeological focus of that approach and strongly believed that it promoted the view that clients were victims of their past. I was rigid in my thinking here, and while I didn't know it, I'm sure I lost plenty of clients because of it. I likely didn't "hear" what these folks were asking for, so I didn't secure an agreement about the tasks of therapy. Then one day, a young woman, Claire, told me that she had been sexually abused as a child and that she wanted to pursue therapy based on a "Courage to Heal" framework, a very popular approach back in the 1980s. I immediately bristled and offered to refer her to therapists who I knew did "that kind of work."

But, to the benefit of my development as a therapist (not to mention Claire's progress in therapy), she didn't accept my refusal. She told me that a close friend of hers (who also had been sexually abused) had seen me, and Claire was convinced that I was the person for the job. Claire asked, "Couldn't you at least look at the book and give it a try?" Essentially, she shamed me into stepping outside of my comfort zone, and it was incredibly rewarding. We followed the workbook, I shared my concerns along the way, and Claire greatly benefited from the work—which was her own idea of how she could be helped. Her toughest task was to get me on board. The Courage to Heal approach provided a rationale for Claire's experience of problems and a remedy to address them. I learned that if the approach resonates with the client, it is the least I can do to believe that it can help. Claire helped me learn that theory has value only in the particular assumptive world of the participants—the client and therapist—and that theory need not be "true" across clients; rather, any theory needs only to be valid with this client in my office now. This realization led me to pursue and incorporate any understanding that made sense to the client.

Client problems also offer a rich area to explore for explanations and solutions. For example, if a client presents with symptoms of trauma, or if you tend to see a lot of clients with that presentation, it makes sense to explore the many approaches that have been successful and offer the one that better fits the client's sensibilities about change, preferences, and culture. You can boil down all of these approaches to their essence, a rationale and remedy, and attempt to apply the ideas. And if it is your first time applying a particular myth and ritual, just tell the client and ask for his or her help. Clients tend to enjoy the collaborative adventure of the endeavor; if they don't, offer to refer them on. Put yourself out there a bit more.

Finally, be proactive in adding theoretical dimensions to your work. Become familiar with many ways of understanding problems and solutions.

Play "on the other hand" games with your colleagues. When someone presents an explanation about a client difficulty, first ensure that the client's perspective is thoroughly represented, and then encourage everyone to present alternative myths and rituals. Then turn the discussion toward which description may represent the better fit with the client. Talking with your colleagues about varied rationales and remedies will benefit everyone's work. It is also fun.

> **Bottom Line:** *Proactively seek an understanding of many different rationales and remedies, in addition to learning some systems in detail. Take theoretical risks. Your theoretical plurality will serve you and your clients well.*

CONCLUSION

It is not the strongest of the species that survive, nor the most intelligent, but the one most responsive to change.
                                                                    —Charles Darwin

This chapter presented the three pathways to Orlinsky and Rønnestad's (2005) empirically derived concept of healing involvement, the therapist's pinnacle of development. Tracking your career development via PCOMS data was presented as taking the guesswork out of your growth and ensuring that you do, indeed, benefit from your experience over time and not merely repeat it. Using your outcomes as the ultimate arbiter of your growth also provides a way to evaluate the different skills and methods you implement to improve your effectiveness. Different methods of calculating your effectiveness were discussed as well as available systems of data collection and analyses. The primary pathway to accelerate your development, your current growth, was also presented. Keeping your finger on the pulse of your day-to-day encounters with clients has a big payoff, influencing not only healing involvement but also your morale and ability to stay vital in the face of the everyday demands of the work. Detailing once again a proactive process in which you need to take charge, I suggested that you systematically examine your work with your current clients and apply a strategy of empowerment and reflection to harvest the lessons of clinical experience. Finally, it was recommended that you drop the belief in the "truth" value of any given approach in favor of adding many valid myths and rituals to your repertoire. When your therapeutic business as usual isn't working for the client, you've been offered a great opportunity to become a better therapist. I encouraged you to pay attention to your client's theories, lose your self-consciousness, and try out differing perspectives and techniques to both find the best fit for the client and expand your theoretical horizons.

CLIENTS ARE THE BEST TEACHERS: THEIR STORIES DOCUMENT OUR DEVELOPMENT

Forget about style; worry about results.

—Bobby Orr

A self-described agoraphobic, Fred left the house only for our sessions, and then only when accompanied by his wife, who stayed in the waiting room. When he was a long-haired, 19-year-old college student, Fred had been arrested in an auto-wrecking yard in rural Texas, trying to steal parts for his broken-down Toyota. In the local county jail, he suffered multiple rapes and beatings, setting in motion a chain of events that led to a term in state prison and a stay in a state psychiatric hospital. He'd been deeply agoraphobic ever since and was the veteran of numerous unsuccessful psychiatric treatments and years of psychotherapy.

In our first session, Fred made only a few brief references to this history. In fact, most of our conversation was devoted to shooting the breeze about basketball—the NCAA finals were in full swing and we were both fans. Fred became very animated as we discussed the various teams, coaches, and players, and I enjoyed his perceptions and his company. In each session, we spent more and more time talking about basketball and less and less about agoraphobia. By the end of the fourth session, though, I was wondering whether we were ever going to talk about anything else. So, primarily because I thought we ought to be doing something, I asked Fred to construct a list (a desensitization hierarchy) of the things he would like to be able to do, ranking them from the most difficult to the least difficult. I was happy now because I thought we had a focus and direction, and I could introduce relaxation, imagery, and covert rehearsal over the next couple of sessions.

Fred returned for the fifth session. The NCAA final game was over and we both played Monday-morning quarterback for about 30 minutes before I asked Fred for the list. He handed it to me, not missing a beat in discussing the game. Out of 20 items, his three most difficult contemplated actions were: going to the bank, going to the dentist, and going to the mall. Although I didn't comment, I noticed that there was a checkmark by each of those items. Finally, in a break in the action, I asked Fred what the checkmarks meant. He casually replied that he'd accomplished all three. I almost jumped out of my chair, but Fred wanted to return to talking about the game. So, in the interstices of our basketball conversation, I asked him what the achievement of these goals meant to him, where he thought these changes might lead, and what might keep them going.

In the following weeks, we kept talking mainly about things we both enjoyed—sports, antiques, camping, and the wilderness. On the margins of these talks, Fred told me he wanted to exercise and started thinking aloud about sports he might take up. He also wanted to contribute financially to his family, which depended on his wife's modest income as a software analyst while he took care of their young daughter. Such discussions took no more than 10 minutes of every session. By the eighth session, Fred had begun a jewelry business in his garage, regularly ran errands in town, and had taken up mountain biking.

In Fred's last session, his 10th, he looked back and talked to me about all the times we'd shot the breeze. He didn't even mention the desensitization hierarchy, which never became part of the work (given Fred's audacity to change before the intervention was implemented). He told me that I was the therapist who had really understood him. The others, he said, had cut off his attempts at conversation to focus on his problems—they were too "clinical." Fred also said that he valued talking to me man to man, and, though he realized that I was not his friend, it felt good to connect in that way nevertheless.

Fred taught me that it was the relationship that counted, and our potential influence on the client's evaluation of the alliance was the magic technique I'd always dreamed of finding. This doesn't mean I'm suggesting enshrining "shooting the breeze" as the newest Holy Grail—not all clients want to spend their sessions talking about basketball. It does mean that it is important to listen to what clients want and to engage them in the process of making a difference in their lives. Previously, I'd thought of this sort of wooing as a precursor to the real business of therapy—much as "foreplay" was once defined as something separate from the real stuff of sex. Now, I realized that the alliance was, in fact, the therapy.

6

THE HEART AND SOUL OF CHANGE

From the moment I picked up your book until I laid it down, I was convulsed with laughter. Someday I intend reading it.

—Groucho Marx

I admit it. I am a snob. Not about money, possessions, wine, food, coffee, social status, or anything like that. I am a snob about psychotherapy, the work I love, and about who teaches me about it. And I always have been. When I was graduate student, a professor proclaimed, "Ninety percent of the patients you see in CMHCs [community mental health centers] are borderlines." I worked at a CMHC at the time and thought his comment reflected a jaundiced view of clients, so I asked him how many clients he had seen in CMHCs. The answer—zero, nada, zilch, none. I wasn't impressed and didn't do much to hide it (which I wouldn't recommend to you graduate students out there). I became very aware of the clinical experience of those teaching me.

I continued my psychotherapy elitism when I was at the Dayton Institute for Family Therapy, a training center where I was privileged to work side by side with some very talented folks, one of whom was my friend and colleague, Greg Rusk. We were both in-the-trenches guys who liked to consider ourselves "thinking therapists," and we often went to workshops together, read the

http://dx.doi.org/10.1037/14392-006
On Becoming a Better Therapist, Second Edition: Evidence-Based Practice One Client at a Time, by B. L. Duncan

same books about therapy, and spent many late evenings after our one-way mirror trainings in vigorous conversation. What emerged from these lively exchanges was the recognition that we were kindred-spirit snobs. We grew weary of folks telling us how to do therapy who really didn't do much of it themselves.

Some of the biggest workshop stars, in fact, have minimal therapy experience, and some have not held one full-time therapy gig—they pretty much went from graduate school to doing workshops based on the luck of associations with celebrities in the therapy field and/or their ability to put on a good show. Entertainment is huge in the workshop business; some presenters play instruments, do magic tricks, and incorporate physical comedy into their schtick. I don't mean there isn't any substance to any of them. In fact, many useful frames for practice have come from these spinmasters. But that's what it tends to look like over time: not evolutions of the work but new performances and frames to sell.

On the other side are the researchers. I have an abiding respect for research and for the folks who do it. I know firsthand that it is indeed a herculean task to conduct research and publish it, especially in top-tier journals. Research should inform practice and be consumed by clinicians—and translated by clinicians. This has been a core goal of mine since I attempted the translation of common-factors research in my first book, *Changing the Rules* (Duncan, Solovey, & Rusk, 1992). So, I'm not saying that there isn't much to learn from researchers. But research needs to pass the through a final clinical filter. When you get two or more people in the room in an endeavor to make a meaningful difference in someone's life, the research needs to resonate with the work itself and the people doing it.

This chapter brings my voice as a therapist to join in hopeful harmony with the best of what research has to offer. This chapter picks up on the discussion of career development and offers empirically based suggestions that have passed through a clinical filter for improving your work. Although traditionally the field has urged us to search for the Holy Grail to enhance our effectiveness, there has not been much return for our efforts here. Psychotherapy is no more effective now, with all our treatment technologies (400 of them) and evidence-based treatments (almost 200 of them), than it was 40 years ago. Nevertheless, although adding models and techniques to your repertoire may show minimal gains on career development in the short run, your accumulation of theoretical breadth will ultimately serve you well.

So it is perfectly fine to put time into learning models and techniques, but it may make more sense to also focus your efforts on the areas that will bring you the biggest return on your investment: on the factors of change commensurate with the amount of variance they account for. Here is where the research about the common factors pays dividends. Recall from Chapter 1 that the client accounts for the overwhelming majority of the variance of outcome, and that the Gassmann and Grawe (2006) study suggested that those therapists who spend more time in resource activation as opposed to problem activation attain better outcomes. Securing clients' participation and rallying their resources are good places to start, and this chapter demonstrates some ways you can harvest client strengths in the service of client goals. This chapter also embraces the enormous body of evidence supporting the power of the alliance, translating that research to deepen your appreciation of its potent impact on outcomes.

In short, Chapter 6 brings you the *heart and soul of change*. The strength of what the client brings to therapy and the impact of the alliance on outcome inspired the title of both this chapter and the book I coedited about the common factors (Duncan, Miller, Wampold, & Hubble, 2010), as well as the organization of therapists, professors, and researchers that I direct. The client's resources and resiliencies and the therapeutic alliance together represent the heart and soul of therapy. Your focus on these primary sources, in conjunction with the Partners in Change Outcome Management System (PCOMS), I believe, is the best way to accelerate your development.

RALLYING CLIENTS TO THE CAUSE: THE HEROIC CLIENT

Until lions have their historians, tales of hunting will always glorify the hunter.

—African Proverb

I hate to tell you, but we have been the hunters in the above proverb. After all, how many books have you read about great clients? As I mentioned in the preface, I chose the word *heroic* for a previous book to highlight the client's contribution to outcome as well as the field's propensity to see the more "unheroic" sides of those we serve (see Duncan, Miller, & Sparks, 2004). I also, via a literary device, wanted to expose psychotherapy's hidden assumptions: the heroic psychotherapist, a knight in shining armor riding high on the white stallion of theory, brandishing a sword of evidence-based treatments, ready to rescue the helplessly disordered patient terrorized by the psychic dragon of mental illness. Hyperbole aside, the client's role in change has been significantly dismissed, whereas the therapist's part in change as the expert steeped in theory and technique has been greatly exaggerated. We *do* play a significant role in change, but we are not knights in shining armor. Using PCOMS allows clients to be the historians of their own change, central players in the psychotherapeutic process, and it permits you to be the historian of your career development.

You can cast clients as the primary agents of change in two ways. The first way is by believing in your clients and expecting that your outcomes will be enhanced when clients take the leading role. The second way is by listening for and being curious about clients' strengths and competencies: hearing the heroic stories that reflect their part in bouncing back from adversity, surmounting obstacles, and initiating action. Although there are many questions you can ask to catalyze such conversations regarding client abilities, as well as several "strength-based" approaches to draw on, there is no formula here; the key is your attitude regarding the client's inherent abilities and resiliencies. Attending to heroic stories requires a balance between listening empathically to difficulties and being alert to evidence of strengths that you *know* are there—to resonate with despair but refuse to succumb to it (Duncan et al., 2004).

This does not mean ignoring pain, being a cheerleader, or glossing over tough issues. Rather, it requires that you listen to the whole story: the suffering and the endurance, the pain and the coping, the desperation and the desire for something different. Listening for heroic stories only suggests that you open yourself to the existence of several competing descriptions about the client's experience. Diagnosis tells but one story; a problem description tells another. Many other tales of survival and courage simultaneously exist. Human beings are complex and have multiple sides, depending on who is recounting them and what sides are emphasized. The folklore of our field has drawn us toward the more pathological account as the only or best version. It is neither.

Consider Sam, a very distressed young man who scored a 7.4 on the Outcome Rating Scale (ORS; Miller & Duncan, 2000).

> *Sam:* I've been in a lot more physical pain lately. . . . No one wants to be around me because of my mental illness. . . . My desire to self-injure has been higher. . . . My financial situation is out of control. . . . My dreams have been increasingly violent toward my stepfather; his mental torture is constant, telling me that I am never going to amount to anything . . . and that I am worthless and do everything wrong. It's hard to argue with him because here I am, I amounted to nothing, he's right. . . . And I fantasize about it every day, different ways of just crushing him. . . . And I feel just hopeless . . . and half the time I am fighting to survive and half the time I am wondering if I should just stop fighting. . . . Part of me hopes that just the whole system will collapse, that society itself will just fold. I am depressed now and the rest of the world is normal. Take an event that would depress anyone. And then being depressed would be normal, so in a way the whole world would come to my level of depression so I wouldn't be abnormal.

What was running through your mind as you read these excerpts from the first 20 minutes of the session? Call 911? Here are stories of self-harm, suicidal ideation, homicidal ideation, and apocalyptic fantasies. While empathic to such dire issues, I refused to cave in to those accounts as the only or truest ones of Sam's identity as a human being. As you read the following excerpts, consider these questions:

- What are the obvious and hidden strengths, resources, and resiliencies?
- What are the competing stories of Sam's identity?
- What is already present that can be recruited to solve the problems?

Barry: Makes a lot of sense. Another way of saying that would be that anyone experiencing what you are—if they were in pain, just came out of surgery, were in a financial hole they couldn't get out of, and didn't have anything going socially—anybody on the planet would be depressed, anybody walking in your shoes would be depressed, and anybody would be struggling with whether or not they wanted to live. That's a long way to say that no wonder you are depressed.

***

Sam: I am one of those leeches on society. I am a negative person. I take away. I think that is one of the reasons why I want to see it all come apart.

Barry: Well, no wonder. It would be like a new beginning if everything came apart—you would have a fighting chance to have a different kind of life. Right now you don't see any hope for there being a different kind of life possible.

Sam: Right, I feel like I could contribute to a society that had decayed to the point where it would need my contribution. I just feel like I would be really good in a situation like that. I could lead a small ragtag band of warriors to lead attacks on the machines or bad guys.

Barry: So it's like there is this inner warrior that wants to come out, you'd be able to take charge of that situation, to contribute in that situation.

Sam: I feel like I would be a good leader.

***

Barry: What keeps you from killing your stepfather?

Sam: The only two things that's keeping him alive is my fear of getting caught and my own personal realization that killing him would not make me feel any better. . . . I am so full of rage when it comes to him. He screwed up all of our lives. Everything he touches is destroyed. I almost feel like it's my responsibility to take him out of the world so he can't do any more harm. But then I would have to do harm to do that, but I can't do that because it's against my religion.

**

Barry: A couple of things occur to me. One is that it's really not surprising that you are struggling now, there are a lot of low spots in your life, a lot of shit has happened in the past, a lot of animosity directed at your stepfather, a lot of bad things have happened to you, to wake up every day and feel like you are a leech on society, your identity, this inner warrior never being able to be expressed, all this stigma that goes along with the mental disability, the physical pain, being in a financial hole—there is just a lot of stuff conspiring to make you feel very bad about yourself. On the other hand, not only do you have this inner warrior aspect of you, that leadership, knowing that there is a lot more to you than this society at this time allows you to express, there are also all these other things about you that are very impressive. You are really a savvy guy, you're smart, you have a dry sense of humor; we didn't laugh much, but you said a lot of things that were funny. And you have a little bit of a twisted way of looking at things, and that's very funny and I think that's a real strength you have. You know a lot of stuff about a lot of things—you're bringing a lot to the table, not the least of which is your insight about your stepfather and your ability to control yourself.

Many stories have emerged: The story of Sam's problems—suicidal/ homicidal ideation, depression, and self-loathing—was real. But it was not the only one and not the most representative of his identity. There was another tale of a remarkably insightful and reflective man who wants to contribute to society, a leader, an inner warrior who controls his impulses. Sam's realization that killing his stepfather wouldn't make him feel any better was more than impressive. Clients' heroic stories pave the way for change by showcasing abilities and making them available for use. You might have been thinking that wishing for the end of the world would provide few resources to harness for change. Consider Sam's concluding statements:

Sam: Somehow, in some way, I'll find a way to give back to society. And it may not be today or tomorrow, but someday, because I am pretty young and I have a lot of time to figure out how I can make society better, and it doesn't have to be the end of the world.

A focus on Sam's more heroic aspects shifted the conversation and seemed to catalyze his enthusiasm for doing something different. And in no way did I gloss over the very serious problems that were on the table. I emphasize this because sometimes people think that when you recruit strengths, it means that you ignore the real problems. Not so: You rally resources so that you can address the real problems.

You can also inquire more directly about strengths and resilience. Recall the discussion in Chapter 1 about problem versus resource activation: The more effective therapists spend more time on the latter. The ORS fits nicely with a strength-based focus. Any mark to the right of the far left can be cause for discussion about why the mark isn't lower. How is the client managing to keep the mark where it is? What resources are being drawn upon? Differences between the domains can spark conversations about what it is about one life area that makes it better than another. Low scores identify areas in which the client is looking for change, but high marks on the different scales also pinpoint client competencies, resources, and social supports. Can strengths in one area that is going well be harvested and used in the arena of the client's troubles?

Several systems of therapy are "strength based" and offer a plethora of ways to inquire about client competencies (de Jong & Berg, 2008; Duncan & Sparks, 2010; Saleeby, 2006; Thomas & Cockburn, 1998; or visit https:// heartandsoulofchange.com). I encourage you to check out these approaches and select questions that are a good fit for you. Finding ones that resonate with you and that you can authentically incorporate is key. Remember that you are the therapy you deliver, so every part of it has to be genuinely you.

One question coming from a narrative tradition that is a good fit for me is, "Who in your life wouldn't be surprised to see you overcome the problem before you now?" Consider Yolanda, a young woman I saw the day after child protective services (CPS) removed her children because she had started using crack again. CPS was not the bad guy here—there was a contract and Yolanda violated it when she started using again. So one story you could tell about Yolanda was that she was the crack-addicted mom who had her kids removed by CPS. But what I am talking about here is believing—no, not believing, but actually *knowing*—that this story is not the only one that can be told, and it is not the one that best reflects who Yolanda really is.

Yolanda was devastated—teary and lethargic—and she had an understandable edge. But far worse was that she barely said anything and didn't even look at me. Though I started "knowing" that there was more to the story, as the old saying goes, that and $3 will get me a cup of coffee. I wasn't getting anywhere with Yolanda, and I was worried. Here were two people who couldn't have been more different from one another—Yolanda was an impoverished 21-year-old African American woman whose world had just split wide open, and I, an old middle-class white guy without a care in the world, relatively speaking. Silence is indeed golden, but it was not leading to any further reflection and comment, so I asked a question to see if I could get Yolanda engaged.

> *Barry:* Yolanda, who in your life wouldn't be surprised to see you stand up to this situation, stop using crack, and do what CPS wants so you can get visitation of your kids back?

> *Yolanda:* *(long pause in which Yolanda looks up at me as if I had suddenly sprouted a new head out of my neck)* Well, my Uncle Charlie wouldn't be surprised.

> *Barry:* If Uncle Charlie was here, what story would he tell me about you that would inspire in me the same confidence he has in you?

> *Yolanda:* *(starting very slowly but picking up steam as she talks)* Uncle Charlie was my favorite uncle and he liked to tell the story of when I used to visit him over the summer with all my other cousins. We would get away from the city and get a taste of country life. I really liked it. One summer when I was 6 or 7, my cousins and I ran deeper into the forest further than we had ever gone before. We were running full blast over a ravine and I was out in front, and then I stepped in quicksand and got stuck and pretty quickly sank to my waist and was slowly sinking. We were way out in the woods and my cousins ran all the way back to get my uncle, who rushed to get me, which seemed to me to be about forever later. Thinking that I would already be dead, Uncle Charlie was so relieved to see me that he cried for joy—by that time I had sunk up to my neck. He never stopped talking about when he found me. I was calm and collected and just as still as I could be—somehow I instinctively knew not to struggle or make a move. He always told me and everybody else what a trooper I was and how I had the heart of a lion. Uncle Charlie would not be surprised by my ability to deal with this stuff. He always told me if I could deal with that situation as a kid, I would be able to deal with anything in my life. He didn't live to see me in the mess I'm in now, but he would still believe in me.

And you know what? Uncle Charlie was right. In fact, there were many other stories about Yolanda that better captured her humanity: Like when she stood up, under great peril, to her crack-dealing, abusive partner and left him and the crack house behind. Despite his continued stalking and the threat of violence, Yolanda acted to protect her children. In addition, under all this duress, she chose to quit crack—and did so for 17 months until a combination of events persuaded her to relapse. So there was a crack-addicted mom who lost her kids, and there was the heroic mother who stood up to abuse to protect her children and who also had made good choices for 17 months regarding her crack use. With these resources and resiliencies to work with, and Yolanda now engaged in the beautiful thing we call therapy, my job was easy. Yolanda started going to NA again, worked with CPS and me to complete their requirements, and started supervised visitation, which ultimately led to regained custody of her children. I am not questioning the validity of the problem stories. Certainly Yolanda was a crack-addicted mom who lost her kids. But that wasn't the whole story, not the one that engaged her in therapy, and not the one that captured her identity as a human being. The stories that allow me to see client resources and resiliencies, those that represent who people are or aspire to be, are the ones that I work to bring to light.

Finally, as Harold (the meticulous engineer who wrote a more satisfying story of his retirement) demonstrated in Chapter 3, change or any difference itself can be a powerful way to encourage further empowerment and client ownership of positive steps. Noting differences, as solution-focused therapy has taught us, can also be a way to harvest and recruit client resources, capabilities, and ideas to overcome the adversity they face—to write a heroic tale of a new start or embarking on a different path in life.

A recent consult client, Bob, was a man who had been struggling with alcohol for most of his life. Looking years older than he should, he was a poster child for all that goes wrong in a life characterized by the long-term abuse of alcohol: periodic homelessness and the loss of family, employment, and self-respect. Bob was a man suffering perhaps the worst effect of all: little hope and destroyed self-esteem, readily revealed by his ORS score of 3.2.

Barry: What do you think would be the most useful thing for us to talk about today?

Bob: I'm not sure, right now I am struggling with staying sober.

Barry: So are you sober today?

Bob: Yes, I am. It's been, uh, what's today, it's been 11 days.

Barry: Wow, that's pretty darn good. Congratulations. How have you been able to do that?

Bob: I have been going to some meetings but maybe I should go to more.

Barry: Okay, so going to meetings is helping. Do you think if you stayed sober, your marks on the ORS would move to the right, that if your mark on the *Individually* scale represented your recovery or your sobriety or the drinking, however you want to look at it, if you continued your sobriety, do you think that mark would move over to the right?

Bob: Definitely.

Barry: It seems like, and correct me if I'm wrong here, your sobriety is central to the way you are experiencing all these domains of your life.

Bob: Yes, it is.

***

Barry: I am always curious about when people make a change, and you are now 11 days sober, and I don't know how you have done in the past, but regardless you have 11 days now. Which means that you got up that first day and you said to yourself in some way, shape, or form, "I am not going to drink today." And I am wondering how you reached that conclusion.

Bob: Like many other times, I wound up in the ER and I just remember how I felt when I woke up. . . . I was feeling pretty low and I think I came to the conclusion that as long as I drink like this that I was going to feel like this. I know it's not going to get any better if I continue to drink. Like over the weekend, I had some alcohol in my apartment, and when I woke up the next day after getting home from the hospital, there was enough alcohol to get drunk— I had spent my whole SS check on alcohol and drank most of it the couple of days before the hospital but there was plenty left to blow myself away. And I was thinking that I could drink this and nobody would know about it. Then I remembered how I felt at the ER . . . *(in a very low voice)* and I poured it out.

Barry: *(smiling)* Wow! *(Bob smiles slightly.)* That was pretty amazing that you did that. No one would have known. . . . Something about this memory in the ER was kind of a wake-up call.

Bob: Yes, it was.

Barry: In a little bit different way than before?

Bob: Yeah, a lot different.

Barry: What was different about it?

Bob: The shame, the guilt, I couldn't shake it. I couldn't look in the mirror, and that's why *(pointing at the ORS)*, on the scale there, on the *Individually* part and that's also why that one is rated so low. I have a lot of shame . . .

Barry: Okay. So you think as you get more sobriety under your belt, you'll feel better about yourself?

Bob: I hope so.

Barry: So that experience was kind of a turning point in some ways.

Bob: I hope so.

Barry: This is pretty amazing when you think about it, you've been struggling with this for a long time, and this time you noticed something different, and it sounds like somehow this has reached the point for you that you did some additional self-search, and you somehow decided that this isn't what you wanted to continue doing.

Bob: (nodding throughout) Yes.

* * *

Barry: But you came home from the hospital and you had alcohol in your apartment. . . . You could have said, "I'll start tomorrow, let me get rid of this first." I am amazed by that and it tells that this time is different. So are your strategies for sobriety like they were before in your times of not drinking? Have you tweaked that or are you doing anything different?

Bob: All the other times I did it on my own. I didn't really do any recovery work.

Barry: So you were able to do it, even for as long as 6 months on your own, but you are thinking now if you do more recovery work you'll make it stick better. And you didn't do that before?

Bob: No, not at all. I didn't go to any meetings.

Barry: Oh, none at all.

* * *

Barry: Really sounds like you know what the recipe for success is.

Bob: (smiles big) I hope so.

Barry: It's not like you have ever given up on this.

Bob: (strongly) No, I haven't! I keep trying.

Barry: You do. That's great. You have a real fighter spirit. It's knocked you down a few times but you are not down for the count. You are not ready to call it over.

Bob: (smiling) Not yet.

Barry: That's great. It makes sense to me and I think it's a great thing that you notice how this time is different for you. There are similarities to the past, but there are some real differences (Bob nods enthusiastically). You noticed something very different in your response to the ER and that led you to a different place. And there's proof that it did because you had alcohol in the house when you came home from the ER. You had to be in a real different place to decide not to start the next day. You sure could have gotten away with starting the next day and drinking everything in your house.

Bob: *(sitting up more)* I could have.

Barry: That would have been easy, and even understandable! But you didn't do that. So this time is different. You have recognized the difference and enacted the difference at the first opportunity you had when you dumped the booze. Then you continued by changing your strategies to include recovery and going to meetings. I think that all this is meaningful.

Bob: I do too.

Barry: Seems like you have some confidence about this time.

Bob: I do.

Bob had had periods of sobriety before, but this time was different: different insights, resolves, and plans to guide him down a path of redemption and recovery. As I verbalized the differences in this occurrence of sobriety and his plan of recovery, including the amazing event of pouring out the booze, Bob became more engaged and ultimately confident. The most striking thing for me was Bob's movement in session from passive and defeated, a man of little hope, to engaged and confident that he was up and still fighting, not down for the count.

> **Bottom Line:** *The quickest way to improve your effectiveness is to engage clients and their resources in service of change. Discovering the client's heroic stories and noting change are but two ways that encourage clients to collaborate from a position of competence and wisdom, as they join you in the purposeful work of change.*

RELIANCE ON THE ALLIANCE

Listening creates a holy silence. When you listen generously to people, they can hear the truth in themselves, often for the first time. And when you listen deeply, you can know yourself in everyone.
—Rachel Remen, *Kitchen Table Wisdom*

The fact of the matter is that the alliance is our most powerful ally and represents the most influence that we can have over outcome. But it's hard not to take it for granted when it gets so little press compared with models and techniques. How often, for example, is the alliance discussed in client conferences? Improving your alliance skills is another way to focus your efforts that will likely lead to progress as you track your career development.

Recall that the best therapists tend to form strong alliances with more people; average alliance scores have accounted for 50% (Owen, Duncan, Reese, Anker, & Sparks, in press) to 97% (Baldwin, Wampold, & Imel, 2007) of therapist differences. Of course, this is what the Session Rating System (SRS) is all about, to help you build better alliances; however, you can also expand and fine-tune your repertoire of relational skills and monitor your career development to see if it matters. I think it will. The alliance is your craft. Practice well the skills of your craft. At some point, your craftsmanship elevates to art.

Bordin (1979) classically defined the alliance with three interacting elements: (a) a relational bond between you and the client—the client's perception of your empathy, positive regard, and genuineness; (b) agreement on the goals of therapy; and (c) agreement on the tasks of therapy, which include all the accompanying details—topics of conversation, frequency of meetings, handling cancellations, payment, etc. The alliance is an all-encompassing framework for psychotherapy. It transcends any specific therapist behavior and is a property of all aspects of providing services (Hatcher & Barends, 2006). The alliance is evident in anything and everything you do, from offering an explanation or technique to scheduling the next appointment, to engage the client in purposive work. In short, it calls for your utmost attention and best clinical skills in each and every client encounter—your conscious, proactive efforts to make it happen. It deserves far more RESPECT (hear Aretha in the background).

The alliance is the central filter of all your words and actions: Is what I am saying and doing *now* building or risking the alliance? Few things are worth risking the alliance. This doesn't mean that you can never challenge clients; it just means that you have to earn the right to do so and must always consider the alliance consequences. At the very least, a discussion with the client about the value of challenge and securing permission is advisable. Our behavior should be designed to engage the client in purposeful work. That is what the alliance is supposed to do.

There are many ways to understand alliance skills (for an excellent review, see Ackerman & Hilsenroth, 2003), as well as many systems to improve your relational abilities—from classic Rogerian (Truax & Carkhuff, 1967) to ways of therapeutically addressing alliance ruptures (Safran, Muran, & Eubanks-Carter, 2011) to specific models that are attentive to relational aspects, such as motivational interviewing (Miller & Rollnick, 2012), to name just a few. And the good news is that there is evidence suggesting that you can improve your ability to form alliances (Crits-Christoph et al., 2006). I encourage you to investigate multiple ways to practice your alliance skills and consider your growth as a therapist to be parallel to the development of your relational repertoire. What follows are a few of my thoughts for your consideration.

The Relational Bond

It is helpful to think of each meeting with a client as a first date (without the romantic overtones, unless you want a very short career-development trajectory), in which you make a conscious effort to put your best foot forward, actively woo the client's favor, and entice his or her participation. This requires listening intently, staying close to the client's experience, not steering the conversation elsewhere unless invited, and just plain being likable, friendly, and accommodating. Because clients vary widely in their experience of what constitutes a good relationship, your flexibility is important. Pay particular attention to what excites clients: When do they lean forward, raise their voices, sparkle their eyes, talk more? What topics and ways of relating raise their activity and engagement? Hold on to the quote from Orlinsky, Rønnestad, and Willutzki (2004; see Chapter 1, this volume) regarding the centrality of client participation.

A useful way to think of your relational responses, as an overall backdrop for your comments, is the concept of *validation*. Validation reflects a genuine acceptance of the client at face value and includes an empathic search for justification of the client's experience in the context of trying circumstances—that they have good reason to feel, think, and behave the way they do (Duncan et al., 1992). Clients are often wary about our judgments. Validation helps them breathe a sigh of relief and know that blame is not a part of our game—we are on their team.

Validation combines three robust empirically demonstrated aspects of the relationship: empathy, unconditional positive regard, and authenticity. Carl Rogers, in his groundbreaking article (1957) that is still well worth the read, defined *empathy* as the therapist's sensitive ability and willingness to understand clients' thoughts, feelings, and struggles from their point of view. It is important to remember that perceived empathy is quite idiosyncratic; there is no single, invariably facilitative empathic response. Empathy, therefore, is work. You can't take it for granted; instead, you have to sort out what the client finds empathic, what engages the client in the work. But it is really worth the effort. A recent meta-analysis of 57 studies looking at empathy and outcome (Elliott, Bohart, Watson, & Greenberg, 2011) found a significant relationship, an r of 31 (r is a statistic different from the d; an r of .31 is a medium effect).

Another idea championed by Rogers, *unconditional positive regard*, characterized as warm acceptance of the client's experience without conditions, a prizing, an affirmation, and a deep nonpossessive caring or love (Rogers, 1957), also exerts a robust impact on outcome. A recent meta-analysis of 18 studies examining positive regard and outcome found a significant relationship, an r of .27 (Farber & Doolin, 2011). Given its importance to outcome, it is surprising how often unconditional positive regard is trivialized and taken for granted.

And, finally, there's congruence/genuineness, "that the therapist is mindfully genuine in the therapy relationship, underscoring present personal awareness, as well as genuineness or authenticity" (Kolden, Klein, Wang, & Austin, 2011, p. 65). Kolden et al. (2011) did a meta-analysis of 16 studies and found a significant relationship between congruence/genuineness and outcome, an r of .24. Lambert (2013) rightly noted that these relationship variable correlations are much higher than those of specific treatments and outcome. Recall that the effect size (ES) of model differences is just a d of .20. So your client's perception of any of the big three relational variables is more powerful than any technique you can ever wield.

Things to consider when validating:

- What are the invalidations contained in the client's story? How is the client blamed for his or her difficulties by him or herself or others?
- What other circumstances have contributed to this situation? How can I place the client's situation in a context that explains and justifies his or her behavior or feelings? How can I give the client credit for trying to do the right thing?

Put the client's experience in the following format:

No wonder you feel or behave this way [*fill in with client circumstance*] given that [*fill in the ways you have discovered to justify his or her responses*].

Consider again my comments to Sam, after hearing all the things troubling him and his desire to see the end of world:

Barry: Makes a lot of sense. Another way of saying that would be that anyone experiencing what you are—if they were in pain, just came out of surgery, were in a financial hole they couldn't get out of, and didn't have anything going socially, anybody on the planet would be depressed, anybody walking in your shoes would be depressed, and anybody would be struggling with whether or not they wanted to live. That's a long way to say that no wonder you are depressed.

These comments replaced the self-invalidations ("I'm a leech, a negative person, etc."), and the invalidations of others (bizarre thinking, etc.). When clients feel validation, different conclusions can be reached and alternative actions can emerge. Sam sighed and relaxed, knowing that I was in his corner, and the next exchange further clarified why he wanted an apocalypse, as well as his recognition of his leadership ability.

Sam: I am one of those leeches on society. I am a drag on society. I am negative, I am a negative person. I take away. I think that is one of the reasons why I want to see it all come apart.

Barry: Well, no wonder. It would be like a new beginning if everything came apart—you would have a fighting chance to have a different kind of life. Right now you don't see any hope for there being a different kind of life possible.

Sam: Right, I feel like I could contribute to a society that had decayed to the point where it would need my contribution. I just feel like I would be really good in a situation like that. I could lead a small ragtag band of warriors to lead attacks on the machines or bad guys.

Barry: So it's like there is this inner warrior that wants to come out, you'd be able to take charge of that situation, to contribute in that situation.

Sam: I feel like I would be a good leader.

Validation (authentic empathy and positive regard) paves the way for client strengths to appear and helps coax the client's participation. Of course, it has to be real, straight from your heart.

In summary, to enhance the relational bond:

- Listen, listen, listen—stay close to the client's experience.
- Be likable, friendly, and responsive (like on a first date).
- Carefully monitor the client's reaction to comments, explanations, interpretations, questions, and suggestions; use your alliance filter and the SRS to keep you on track.
- Be flexible: Do whatever it takes to engage the client and ensure his or her experience of empathy, positive regard, and congruence. Use *your* complexity to fit clients.
- Validate the client. Legitimize the client's concerns and highlight the importance of the client's struggle. Appreciate your clients. Let them know that you do.

The SRS (or any alliance tool) is the only way to know for sure whether you are accomplishing your relational efforts.

> **Bottom Line:** *There are a lot of ways of understanding and applying relationship skills, and research offers key guidelines regarding what is important to outcome from the client's point of view. Take on your relational skills as a project and as perhaps the central symbol of your development as a therapist. Try the different systems of skills on for size and watch your outcomes improve as you refine ways to purposefully involve your clients in the work.*

Accepting the Client's Goals

The second aspect of the alliance is the agreement on the goals of therapy. Chapter 3 covered this ground in the discussion about the SRS, so here I will just make a few quick points. When we ask clients what they want to be different, we give credibility to their beliefs and values regarding the problem and its solution. Regardless of how unreasonable they may sound, as illustrated by Carly and her desire to go to school in the midst of a hospitalization crisis, you should accept client goals at face value, because those are the desires that will excite and motivate—that will engage him or her in purposive work. If we are straining our actions through the alliance filter, goals other than those of the client will likely not fit through. Collaborative goal formation begins the process of change, wherever the client may ultimately travel. Both the ORS and the SRS keep us on the same page with clients regarding their goals. As Carly aptly illustrated, clients are not likely to show benefit on the ORS if they are not working on their goals, and to ensure our attention, the SRS directly solicits the goal issue.

It is sometimes helpful to encourage clients to think small (Fisch, Weakland, & Segal, 1982). A change in one aspect of a problem often leads to changes in other areas as well. The wonderful thing about thinking small is that the most easily attainable sign of change becomes symbolic of resolving the entire problem; it creates a momentum and energy like the first domino falling in the seemingly never-ending line of the problem. This is why it is useful to ask clients what it will take for the mark on a given scale to move just one centimeter to the right. The client's subjective experience of early change, as noted earlier, is predictive of continued change and sets an expectation for progress and smooth sailing. Do not underestimate the power of thinking small. The first glimmer of light can turn into a neon sign shining the way to the ultimate destination.

But, once again: Don't stress. Some clients just don't think of what they want from therapy in concrete behavioral terms and perhaps don't slice up the world in tangible observables. That's okay. But you can always connect whatever experience clients are describing, no matter how vaguely, to the marks on the ORS. The ORS will measure their benefit in the major domains of life, regardless of the client's propensity to set clearly defined goals.

Bottom Line: Work on client goals. Period.

Agreement About the Tasks of Therapy

The final aspect of the alliance is the agreement on the tasks of therapy. Tasks include specific techniques or points of view, topics of conversation, interview procedures, frequency of meeting, and all the nuts and bolts of doing the work. Don't underestimate the importance of the seemingly mundane issues of scheduling, cancellation, payment, and between-sessions contacts. These are all aspects of the task dimension and can count for or against you in the alliance. All of your behaviors need to go through the alliance filter; each of your actions is a manifestation of the alliance. As noted in Chapter 4, in our follow-up study of the Norway Feedback Trial, we found that the category with the most complaints was just this aspect of the alliance—the everyday aspects of providing the service (Anker, Sparks, Duncan, Owen, & Stapnes, 2011).

Asking for help to set the tasks of therapy further demonstrates respect for client capabilities, as well as our efforts to enlist participation in a collaborative endeavor. This is probably our biggest alliance blind spot. After all, we're supposed to be the experts, right? (Recall Dan Ariely and the nurses ripping off his bandages.) The beauty of collaboratively setting the tasks of therapy is that we ensure not only that the alliance is on track with an approach that resonates with everyone involved, but also that this process provides a continual impetus to broaden our theoretical horizons. Negotiating the tasks of therapy sets the stage for expanding your conceptual repertoire, your theoretical breadth, as discussed in the previous chapter.

So you can't have a good alliance without some agreement about the goals and how therapy is going to address the issues at hand. Tryon and Winograd (2011) conducted two meta-analyses related to the agreement on tasks—goal consensus (which included agreement on tasks) and collaboration—and their relationship to outcome. Looking at 15 studies, they found a goal consensus–outcome d of .34, indicating that better outcomes can be expected when client and therapist agree on goals and the processes to achieve them. Based on 19 studies, the collaboration-outcome meta-analysis found a d of .33, suggesting that outcome is likely enhanced when client and therapist are in a cooperative relationship. Once again, these alliance variables are more powerful than the impact of model and technique.

In an important way, the alliance depends on the delivery of some particular technique or treatment—a framework for understanding and solving the problem. If technique fails to engage the client in purposive work, it is not working properly and a change is needed. In essence, technique is the alliance in action, carrying an explanation for the client's difficulties and a remedy for them; it's an expression of the therapist's belief that it could be helpful, in hopes of engendering the same response in the client. Indeed, you cannot have an alliance without a treatment, an agreement between the client and therapist about how therapy will address the client's goals. Similarly, you cannot have a positive expectation for change without a credible way for both the client and therapist to understand how change can happen.

Here is where the variety of models and techniques pays off. The question is: Does the model or technique resonate? Does it fit client preferences? Does its application help or hinder the alliance? Is it something that both you and the client can get behind? You matter here, too. If you don't believe in the restorative power of any selected approach—if you don't have allegiance to it—then not much good will come of it. Can you get on board with the client's notions about how he or she can be helped? Or perhaps some idiosyncratic blend of client ideas, yours, and theoretical/technical ones might ultimately be just the ticket. Your alliance skills are truly at play here: your interpersonal ability to explore the client's ideas, discuss options, collaboratively form a plan, and negotiate any changes when benefit to the client is not forthcoming.

The issue of resonance and the agreement about tasks—finding a framework for therapy that both you and the client can believe in—is why it makes a lot of sense to ask clients about their ideas on how to proceed, or at the very least get client approval of any intervention plan. Such a process has not been highly regarded in traditional psychotherapy; the search has been instead for interventions that promote change by validating the therapist's favored theory. Serving the alliance requires taking a different angle: searching for ideas that promote change by validating the client's view of what is helpful, the *client's theory of change* (Duncan et al., 1992; Duncan & Miller, 2000b; Duncan & Moynihan, 1994). Frank and Frank (1991) said it best: "Ideally, therapists should select for each patient the therapy that accords, or can be brought to accord, with the patient's personal characteristics and view of the problem" (p. xv).

Perhaps the most important aspect of this collaboration is whether the favored explanation and ritual of the therapist fit client preferences. Swift, Callahan, and Vollmer (2011) conducted a meta-analysis of 35 studies of client preference, breaking client preferences into three areas: role, therapist, and treatment preferences. They found that clients who received their preferred conditions were less likely to drop out and that the overall ES for client preference was $d = .31$ (once again, more potent than model and technique). So it makes sense to ensure that whatever explanation and ritual are chosen are ones that the client can get behind.

Asking about the client's theories or preferences does not preclude your ideas, suggestions, models, methods, or in any way mean that you do not contribute. Instead, it speaks to the more collaborative aspects of formulating a plan, with the degree and intensity of your input determined by the client's expectations of your role. Securing an agreement about the tasks is all but guaranteed when a given therapy framework—explanation or solution—implements, fits, or complements the client's ideas and beliefs. Examples are found throughout this book (see also Duncan, Hubble, & Miller, 1997; Duncan et al., 2004). Once again, the SRS can help us not only to focus on this issue but also to catch ourselves when we are missing the mark, as it did with Ken, the construction supervisor having panic attacks, in Chapter 3.

> **Bottom Line:** *Agreement about the tasks of therapy is a critical component of the alliance. The application of any agreed-upon explanation or technique represents the alliance in action. The litmus test of any chosen rationale or ritual is whether or not it engages the client in purposive work and makes a meaningful difference determined by the client.*

The Alliance: Why Do You Think They Call It Work?

My dad had a stalwart response to any complaint I ever made about doing any job. Whether it was painting or roofing a house, working in a tire factory, studying for a test, or working in my private practice, his response was consistent: "Why do you think they call it work?"

We all have clients who rapidly respond to us, with whom we connect quickly. But what about the folks who are mandated by the courts or protective services or who just plain don't want to be there (like almost all kids)? What about people who have never been in a good relationship or have been abused or traumatized? What about folks to whom life just never seems to give a break, or who have lost hope? Well, the therapist's job, our job, is exactly the same regardless. If we want anything good to happen, it all rests on a strong alliance—we have to engage the client in purposeful work. The research about what differentiates one therapist from another, as well as my personal experience, suggest that the ability to form alliances with people who are not easy to form alliances with—to engage people who don't want to be engaged—separates the best from the rest.

It's hard work. We often think that "therapeutic work" only applies to clients; it actually applies to us too. We have to earn this thing called *the alliance*. We have to put ourselves out there with each and every person, each and every interaction, and each and every session. It is a daunting task, to be sure, but one that is perpetually minimized in its importance and difficulty. It gets such little press compared with models and techniques and is often relegated to statements like "first gain rapport and then . . . " or "form a relationship and then . . . " as if it were something we effortlessly do before the *real* intervention starts. The alliance is not the anesthesia to surgery. We don't offer Rogerian reflections to lull clients into complacency so we can stick the real intervention to them!

When Lisbeth was introduced to me in the waiting room, she told me to go f—k myself. I was doing a consult because this 16-year-old was refusing to go to school and had assaulted four foster parents, with resulting psychiatric hospitalizations. Lisbeth was one angry adolescent, and my initial thought was, "Wouldn't it be sweet if she told me what she was angry about?" because I knew there had to be a good reason.

In the opening moments, I asked Lisbeth what she thought would be most useful for us to talk about and she said, "What I think of you is that you are a condescending bastard with no understanding of your clients whatso-ever!" Whew, she knew how to hit where it hurt! But I admired her chutzpah. In essence, if you take out the anger, she was telling me to not condescend to her because she was a kid, and that I'd better take the time to understand her. This helped me maintain my conviction that if I understood her story, everything, especially her anger, would make complete sense.

Lisbeth: I'm just angry all the time, you stupid!

Barry: I'm getting that you are pretty angry.

[After all, I am a trained observer of human behavior!]

Lisbeth: All because of that psychiatrist or should I say mind-f—ker . . . Just because I threatened to break her knees because she tried to give me medication. Break her knees, mind you, not break her neck *(raising her finger)*.

Barry: Right, it's not like you wanted to kill her or anything, you just wanted to permanently impair her. There's a big difference.

Lisbeth: *(smiles)* Right.

She told me how she refused medication in one of her many hospital-izations and had threatened to break the kneecaps of the psychiatrist who attempted to force her to take meds. This likely stimulated replies ad nauseam about the inappropriateness of her violent tendencies. I responded differently, got a smile and more conversation.

Lisbeth told me that she had been removed from her home at age 13 because of multiple sexual abuses by her mother's boyfriends and that, since then, she had been in four foster-care homes, including that of the fourth foster parent, Sophie, who sat before me now. She also told me that the previous 18 months of therapy had not addressed her goal of telling her mother off, once and for all. In fact, no attempt had been made to allow any approximation of this to happen.

Lisbeth: All I want to do is see my mom once. And then I'm going to wring her neck verbally and never see her again after that.

Barry: What's preventing that from happening?

Lisbeth: They think I'm going to get all stressed out and weird. Of course, I've been on edge ever since I left her.

Barry: So you want to tell her off once and for all, you think that will help you let it go?

Lisbeth: I ain't letting it go. You stupid?

Barry: *(laughs)* Most of the time.

***

Sophie:	Lisbeth was in several foster homes before she lived with us and she's been with us the longest.
Barry:	So, Lisbeth, how has it lasted with Sophie?
Lisbeth:	I stick to her like a barnacle. *(Everyone laughs.)*
Barry:	You've had quite the storied life. You're like this crusty old sailor—you curse like a sailor, and you've had many harrowing adventures with all these different experiences, so you're salty.
Lisbeth:	*(big smile)* Salty?

Given that Lisbeth's goal had been ignored, her lack of engagement in therapy seemed a reasonable response. After a while of allowing her story to wash over me, I ventured a comment that Lisbeth was like a salty old sailor, crusty at the ripe old age of 16. She smiled in a way that acknowledged that I both understood and appreciated her. Lisbeth rewarded me with an explanation of her anger—what I was really hoping to accomplish. She told me how she was relieved to be removed from her home and that her first foster-care parent had expressed intentions to adopt both Lisbeth and her 5-year-old brother. But instead, her brother was adopted and Lisbeth was dumped. That's when the assaults started and when she began to completely dismiss school. So the first adult that she trusted, after having none in her life worthy of her trust, betrayed her totally and completely.

Lisbeth:	I just got out of my f—kin' mom's house and I went to live with Tara Traitor.
Barry:	I like your names for folks.
Lisbeth:	She took me into her home. We lasted about 2 months . . . she used me, I don't know, as a get-my-brother-and-toss-me-away ploy.
Barry:	You were going to school at the time?
Lisbeth:	Yes. I was going to school full-time.
Barry:	You were doing the regular kid thing.
Lisbeth:	Yeah. Then she kicked me out and adopted the little abomination . . .
Barry:	That really changed things. And you became really pissed off.
Lisbeth:	Yeah, and then I stopped going to school, and attacking people, going to the hospital.

Barry: It's too bad that you took the fall for her being a traitor. That really cranked you up to a real righteous anger.

Lisbeth: Righteous anger?

Barry: Yes. Your anger is certainly righteous, given how much you have been screwed around.

There is no more righteous anger than this kid felt. I said that, we connected, and the work of therapy could proceed—Lisbeth was purposefully involved. Our interaction took on a more bantering quality, more as peers, and one in which I could playfully challenge her a bit.

Barry: Sophie, you've made it through the trials and tribulations here and, you know, she is a tough row to hoe. . . . How have you done it?

Sophie: Well, I love her . . . and she keeps me on my toes. She keeps me going. I like that.

Barry: So you two have been able to connect and have a relationship . . .

Lisbeth: *(interrupts)* No, I am just stickin' to her.

Barry: That's a connection I'd say.

Lisbeth: That's not a connection, buddy! That's just me being a leech, a parasite.

Barry: Isn't that a connection?

Lisbeth: No, it's just a feeding thing. . . . I am a parasitic being by strategic means.

Barry: Okay, strategic parasite, you're still connected to Sophie, and you're suckin' it for everything you can get, the life blood out of her. But she's holding up pretty well *(Sophie and Lisbeth look at each other)*, because she is holding on to this thing that she loves you.

Lisbeth: No, no, motherf—king no!

Barry: *(smiles)* Love, the dreaded four-letter word! I think there is really something there, that connection, and I am not going to say the other word . . .

Lisbeth: *(interrupting)* I gonna f—kin' rip your ass off, and feed it to you!

Barry: Wouldn't taste very good.

Lisbeth: I know, because you are a crusty old man.

Now don't get me wrong, this wouldn't be my preferred way to interact with a teenager. But I hope the printed word conveys the difference of our interaction. What started out as anger and somewhat mean-spirited attacks evolved into a more playful banter. This interchange ended with Lisbeth calling me crusty, the same adjective I had used to describe her. So now we were crusty together—a crusty old sailor and a crusty old therapist.

I couldn't have written a better script for the ending because the session closed with Lisbeth going one up on me, getting in a final zinger.

Barry: If you want, you can get feedback from the team in the other room about what they observed here today.

Lisbeth: Shakes her head and gives the camera the finger.

Barry: (to Sophie) I really respect that you have been able to hang in here with Lisbeth. You are the best thing that ever happened to her. Her previous experiences were either just plain awful or people didn't stay with her through the bad stuff. And you've done that and I think in the long run it will pay off.

Sophie: I do too. I know we are close despite what she says. I don't pay any attention to her language.

Barry: (to Lisbeth) You know, I like you, Lisbeth, and I know you have been through a lot of shit, way too much, actually, and I do think of you as a crusty old, salty sailor . . . and I think you are going to figure this out.

Lisbeth: Figure this out?! Now you're just being like Dr. Phil, and I don't particularly like Dr. Phil!

Barry: (grabbing his heart and smiling) I don't either! You just cut me to the quick with that one. (Lisbeth beams throughout the entire interchange.) You got me with that one—I hate that guy!

(Everyone gets up to leave.)

Lisbeth: Pointing to the camera. Be sure to tell them that I hate them!

Barry: You want to give them the finger one last time? (Lisbeth does so with enthusiasm and playfulness.)

Perhaps it seems over the top to encourage an adolescent to give the finger to a group of therapists watching in another room. And maybe it is. But it demonstrated quite a shift from the beginning of the session, a shift that occurred via the power of the relationship and a deliberate, conscious effort to forge an alliance to engage a troubled teenager in a process that just might be helpful via the magic of this thing we call *psychotherapy*.

CONCLUSION

What is important . . . is not the right doctrine but the attainment of true experience. It is giving up believing in belief.
    —Alan Keightley, *Into Every Life a Little Zen Must Fall*

Harvesting client resources and securing strong alliances, in all of the varied ways available, is a great place to start (and continue) to grow as a therapist. This chapter offered suggestions about how to get started, and it boils down to two attitudes. First is a dependence on clients and what they bring as the most potent aspect of change—to rally, recruit, or harvest client's existing resources in the service of client goals. The second attitude is the understanding that the alliance is the therapy and that everything you do must be strained through the alliance filter. Does your behavior build or risk the alliance? Do your model and technique engage or not engage the client in purposeful work? And, of course, the proof of the pudding is in the eating. The answer can only be derived from the client's response to any treatment delivered: the client's feedback regarding progress in therapy and the quality of the alliance.

CLIENTS ARE THE BEST TEACHERS: THEIR STORIES DOCUMENT OUR DEVELOPMENT

Facts don't cease to exist because they are ignored.
    —Robert Louis Stevenson

This is a bit of a tawdry tale, but nevertheless it is an invaluable marker in my development as a therapist. Richard, a 29-year-old systems analyst, was referred by his company doctor because of his increasing distress and frequent absences. When I greeted Richard in the waiting room, he jumped out of his chair, got right in my face—not 3 inches away—and demanded, "What are you going to do for me?"

Richard didn't look too good. The 60-cent therapy words would be *agitated* and *disheveled*. Tension and distress characterized his every move, and he looked as if he hadn't slept in days—if he had slept, it was surely in the clothes he was wearing. I tried to stay calm and just invited him to accompany me to my office, whereupon Richard raised his voice another notch and repeated his question, and he was once again too close for comfort. I was definitely freaked at this point, but I believed that if I could just get Richard to tell me what was up, all this agitation and hostility would make sense.

I simply replied that I didn't know if I could do anything for him but that I would try my very best, and would he please have a seat and tell me what was going on. After staring intently at me for what seemed like days, Richard finally sat down on my couch and told his story, and the floodgates opened. Richard began suspecting his wife, Justine, of having an affair after he discovered footprints in the snow in his backyard. Other bits of evidence (telephone hang-ups, Justine staying out later than expected) resulted in Richard's becoming increasingly convinced of her infidelity. He followed her, meticulously searched her belongings, and kept track of her whereabouts. But he could not find the incontrovertible evidence that he was sure existed.

Throughout Richard's growing mistrust, Justine emphatically denied the affair and told him he needed help. Perhaps in desperation, Richard began to secretly check Justine's underwear for signs of semen, which would provide ironclad evidence of her unfaithfulness (given that there was no sex with him). Finally, Richard found stains on her underwear and took it to a laboratory, which confirmed the presence of semen. Justine still denied his accusations and insisted the semen was his. She stepped up her efforts to involve others, telling friends, family, his employer, and their own children, that Richard was sick and in need of hospitalization. Justine rallied many to her cause and filed for divorce. The company doctor concurred with her assessment, as did the first provider that Richard saw, a psychiatrist who offered an antipsychotic to ease Richard's pain. Richard didn't do much to disconfirm everyone's assessment of his sanity. He was doing some pretty wacky things and looked more distressed and haggard with each passing day.

Richard told me that he was obtaining a DNA analysis of the semen to see if it was a match with his. While scrutinizing my every reaction, not in a threatening way but rather like a condemned man waiting for a sentence, he nervously asked me if I believed him.

So was Richard psychotic or was Justine a liar? Subsequently, I talked with Justine and invited her to therapy, but she declined. She was very persuasive and pulled out all the stops to describe Richard as hopelessly psychotic and in need of medical help, noting that Richard's sister was also schizophrenic and lived in a group home. What would you say to Richard?

I told Richard that I did believe him. Richard allowed himself a moment of relief but pressed on and told me that the DNA test was going to cost a lot of money, money that he had to borrow. He then leaned forward, stared uncomfortably, and asked me the big question: Did I think he was crazy for spending all that money?

I responded that peace of mind is cheap at any price. Richard broke down and cried long and hard. He had been through a lot, and he was starting to believe what many had told him: that he was paranoid and needed medication. After a while, we started talking about what he needed to do to stop looking crazy while he waited on the DNA results. If we took the affair as a given and also a given that Justine's intent was to make him look crazy as a loon, then everything he was doing was playing right into her hands. Richard and I worked out a plan to get normalcy back in his life: return to work, start spending time with his kids, and take better care of himself. He did all of those things and continued to bide his time as best he could.

Finally, the results came in. Although Richard was greatly saddened when the DNA results confirmed that the semen was not his, he was not surprised. Ultimately, the whole seamy business came to light, and Richard went about rebuilding his life. I was both relieved and heartened by the results. I had taken a bit of a risk to believe Richard. Justine had threatened legal action against me for not insisting on medication, and the company doctor had suggested that I was acting unethically. In a sense, I was vindicated along with Richard, but, more to the point, I was heartened that my belief in him seemed to make a difference regarding getting Richard back on track in his life—regardless of the ultimate truth of his story.

In retrospect, by encouraging Richard to tell his story and not getting sidetracked by his initial presentation or by attributions of pathology, I had the opportunity to make sense of Richard's hostility and agitation. No wonder he was hostile, given that others had essentially told him he was crazy and was wasting his family's money. In the context of our relationship, Richard found validation of his concerns to replace the invalidation of others.

I was so moved by the depth of Richard's suffering, and by his response to my simple act of believing him and understanding his desire to know what was going on, that I have never forgotten it. Honestly, while Richard told me his story, I struggled with believing him, which I knew was risky to our alliance. But I ultimately made a conscious choice, during that session, to believe Richard—it didn't matter how bizarre he seemed or how classically paranoid he looked. I decided, at the very least, that my clients deserve to be believed. That was a significant event in my development as a therapist. From that day on, I no longer struggled with being a reality police officer. Such an attitude does not fit through the alliance filter. And while it's true that sometimes people do lie, even maliciously, like Justine, I am willing to suspend disbelief until the "facts" appear, or maybe even into perpetuity.

7

WIZARDS, HUMBUGS, OR WITCHES

What we do is a measure of who we are. If we imagine our work as labor,
we become laborers. If we imagine our work as art, we become artists.
—Jeffrey Patnaude

Although there were many positives about my graduate school training for which I am grateful, I was never encouraged much to reflect about
my identity as a therapist. The emphasis, instead, and surely well-meant,
was on my professional role as a psychologist—expert, empirical, objective,
and better than anyone else—like a medical doctor but more scientific and
without the white coat. In fact, "professional" was stuffed down our throats
so much that some of us mirthfully called our program "The School of *Real*
Professional Psychology." Perhaps you had to be there, but the point is that
reflection about my identity as a helper didn't happen much in school.

So confused was I that I avoided the question of what I did for a living
like the plague. I didn't really like saying I was a psychologist or a therapist
and hearing remarks like, "Are you going to psychoanalyze me?" or other
harmless looks or comments that people give or say off-the-cuff. The reason
I didn't like it was that I didn't have an authentic way to describe what I

http://dx.doi.org/10.1037/14392-007
On Becoming a Better Therapist, Second Edition: Evidence-Based Practice One Client at a Time, by B. L. Duncan
Copyright © 2014 by the American Psychological Association. All rights reserved.

did that captured what being a therapist meant to me. Instead, I really just wanted to tell people I was a machinist in a tool-and-die shop and be done with it.

With other mental health professionals, I would mostly just call myself a therapist, with no particular description of what that meant. Often, encounters with other therapists included a mutual and obligatory identification by discipline or orientation. Sometimes I might say that I was "a psychologist, but please don't hold that against me"—it's funny how many have smiled in response. There is definitely bad blood among the disciplines. You know the old joke: Psychiatrists don't like psychologists, who don't like social workers, who don't like counselors, who don't like marriage and family therapists, who don't like addiction specialists, who don't like their clients. But it is sad, really, that we start off with an "us versus them" mentality, holding steadfastly to what distinguishes us from one another until we figure out that we are all joined by this common thing called *psychotherapy*. We all bring a little something different to the table, but our identity as therapists and desire to help, as demonstrated in the Orlinsky and Rønnestad (2005) study, transcend disciplinary wars and theoretical fractionation.

What is your identity as a therapist? How do you describe what you do? At your very best, what role do you play with your clients? What recent work with a client represents the essence of your identity, illustrating what you embrace most about what you do?

In our book, *Heroic Clients, Heroic Agencies: Partners for Change*, now in its third rendition (Duncan & Sparks, 2010), Jacqueline Sparks and I assembled an eclectic collection of essays from counselors and therapists of all flavors and seasonings concerning their identity. We hoped to encourage therapist introspection about this important topic. Figure 7.1 is Douglas McFadzean's (2010) contribution, a clever drawing of the range of possible metaphors for our identity as therapists. One of the essays was "Wizards, Humbugs, or Witches," by Greg Rusk (2010). I still enjoy using this well-worn but compelling tale to stimulate therapist reflection, hence the title of this chapter.

This chapter keeps the focus on you, encouraging you to envision your identity as a helper and to further contemplate this complexly human enterprise called therapy. It takes a whimsical look at therapist identity, using the classic fable *The Wizard of Oz* to illustrate three different therapist personas. While each of the proposed identities—wizard, humbug, or witch—has advantages, the therapist identity akin to Glinda, the Good Witch of the North, is recommended for consideration. Closely related to reflection about your identity is your personal description of what therapy means to you. This chapter encourages you to define and continually revise your personal account of what you do as a therapist. I offer my description and suggest that embracing the inherent uncertainty of therapy is an important

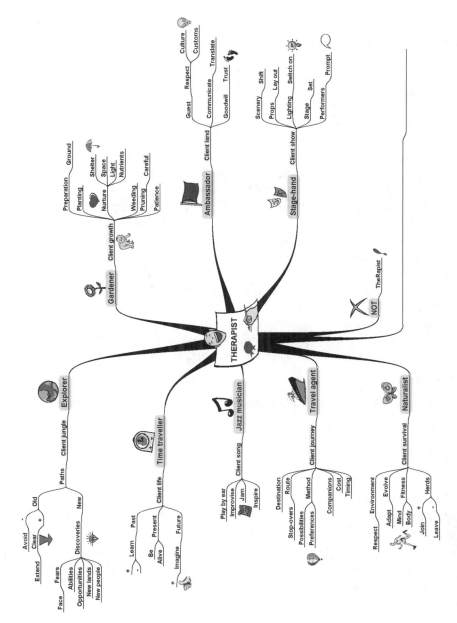

Figure 7.1. Metaphors of therapist identity. From *Heroic Clients, Heroic Agencies: Partners for Change* (2nd ed., p. 199), by B. Duncan and J. Sparks (Eds.), 2010, Jensen Beach, FL: Author. Copyright 2010 by Douglas McFadzean. Reprinted with permission.

developmental milestone. Psychotherapy is presented as a discovery-oriented process, a non-cookie-cutter search for what works for each unique client. The Partners for Change Outcome Management System (PCOMS) provides a comforting compass, a way to manage the uncertainty that is just as characteristic of therapy as it is of life.

THERAPIST IDENTITY AND *THE WIZARD OF OZ*

> The value of identity of course is that so often with it comes purpose.
> —Richard R. Grant

L. Frank Baum's (1900) wonderful story, *The Wizard of Oz*, brought to the screen in 1939 (Metro-Goldwyn-Mayer; directed by Victor Fleming), is a charming metaphor for the journeys people take to resolve problems and, believe it or not, the identity of psychotherapists.[1] The familiar tale involves four characters who perceive something missing in their lives. Each believes that a wizard is necessary to help them find completeness. The Scarecrow sorrowfully exclaims, "Oh, I'm a failure, because I haven't got a brain." The Tin Man laments "that I could be kinda human, if I only had a heart." The Cowardly Lion whines, "My life has been simply unbearable . . . if I only had the nerve." Finally, there is Dorothy, who simply wants to return home to Uncle Henry and Auntie Em. As the unusual quartet, plus Toto the dog, skip down the Yellow Brick Road in search of the Wizard of Oz, they sing:

Dorothy: If the Wizard is a wizard who will serve.

Scarecrow: Then I'm sure to get a brain . . .

Tin Man: . . . a heart

Dorothy: . . . a home

Lion: . . . the nerve!

In time, despite calamity and distance, they arrive at the Emerald City and are finally granted an audience with the Great Oz. Impressively framed by fire and smoke, he proclaims in a thunderous voice:

> The Great and Powerful Oz knows why you have come! . . . The beneficent Oz has every intention of granting your requests! But, you must prove yourselves worthy by performing a small task. Bring me the broom-

---

[1]This section has been adapted from "Wizard, Humbug, or Witch," by G. Rusk, 2010, in B. Duncan and J. Sparks (Eds.), *Heroic Clients, Heroic Agencies: Partners for Change*, (2nd ed., pp. 211–212). Jensen Beach, FL: Author. Adapted with permission.

stick of the Wicked Witch of the West . . . and I'll grant your requests. Now go!

Disappointed, the four friends depart on the journey prescribed by the Great and Powerful Oz. Overcoming insurmountable odds, the four heroically prevail over the Wicked Witch and return with the broomstick. Despite their accomplishment, the mighty Oz is reluctant to grant their wishes. While the Wizard stalls, Toto pulls aside a curtain and exposes him as a Humbug. The humbled Humbug quickly recovers and grants boons to the Scarecrow, Lion, and Tin Man. He gives the Scarecrow a diploma—a doctorate in thinkology—to substitute for a brain. The Cowardly Lion is awarded a "Triple Cross" for valor, signifying his courage. And, finally, the Tin Man receives a testimonial and a watch that looks and sounds like a human heart.

The Humbug also agrees to fly Dorothy back to Kansas by way of a hot-air balloon. Yet, when Dorothy jumps out of the basket to retrieve Toto, the balloon unexpectedly takes off, apparently stranding Dorothy in Oz. Just when all seems lost, Glinda, the beautiful Good Witch of the North, suddenly appears and says, "You don't need to be helped any longer. You've always had the power to go back to Kansas." Dorothy wonders aloud, "I *have*?"

The Scarecrow and Tin Man ask Dorothy what she has discovered on her journey. Dorothy thoughtfully responds, "Well, I . . . I think that it . . . wasn't just enough to want to see Uncle Henry and Auntie Em . . . and it's that if I ever go looking for my heart's desire again, I won't look any further than my own backyard; because if it isn't there, I never really lost it to begin with!"

Glinda, nodding and smiling, "That's all it is . . . she had to find out for herself. Now those magic slippers will take you home in two seconds!"

Are you a Wizard, Humbug, or Witch? I have been all three. The Great and Powerful Oz, the expert faced with overwhelming problems (e.g., a Scarecrow wanting a brain or Dorothy trying to return to an unknown place), did what I was trained to do. He prescribed a protracted journey for them to acquire something *he* thought they needed—just as I have assessed clients' problems ("The Great and Powerful Oz knows why you have come!"), framed them in my favorite theoretical terms, and constructed therapeutic tasks and interventions, without collaboration, to provide clients with things I thought they needed to improve their mental health or address their problems. Clients proved themselves worthy, not resistant, by complying with my interventions.

For their part, Dorothy and her companions were so focused on seizing the Wicked Witch's broomstick that they did not see how wise and heroically they had acted in accomplishing the task. When we send clients on trips through our own theory-land to find our model's broomstick, their contributions tend to fall through the cracks and clients often attribute their successes to us—our guru or wizard status. Sending Dorothy off on the quest for the broomstick represents the kind of therapy that is theory-directed; the therapist persona is one of expert.

After his embarrassing exposure, the Humbug cleverly addresses the requests of the Scarecrow, Tin Man, and Lion, granting each something tangible. Although not quite what they expected, our heroes are pleased to receive validation of their experiences and desires for completeness. Literally, the Humbug pulls the solutions from his black bag—just as I have listened to clients' problems, without much collaboration, and dutifully delivered interventions from my black bag of reframes, techniques, and evidence-based treatments. Sometimes it helped, just as the Humbug's efforts did. But as the rock band America's old song goes, "Oz never did give nothing to the Tin Man/ That he didn't, didn't already have." The Humbug and black bag embody the kind of therapy that is technique driven—therapist identity is that of a skilled technician delivering the latest evidence-based treatment and of a salesman of sorts, enthusiastically convincing the client that the intervention is just what he or she needs.

Should the therapist identities of Wizard or Humbug be condemned for the presumption that a journey was required or a solution needed to be pulled from a black bag? Hardly. We have all been there and done that, mainly fueled by our desires to be helpful and by the hangovers from our training. In truth, we have all felt the burden of clients' expectations that we fix their problems. And, of course, these identities, not in their caricatures depicted here but in terms of our theoretical expertise and technical savvy, are useful at times. But we don't have to function as "false wizards," who send clients with difficult problems on protracted theory driven pilgrimages. Neither do we have to reach in a "humbug's bag of tricks" to face clients in dire circumstances. Understandably, though, we adopt these therapeutic roles because that is how we've been trained, or we just don't know what else to do. Our limited tolerance for uncertainty, together with clients' expectations of us, also restricts our sense of adventure and co-discovery, influencing us toward cookie-cutter practices and away from the great, beautiful, and largely unknown territory of a client's path to change.

Dorothy's experience was not like the experiences of her friends. Neither Wizard nor Humbug was of any service. Glinda offered something decidedly different. She helped Dorothy to discover her own meaning about her perilous quest to Oz and her own resources to return home. Glinda was always there throughout Dorothy's trek through the magical land, in the background, offering help when needed and playing an important role. Although I'm not as pretty as Glinda, and regrettably possess neither a magic wand nor bubble transportation, I do strive to adopt Glinda's persona in my work with clients, helping them to harvest resources and find solutions and to discover what works.

How do you see your identity? *The Wizard of Oz* is a fun way to start or continue your introspection. Consider all the metaphors presented in Figure 7.1 and think of your own as well. Do it any way you like, but do it. Your reflections about being a therapist are important.

Although designed to stimulate your thoughts, the different caricatures of therapist identity are not without merit and are not mutually exclusive. The role you assume can be quite different with different clients, depending on what you and the client negotiate as being most useful. Finding out explicitly what clients expect from you is important to nail down as quickly as possible. It gives you a heads-up about what you can do to be most helpful. Some clients want a sounding board, some want a confidant, some want to brainstorm and problem solve, many want a collaborator, and some want an expert to tell them what to do, or at least take charge and chart a therapeutic course. Explore the client's preferences about your role by asking:

- How do you see me fitting into what you would like to see happen?
- How can I be of most help to you now?
- What role do you see me playing in your endeavor to change this situation?
- In what ways do you see me and this process as helpful to attaining your goals?
- Let me make sure I am getting this right. Are you looking for suggestions from me about that situation?

Flexibility is not without pitfalls. It means that we don't know what role, a priori, will be most helpful. We have to *discover* it with each individual client. This doesn't mean you have to be something that you are not, or be inauthentic in any way. What it does mean is that, just as you know that there is no single facilitative therapist response for empathy, you know that you must accommodate the role that the client believes will be most helpful. When clients want a more expert stance from me—Dr. Duncan instead of Barry—I can do that. Although I can never genuinely know the definitive way to solve or "cure" any problem, I can stretch myself, within the limits of authenticity, to fit what the client is looking for. At the very least, I can be more expert-like. I can authoritatively suggest that there are many ways of addressing the client's circumstance and rely on him or her to let me know which one resonates the most after I have presented viable explanations. I can cite research and assume a more expert role but without the fire and smoke. Similarly, if a client cuts to the chase, asking for suggestions, I can offer remedies or rituals, pull them out of my black bag, and perform a more technical role but ultimately implement the one that the client gets on board most with. Then the client's response or benefit will show the way.

Keep in mind that this wide range of different roles is nothing compared with the diversity of parts you already adeptly and genuinely play in your life: adult, child, parent, friend, sibling, peer, partner, student, supervisor, mentor, etc. You are multidimensional and can utilize your own complexity for your clients by fitting their perceptions of what they want from you.

> **Bottom Line:** *Take the time to reflect about your identity and the roles you play with clients. Evolve a description of your identity that captures the essence of what it means to be a helper and that you can feel good about sharing.*

A WORK IN PROGRESS

Identity is such a crucial affair that one shouldn't rush into it.
—David Quammen

In their compelling book based on their extensive empirical investigations, Rønnestad and Skovholt (2013) described a six-phase model of therapist development, from lay helper to senior professional, and spoke of the importance of continuous reflection. They asserted that continuous reflection and an attitude of openness to new learning is a prerequisite for professional development at all levels of experience. As we develop as therapists, then, it is also useful to contemplate how we describe what we do—to define, edit, refine, expand, or outright change it altogether. Recall the discussion about allegiance and the importance of the therapist believing in whatever explanations and solutions are employed; or, in Frank's paraphrased words (Frank & Frank, 1991), our belief in the restorative power of our methods. Given the impact of our expectations—our allegiance to what we do with clients—it makes sense to describe our work in ways that we can believe in and that also do not restrict our flexibility.

Although we originally described our work as "strategic eclecticism" (Duncan, Parks & Rusk, 1990), my colleagues (mainly Greg Rusk and Andy Solovey) and I later started calling what we did *client directed* (Duncan et al., 1992) to focus attention on the common factors, especially clients' contribution to outcome: their resources, ideas, and views of the alliance. In 2000, because of the influence of Lambert's work on client-based assessment, the term *client-directed, outcome-informed* (CDOI) emerged:

> Our vision . . . embraces change that is client-directed, not theory-driven, subscribes to a relational rather than a medical model, and is committed to successful outcome instead of competent service delivery. (Duncan & Miller, 2000, pp. 217–218)

Expanding and refining the description, and making it more value based, Duncan and Sparks (2007) defined the work:

> CDOI contains no fixed techniques or causal theories regarding the concerns that bring people to treatment. Any interaction can be client-directed and outcome-informed when the consumer's voice is privileged, recovery is expected, and helpers purposefully form partnerships to: (1) enhance the factors across theories that account for success; (2) use client's ideas and preferences (theories) to guide choice of technique and model; and (3) inform the work with reliable and valid measures of the consumer's experience of the alliance and outcome. (p. 14)

Although the CDOI description is one to which I can truly pledge my allegiance, in reflecting about the work over the past few years, I now add three additional descriptors or values: *alliance focused, discovery oriented* and *socially just*. This continues to be a work in progress that I hope never stops. Although addressed above (i.e., "partnership" and "enhancing the factors across theories"), I now include *alliance focused* to ensure it is not given short shrift. As articulated in the last chapter, the importance of the relationship/alliance is immense and its empirical support overwhelming, especially as compared with the more revered aspects of psychotherapy—model and technique. I emphasize this as a reminder to myself that the alliance is job one in each and every encounter and requires my continued effort and focus. It is superordinate to everything else. The Session Rating Scale (SRS) is central to this endeavor. It just doesn't happen on its own, and it can be damn hard work.

It can be fun, too. I saw a young woman, Miriam, whose description of herself as extremely depressed was verified by a score of 10.3 on the Outcome Rating Scale (ORS). I was unable to engage her much, and she spent most of the time looking down and giving very sparse answers to questions. I was not at all happy with the session and was concerned that Miriam would not return for another try. I gave her the Session Rating Scale, and she gave me high marks. I was hoping for at least one low mark that could potentially spark a helpful conversation about what was missing. As I perused her marks on the SRS, I noticed that her name was Marion, not Miriam, the name I had called her at least six times in the session. I apologized profusely, and said, "Marion, if you decide to forgive me for my blunder and come back and see me, would you be willing to please call me Larry throughout the session so we can try and even out my stupid mistake?" Marion started chuckling, and then I joined her, and we enjoyed a healthy laugh together. Marion started the next session calling me Larry, participated in therapy, and ultimately benefited.

The term *discovery oriented* isn't mentioned in the above quote, although it is implied in the statements referring to the client's ideas, preferences, and theories. I have thought about the discovery aspects of psychotherapy, as have others, for some time (see Duncan, Hubble, & Miller, 1997). But the notion of discovery has taken on a different meaning for me. In addition to unfolding clients' ideas and theories to secure resonance with any rationale and remedy or, said another way, their agreement about the tasks of therapy, the discovery process now has a definitive purpose, a measurable end. It isn't vague or theory driven; there is a tangible treasure to be found. It is the hunt for what works, for what results in an increased ORS score culminating in the client's reaching the expected treatment response. Psychotherapy is an expedition into what will ultimately prove to be beneficial to clients, an exploration of client beliefs, values, and theories, as well as cultural and therapy myths and rituals, using client feedback about progress and the alliance as the ultimate arbiter.

And the term *social justice* isn't mentioned in the CDOI definition, although it is implied in the statement about privileging client voice. Providing socially just services has always been a part of my work, especially since Jacqueline Sparks became a colleague, but it is now included more explicitly. Basically, social justice involves working with clients in ways that privilege their social and cultural locations and ensuring their self-determination in the process, and it also requires therapists to play an advocacy role in changing conditions of oppression in the broader society that are seen as sources of the many clients' difficulties (Crethar & Winterowd, 2012; Vasquez, 2012). The broader implications of how PCOMS relates to social justice are discussed in Chapter 8.

My description of what I do reflects my value system as a therapist. I encourage you to come up with your own, while keeping client benefit as the overseer. But, first, a brief foray into the scary land of uncertainty, a terrain more frightening than the likes of lions and tigers and bears (Oh, my!).

UNCERTAINTY AND DISCOVERY

Certainty? In this world nothing is certain but death and taxes.
—Benjamin Franklin

Franklin's comment applies equally to psychotherapy, in which nothing is certain but termination and the fee for service. But this can raise our anxiety levels about the work, especially, perhaps, among students and newer therapists, although many of the more experienced are none too comfortable with it. We long for the structured, the scripted, the predictable, the manualized, the surefire way to conduct a session—maybe not even to sequester success but at times just to get through it, staring eye-to-eye with a person experiencing significant distress. Who can blame us? But uncertainty and complexity are endemic to the work, as they are to life, and therefore are important to embrace for therapist development.

Of course, there's nothing wrong with wanting a little certainty or routine. In fact, I like the routine of doing the ORS and SRS and discussing progress and the alliance with clients. All routine or structure is not bad. If you are like many people, you appreciate having something you can hold on to when you are on unfamiliar ground—like when you meet clients for the first time or feel cast adrift in the sea of information that clients give. But you want to leave space for the inexplicable. You want uncertainty to always be lingering.

Why? As frightening as it feels, uncertainty is the place of unlimited possibilities for change. It is this indeterminacy that gives therapy its texture and infuses it with the excitement of discovery. This allows for the "hereto-fore unsaid," the "aha moments," and all the spontaneous ideas, connections, conclusions, plans, insights, resolves, and new identities that emerge when you put two people together in a room and call it *psychotherapy*. This doesn't mean, of course, that it's all fireworks (just watch an entire session, rather than edited video clips, to see what I mean); it just means that your tolerance for uncertainty creates the space for new directions and insights to occur to both the client *and* you.

Uncertainty stokes the flames of such occurrences. Good therapy capitalizes on these opportunities. Perhaps, helping at its very best sets the context for these unique discoveries. The tolerance for uncertainty, however, requires faith—faith in the client, in yourself, and in psychotherapy. It also requires patience. I am certain of one thing: Uncertainty is the key that unlocks the potential for discovery. It is hard to discover something if you already know what it is that you are looking for and where it is.

DISCOVERING WHAT WORKS

I offer an account of what I do to encourage you to articulate what it is that you do—to continue your ongoing professional reflections. If you find it compelling, I invite you to sample discussions elsewhere (especially Duncan et al., 1997; and Duncan, Miller, & Sparks, 2004), where you will find detailed client examples and transcripts.

Milton Erickson (Erickson & Rossi, 1979) addressed the process of discovery in what he called *utilization*:

> Exploring a patient's individuality to ascertain what life learnings, experiences, and mental skills are available to deal with the problem . . . [and] then utilizing these uniquely personal internal responses to achieve therapeutic goals. (p. 1)

Discovering what works entails embracing the strong probability, as the Erickson quote suggests, that clients not only have all that is necessary to resolve problems but also may have already solved them, started to solve them, have a very good idea about how to do it, or are just about ready to figure out something important. And you are in the mix as well—it requires your reactions, ideas, musings, favorite myths and rituals, and consideration of the rationales and remedies you've never tried. Every conversation sets the occasion for unearthing new avenues out of the client's dilemma. Because this work is unencumbered by rote application of any particular theoretical or explanatory concepts, there is freedom to speculate. Some ideas grow into relevant discussion, while others fade away as it becomes apparent that they are not helpful to pursue. Conversing with clients unfolds and expands experiences and can result in new meanings and plans for action. This process seeks to chart a different course (connections, conclusions, solutions, etc.) in any form that permits a way to address the client's goals, to encourage an increase on the ORS and the client's benefit from therapy—to discover what works.

From a discovery-oriented perspective, the word *intervention* does not adequately describe the collaborative process that emerges (Duncan et al., 1997). To *intervene* is "to come into or between by way of hindrance or modification" (Merriam-Webster's OnLine; http://www.merriam-webster.com). It implies something done to clients rather than with them, and it consequently overemphasizes the technical expertise of the therapist, inaccurately portraying what makes therapy successful. The word *intervention* does not capture the interdependence of technique on the client's resources and ideas or how technique is successful to the extent that it emerges from the client's positive evaluation of the alliance. The words *invent* and *invention* seem more apropos. To *invent* is to "find or discover, to produce for the first time through imagination or ingenious thinking and experiment" (Merriam-Webster's OnLine; http://www.merriam-webster.com). Every technique is used for the first time, invented by clients and therapists to fit the client's unique attributes and circumstance.

My description of psychotherapy casts the client and therapist as co-explorers, searching the client's world for the map that provides a route of restoration. As coadventurers, we encounter multiple opportunities for sharing our respective vantage points while crossing the terrain of the client's world, periodically stopping to consult our ORS/SRS compass to ensure we are headed in the right direction. When lost along the way, we regroup to look for alternate routes on our maps, as well as the maps of others we encounter on the journey. Such expeditions often uncover trails that we never dreamed existed. The clients whom you met in this book exemplify the proposed discovery-oriented perspective of psychotherapy.

CONCLUSION

"Who are you?" said the Caterpillar. Alice replied rather shyly, "I—I hardly know, Sir, just at present—at least I know who I was when I got up this morning, but I must have changed several times since then."
—Lewis Carroll, *Alice's Adventures in Wonderland*

This chapter kept the spotlight on you—your identity as a helper and how you describe what you do. I offered the enchanting tale of *The Wizard of Oz* to stimulate your introspection and encouraged you to think of your own metaphors. Your continued reflection about your identity fits hand-in-glove with your description of what it is that you do as a therapist. Your ongoing reflections about your identity and what you do fuel the developmental process. Articulating a description that you can authentically believe in brings your allegiance to the therapeutic table; it reinforces your expectation that what you are doing with clients will be helpful. You were encouraged to have your cake and eat it too, to be flexible in your description of your work to enable a broad range of possibilities for you and your clients to sample. A good place to start may be to grapple with and embrace uncertainty as a prerequisite for your continued development. I presented my description of what I do as a springboard for your consideration of what you do. A discovery-oriented description was offered that has been illustrated by the clients presented in this book.

CLIENTS ARE THE BEST TEACHERS: THEIR STORIES DOCUMENT OUR DEVELOPMENT

When one admits that nothing is certain, one must, I think, also admit that some things are much more nearly certain than others.
—Bertrand Russell

Natalie told me she'd been a multiple personality since childhood, when her different alters provided protection from a brutally abusive environment. She felt she had already dealt with the abuse and didn't want to become integrated into a single self but, rather, wanted "co-consciousness," a state in which the alters would be aware of each other's experience without losing their separate identities. Natalie entered therapy because she had lost access to some of her most intuitive sub-selves.

Talk about uncertainty. I didn't have any idea of how to help Natalie recontact her missing alters or promote co-consciousness. I shared my lack of experience in these matters, and Natalie responded that her doctor had referred her and had said good things about me and that she trusted her completely. Besides, she added, the previous therapist, a dissociative identity expert, had all but demanded that Natalie give up her alters in service of an integrated personality. Natalie wanted nothing to do with that. Natalie told me that she didn't fit the mold of that therapist's thinking about multiples, and added, "I can't help that!"

But I was willing to not know—to explore her world, to find out how her system worked, to validate it, and try to discover a way to help her reaccess her alters. Natalie was quite remarkable: witty, obviously bright, and very artistic. She worked as a copy editor for a magazine by day and by night was an accomplished oil painter. Over the next few sessions, Natalie and others in her system explained to me that her alters lived in various rooms in a visualized house. Some were practical, others intuitive, and others tough as nails. She would visualize the pathway to the different alters' rooms to access them; whoever had the best skills then emerged to deal with whatever life dished out—except for now, when some of them had mysteriously gone missing. I sincerely told Natalie—an extremely intuitive woman, or collection of women—that I thought she had a "wonderful system" and suggested she think of all the ways she had gained access to her alters before.

A possible source to the problem was finally discovered. Natalie said she thought that the alters were hiding because her boyfriend, Joe, was embroiled in extreme, ongoing arguments with a brother and sister over the impending sale of their grandparents' farm. Natalie believed that the alters were frightened and hiding, much as they did when she was a child. Once Joe became less unpredictably volatile, Natalie thought, access to her missing alters would return. With this discovery made, we focused on ways to address Joe's anger and otherwise, in Natalie's words, "deflect it" and diminish its impact on her alters. Natalie implemented our inventions and Joe responded by calming down and becoming more attentive to Natalie's needs. Subsequently, over the next days, several alters "came home."

But my confusion and the uncertainty didn't stop there. With the crisis with Joe averted, Natalie identified a new goal of addressing her Epstein-Barr virus. In the next session, a wise, spiritually centered martial artist alter named Nora showed up. Since Natalie was already adept at visualization, I had planned to suggest that we fine-tune her skills to rally her resources against the virus. I suggested this to Nora instead, and we worked on various martial arts images to combat the virus. I wondered aloud if it were possible to teach the others the same skills, and Nora said she would try.

Perhaps in my most speechless encounter with a client since Tina (my first-ever client who dispassionately disrobed despite my dismay), Natalie appeared in the next session and with great enthusiasm exclaimed, "I'm a me!" My experienced and tempered empathic therapeutic response: "Say what?" I was so dumbfounded, so confused—I clearly didn't know what the hell was going on. Hemming and hawing and undeniably lost, my clueless response to Natalie's revelation often brings down the house when I show the video in my trainings. But as I always say, at least I was authentically stupid!

Then Natalie explained: Nora had called a meeting in a visualized library to communicate to the alters what she had learned about Epstein-Barr. It was the first time they had all been in the same room together. Natalie reported that each alter had come forward, naming her special gifts to the overall system. After praying together, each alter had said, "I belong."

Natalie told me, "Now I'm a 'me,' and I'm different. I am the collage of their gifts. Everybody's there. And if they want, they could still come out, but I'm a me. This me is finding out a lot of things. It's like I'm looking through a pair of new eyes that have never been touched or scarred." Again, I was dumbstruck! She had gone beyond co-consciousness to a form of integration that she welcomed. I sat stunned for some time before Natalie asked me if she could give me a hug. I am not sure, in retrospect, whether it was a celebratory hug or one designed to comfort me and reel in my confusion.

Natalie stands out to me because I never have felt more cast adrift. I didn't have a clue about what to do—no theoretical or technical training prepared me for this client and how therapy progressed over time. But I was there hunting for what could work, adding something when I could—the anger suggestions and the imagery to help combat the virus—until the unexpected occurred. Natalie also illustrates how difficult it can be to *write* about psychotherapy. At one extreme, it can sound like I'm hawking a new improved cookie cutter while condemning cookie-cutter solutions. At the other extreme, I probably risk offering vague camp counselor platitudes about the importance of a good alliance. I believe it is best described, for me, as a collaborative expedition for the magic of the moment: not the magic of the sweeping, dramatic gesture or an isolated technique or any other novelty but, rather, the magic that grows out of exploring the client's world, validating their experiences, and discovering what works.

8

BECOMING A BETTER AGENCY

America's mental health service delivery system is in shambles . . . [and is] incapable of efficiently delivering . . . effective treatments.
—President's New Freedom Commission
on Mental Health, Interim Report

Although the efficacy of psychotherapy has been unequivocally demonstrated in randomized clinical trials (RCTs; Lambert, 2013), the jury is still out regarding its effectiveness in everyday clinical settings, especially in the public domain. This is noteworthy because 61% of mental health and substance abuse care in the United States is publicly funded (Kaiser Commission on Medicaid and the Uninsured, 2011).

Great strides, however, in determining the effectiveness of services in natural settings have recently been made through the methodology of *benchmarking*, which permits comparison with a reliably determined effect size (ES) from clinical trials. For example, using benchmarks from RCTs of psychotherapy for depression, Minami et al. (2008) found that clients who received psychotherapy in a managed care setting received treatment as effective as those clients receiving evidence-based treatments (EBTs) in clinical trials. Similarly, Minami et al. (2009) evaluated services provided at a university counseling center (UCC) and found treatment effects equivalent to those observed in RCTs.

http://dx.doi.org/10.1037/14392-008
On Becoming a Better Therapist, Second Edition: Evidence-Based Practice One Client at a Time, by B. L. Duncan
Copyright © 2014 by the American Psychological Association. All rights reserved.

For those receiving, providing, or funding public behavioral health (PBH), however, the question is not whether psychotherapy works in RCTs, private insurance settings, or UCCs but, rather, whether the benefits of psychotherapy routinely provided by therapists on the front lines extend to the impoverished, disempowered, and disenfranchised. Studies designed to answer this question have, so far, painted an ugly picture. For example, looking at childhood depression, Weersing and Weisz (2002) compared outcomes in six community mental health centers (CMHCs) in the Los Angeles area with a clinical trial benchmark. They found the outcomes of depressed youth treated in CMHCs approximated those of control groups in RCTs.

Another way of evaluating effectiveness, as discussed in Chapter 5, is by examining the rates of reliable and/or clinically significant change (CSC; Jacobson & Truax, 1991). Perhaps the most damning data regarding PBH effectiveness was presented by Hansen, Lambert, and Forman (2002), who reported a paltry 20.5% reliable change rate and 8.6% CSC rate, a combined reliable and clinically significant change (RCSC) rate of just 29.1% at a CMHC. This study seemed to only confirm the conclusion, noted in the epigram above, reached by the President's New Freedom Commission on Mental Health, Interim Report (2002). Hansen et al. (2002) also reported an unimpressive 35% RCSC rate across six different types of outpatient settings. In other words, almost two thirds of the 6,072 clients did not benefit from psychotherapy.

Can PBH redeem itself? Can outcomes be improved in any organization for that matter? This chapter addresses these questions and demonstrates that the Partners for Change Outcome Management System (PCOMS) can raise the bar of PBH performance as well as any setting willing to take the plunge of systematically identifying clients at risk for a negative outcome. First, the chapter reports the results of our recent study (Reese, Duncan, Bohanske, Owen, & Minami, 2014) that evaluated the effectiveness of a large, multicultural PBH agency that had implemented PCOMS against clinical benchmarks from RCTs—a story of redemption and success. But there is no free lunch. Implementation of PCOMS so that gains in effectiveness are realized at the individual therapist and agency levels takes a concerted long-term commitment that integrates PCOMS in all aspects of service delivery. The chapter also details the four secrets of implementing PCOMS and the supervisory process that sustains its impact.

ONE AGENCY'S STORY OF REDEMPTION AND SUCCESS

Those who wish to sing always find a song.

—Swedish Proverb

Just as now is not an easy time to be a therapist, as noted in Chapter 1, it is not a stroll in the park to be a public agency either. Paperwork and continual oversight is a way of life. In addition to state requirements, managed care companies are frequently retained to handle the distribution of public funds and ensure accountability. Add more forms. Then, each agency has its own policies and procedures necessitated by national regulatory and accrediting bodies. Add still more paperwork. If that were not enough, the rush to limit service provision to EBTs has added new layers of management, policies, and procedures. It is easy to see why outcomes and the quality of service delivery can get shuffled to bottom of the paperwork pile.

But this is not the case at Southwest Behavioral Health Services (SBHS), a large ($70 million annual budget) nonprofit, comprehensive community behavioral health organization providing services to people living in Maricopa (Phoenix), Mohave, Yavapa, Coconino, and Gila counties in Arizona. SBHS provides clinical services to a diverse group of Medicaid-insured clients at or below 100% of the federal poverty level through a wide variety of programs, including mental health and substance abuse treatments for youth and adults. SBHS is also the professional home of the Heart and Soul of Change Project (hereafter the Project) leader, Bob Bohanske. Because of Bob's efforts, SBHS embarked on a journey of transformation and implemented PCOMS beginning in 2007, eventually rolling it out across all clinical services (see Bohanske & Franczak, 2010, for a full description).

The data for the Reese et al. (2014) benchmarking study were collected from adult clients attending at least two sessions who were discharged between January 2007 and December 2011. Given that clients completed the measure at each session, a larger inclusion rate was enabled because the data from last session were always collected. Although some data sets include only those functioning in the clinical range at intake (e.g., Minami et al., 2009), we also included clients who scored over the clinical cutoff at intake (27% of final data set) to be more representative of typical PBH data. Using these criteria, we identified 5,168 clients seen by 86 therapists. This total data set was used to compare with the benchmarks derived from RCTs of client feedback (both the Outcome Questionnaire [OQ] and the Outcome Rating Scale [ORS]).

The clients were predominantly female (60.7%) and Caucasian (67.8%), with their ages ranging from 18 to 87 (M = 36.7) and mostly between the ages of 18 and 40 (61.8%) or 41 and 64 (37.3%). Hispanics were the largest minority (17.7%), followed by African Americans (9.3%), Native Americans (2.8%), and other ethnic groups (2.4%). Clients attended a mean of 8.9 sessions. Regarding the primary diagnosis, depression, mood, and anxiety disorders (excluding bipolar disorder) were the most common (46.0%), followed by substance abuse disorders (18.8%), bipolar disorder and schizophrenia (14.4%), and adjustment disorder (10.0%). A mix of other diagnostic categories accounted for the remainder. Exploratory analyses were conducted on client demographic variables such as race/ethnicity, gender, and diagnoses. As many other studies have found, the demographic variables had little impact on effectiveness. An interesting "nonfinding" was that diagnosis also had little impact on outcome, yet another confirmation that it should be given little importance in the clinical process.

Although the total sample was representative of typical agency practice, the data were trimmed by eliminating those clients who scored over the clinical cutoff and who had a diagnosis of any disorder other than a depressive disorder, to approximate the methodology used in the benchmarking studies of managed care and university counseling settings. This reduced the sample to 1,589 clients for the second benchmark comparison.

And our results: The total sample ES estimates of SBHS were comparable with those of RCTs evaluating systematic client feedback (OQ system and PCOMS combined). In addition, a comparison of ES estimates revealed that psychotherapy for adult depression provided at SBHS generated ES estimates that were similar to those observed in clinical trials of major depression treated by EBTs. Therefore, despite differences in clinical and demographic characteristics between this agency and clinical trials included in the benchmark, it is reasonable to conclude that psychotherapy services provided at SBHS by the rank and file are effective. This is noteworthy because the conditions of RCTs are quite different, often far more posh compared to those in the trenches. Clinicians in PBH settings must take all comers, many of whose complicated lives and histories would be an immediate cause for exclusion in most research settings.

Comparisons to the two noted benchmarking studies (Minami et al., 2008, 2009) also revealed similar ES estimates. This too is noteworthy, given the representative nature of the SBHS sample. Both of the other benchmarking studies lost considerable portions of data. For example, Minami et al. (2008), the study conducted in a managed care setting in which the OQ was administered by only 65% of therapists and was required only at the first, third, fifth, and every fifth session thereafter, lost over 55% of the data for lack of two data points. The current sample lost only those who didn't return for a second visit, again raising the issue of feasibility discussed in Chapter 2.

So why are services at SBHS superior to previous dismal reports of outcomes at CMHCs (Hansen et al., 2002; Weersing & Weisz, 2002)? Perhaps the most obvious answer is the dose of treatment, the issue highlighted by Hansen et al. (2002), who argued that the dose of treatment (4.3 sessions) was inadequate exposure to psychotherapy for improvement to occur. Our study provided some support for their argument, given that the average was 8.9 sessions. Not supportive of the dose explanation, however, and revealed in Table 8.1, in as few as three sessions, over 50% of clients achieved either reliable (21.7%) or clinically significant (32.8%) change. The addition of

TABLE 8.1

Clinically Significant Change by Session of SBHS and UCC

Total *N*		*N* in clinical range		% CSC (*n*) of eligible		No. of sessions
SBHS[a]	UCC[b]	SBHS[a]	UCC[b]	SBHS[a]	UCC[b]	
550	NA	420	NA	26.2 (110)	NA	2
702	1195	527	706	32.8 (173)	35.8 (253)	3
549	843	401	520	38.2 (153)	40.4 (210)	4
467	597	370	381	47.3 (175)	40.4 (154)	5
360	418	251	270	43.8 (110)	42.2 (114)	6
317	311	226	208	46.9 (106)	43.3 (90)	7
280	257	186	182	51.6 (96)	46.5 (80)	8
260	229	181	153	49.7 (90)	47.7 (73)	9
213	152	155	100	51.6 (80)	50.0 (50)	10
160	128	111	92	41.4 (46)	46.7 (43)	11
144	110	101	76	54.5 (55)	47.4 (36)	12
114	93	81	60	58.0 (47)	41.7 (25)	13
107	82	68	63	45.6 (31)	49.2 (31)	14
87	43	63	32	54.0 (34)	53.1 (17)	15
91	41	63	34	50.8 (32)	47.1 (16)	16
77	32	56	23	48.2 (27)	31.1 (9)	17
586	145	435	95	49.7 (216)	43.2 (41)	18–40
104	NA	79	NA	46.8 (37)	NA	41+
5168	4676	3774	2985	42.9 (1618)	41.6 (1242)	TOTAL

Note. SBHS = Southwest Behavioral Health Services; UCC = university counseling center; NA = not available.
[a]Data from Reese, Duncan, Bohanske, Owen, and Minami, 2014.
[b]Data from Baldwin, Berkeljon, Atkins, Olsen, and Nielsen, 2009.

systematic client feedback provides a better explanation. Considering both the OQ system and PCOMS, identifying clients at risk via the routine use of outcome measures has now been shown in 11 RCTs to improve outcomes. SBHS started implementation of systematic client feedback in 2007 and now integrates routine consumer feedback in all services. In other words, PCOMS is the reason.

Very few studies have systematically looked at large naturalistic data sets. We were able to find only one other U.S. study in addition to the benchmarking studies discussed above, the study by Baldwin, Berkeljon, Atkins, Olsen, and Nielsen (2009) of a UCC, discussed in Chapter 2. Comparisons with the current PBH sample (see Table 8.1) revealed a surprising similarity of the two data sets, measured by different outcome instruments (the ORS and OQ), in the rates of CSC by session as well as the overall CSC rate (42.9 in the PBH sample vs. 41.6 in the UCC sample). There were perhaps some expected differences as well. Regarding clients entering therapy in the clinical range, 63.8% of the clients in the UCC study entered in the clinical range compared with 72.9% in the SBHS sample. The prevailing assumptions regarding the two sites may be that university counseling clients are likely to be more functional than PBH clients (e.g., more available resources, education) and therefore more likely to achieve better outcomes. While there is some support for the first assumption, given the percentage of clients entering in the clinical range, the difference (9.1%) may be less than expected. The second assumption (better outcomes) was not borne out by our study.

Finally, in addition to the improvements in outcomes resulting in the noted similarities to RCTs, a UCC, and a managed care setting, SBHS also realized significant gains in efficiency. After PCOMS implementation, there was a significant reduction in length of stay across programs, a decrease in cancellations and no-shows, and an increase in overall therapist and agency productivity—serving more clients with the same number of staff. The story of redemption and success was complete. SBHS improved both the effectiveness and efficiency of services, leaving the dismal report of President's New Freedom Commission far behind.

FOUR SECRETS OF SUCCESSFUL PCOMS IMPLEMENTATION

I haven't failed. I've found 10,000 ways that won't work.
—Benjamin Franklin

The Heart and Soul of Change Project (https://heartandsoulofchange. com) is a practice-driven training and research initiative that focuses on improving outcomes via client-based outcome feedback, or PCOMS. The website is a major dissemination vehicle for PCOMS with over 250 free downloads (articles, handouts, slides, videos, and webinars) as well as a "member" site with additional training resources, including client videos. While PCOMS is not tied to any model-based assumptions and can be incorporated in any treatment, it does promote a set of service delivery values: client privilege in determining the benefit of services as well as in all decisions that affect care, including intervention preferences; an expectation of recovery; attention to those common factors that cut across all models that account for therapeutic change; and an appreciation of social justice in the provision of care—or client-directed, outcome-informed clinical work (Duncan, 2010a; Duncan, Miller, & Sparks, 2004; Duncan, Solovey, & Rusk, 1992; Duncan & Sparks, 2002, 2007, 2010).

PCOMS offers a way to operationalize interrelated ideas that often sound like platitudes: individually tailored services, consumer involvement, recovery, and social justice. Despite well-intentioned efforts, the infrastructure of therapy (paperwork, policies, procedures, and professional language) can reify descriptions of client problems and silence client views, goals, and preferences.

Routinely requesting, documenting, and responding to client feedback transforms power relations in the immediate therapy encounter by privileging client beliefs and goals over potential culturally biased and insensitive practices.

Outside the therapy dyad, client-generated data via PCOMS help overcome inequities built into everyday mental health service delivery by redefining whose voice counts. Use of client feedback applies the principles of social justice that, until now, have largely existed only in the pages of training manuals, textbooks, and academic journals (Sparks, 2013). PCOMS seeks to level the psychotherapy process by inviting collaborative decision making, honoring client diversity with multiple language availability, and valuing local cultural knowledge; PCOMS provides a mechanism for routine attention to multiculturalism and consumer involvement.[1] Finally, PCOMS helps to enable recovery-oriented services (Bohanske & Franczak, 2010; Sparks & Muro, 2009) via attention to facilitating individually defined change rather than the treatment of "mental illness."

Transporting PCOMS to everyday organizational practice by the Project emphasizes these values in addition to the mechanics and clinical nuances of using the ORS and the Session Rating Scale (SRS). Over the course of the past decade, four secrets to successful implementation of PCOMS have emerged: In it for the long haul; Love your data; Inspire the frontline clinician; and Supervision for a change.

In It for the Long Haul

Organizational change is hard, and many things can sabotage well-intentioned efforts. People at all levels from the CEO to support staff tire of hearing about the next great thing (the next paradigm shift is always just around

---

[1]Sometimes the question arises regarding whether PCOMS imposes Western thought on nondominant cultures. Jacqueline Sparks, Project Partner and social justice advocate, believes that the measures are designed specifically *not* to impose Western ideology on those who come from non-Western cultures. On a recent post to the Project listserv (https://groups.google.com/forum/?fromgroups#!forum/heroicagencies), she wrote:

> Our mental health system is Western-based, particularly its emphasis on the objective expert apart from the client who can determine the process and procedures that will "cure" the client, based on Western norms of [fill in the blank—what is a healthy man, woman, couple, family, etc.]. There are many tragic histories of how this model has produced oppressive practices. PCOMS, instead, fundamentally alters this dynamic, inviting a collaboration where the distinction between us and them is broken down and where client views, including cultural and spiritual preferences, are honored first and foremost. PCOMS is an antidote to Western oppression of indigenous and non-European cultures. Granted, the forms, despite being translated into 22 languages, come from systems of measurement that are rooted in Western thought. However, the visual analog continua and lack of specific content questions allow a broad range of flexibility for the client to communicate his or her unique experience. They, not a diagnosis or theoretical lens, provide the starting point for the conversation that unfolds the client's unique story, views, and preferences. I make the assumption that the desire to not be "done to" but to do (for self/family however conceived), to have a voice that is heard, is valued cross-culturally.

the corner), and, as discussed in Chapter 2, measuring outcomes has its own set of obstacles and fears. Over time, many learn to cope by battening down the hatches and waiting out the storm, the latest edict dictated by management. Consequently, it is often best to think small and go slow, garnering support over time and winning people over. For example, conducting a pilot project in one site or program can offer a way to get things started in a manageable way, especially if the pilot is with the easiest implementations first, like outpatient psychotherapy services. This is how Bob Bohanske at SBHS went about it. Another approach is to start with so-called early responders or volunteers who embrace the ideas from the beginning. Then, the findings and enthusiasm from the pilot can be used to secure ongoing commitment from others. This is how Dave Hanna at Bluegrass Community Mental Health in Kentucky got things rolling.

Successful transportation of PCOMS requires commitment at all levels (Exhibit 8.1 is a readiness checklist). Implementation is not a sprint, it's a marathon. I learned this the hard way. Some trainings that I had hoped would inspire implementation were doomed from the beginning. For example, sometimes an enthusiastic person who had read about PCOMS or attended a workshop attempted to champion its implementation by bringing me in to

EXHIBIT 8.1
Partners for Change Outcome Management System (PCOMS)
Organizational Readiness Checklist

1. The Agency/Organization/Behavioral Health Care System has secured Board of Director approval and support for PCOMS.
2. Has consensus among the agency director and senior managers that consumer partnership, accountability, and PCOMS are central features of service delivery.
3. Has a business/financial plan that incorporates PCOMS, training, and data collection.
4. Promotes regular communication with funders about PCOMS data as they apply to agency effectiveness and efficiency.
5. Has a human resource training and development plan that supports ongoing PCOMS education at all levels, including a core group of internal trainers, and that integrates PCOMS into individual development plans, performance appraisals, and hiring practices.
6. Has the infrastructure (e.g., support staff, IT, computer hardware, software) to support the collection and analysis of PCOMS data at the individual consumer, therapist, program, and agency levels.
7. Has a supervisory infrastructure that allows PCOMS data to be used to individualize treatment planning, identify at-risk clients and proactively address treatment needs, and improve therapist performance.
8. Has a structure to support and a policy for addressing clients who are not progressing that ensures rapid transfer and continuity of care.
9. Has a Mission Statement that incorporates consumer partnership and accountability as central features of service delivery.
10. Has a Client Rights and Responsibilities Statement that emphasizes consumer feedback and partnership to guide all treatment services.

do training, but without agency support and the infrastructure to maintain it, implementation quickly fell flat. More often, an agency director would arrange a training because he or she wanted to steer the organization toward measuring outcomes because of state requirements but would not have anyone else on board or any plan of implementation beyond my 1-day overview. Sometimes these trainings were mandated without any groundwork, resulting in my surprise to find a somewhat hostile audience in fear of management "big brother" and the "real" purpose of measuring outcomes. Fueling these fears, sometimes managed care entities employed my training services with the intention of using PCOMS to do provider profiling. Of course, once I figured that out, it didn't go any further.

Implementing PCOMS requires much more than attendance at a workshop because it involves all aspects of service delivery. I finally learned that certain things have to be in place for any chance of success. No doubt, organizing services around client preferences and progress challenges conventional wisdom about how to provide treatment—new staff orientation, intake process, documentation, treatment plans, case staffing, and supervision all need revision. Without the infrastructure to support such changes, they are unlikely to happen. Although all of the items on the checklist are important, I focus here on a few key items.

- *Consensus among the agency director and senior managers that consumer partnership, accountability, and PCOMS are central features of service delivery.* Unless everyone is on board, implementation is likely to fail because those who are under the skeptical/ indifferent manager in the organizational tree will not follow through with what is required. This is the first legwork that needs to occur to ensure success. Having the management team on board who can speak the language allows the conversation to start with frontline clinicians and assuage their concerns about what management is up to.
- *A business/financial plan that incorporates PCOMS.* While implementing PCOMS is very low cost compared with EBTs because it applies to all clients and not just to one specific diagnosis, it's not free. The plan must include the initial and follow-up training and consultation expenses as well as ongoing data collection and dissemination costs. I also recommend that the plan include the training of a core group of internal champions who can replace the need for outside consultation. Organizations that commit to these internal folks have a much greater chance for success, not only because of their increased expertise with PCOMS but also because of their ability to use available resources on the website to train others.

- A *supervisory infrastructure that allows PCOMS data to be used to individualize treatment planning, identify at-risk clients and proactively address treatment needs, and improve therapist performance.* Early on, I encountered many agencies that did not include clinical supervision as part of their routine functioning. Reasons for this included: no available time because of therapist productivity requirements, administrative supervision regarding funding and reporting issues took priority, or only unlicensed therapists required supervision. The latter is ironic, given that it implies that licensed therapists are successful with all their clients.
- Successful implementation is not possible without ongoing supervision to ensure data integrity, allowing clients at risk to be identified and addressed proactively. Over time, and faced with relentless competing demands, staff enthusiasm for any new approach naturally wanes. The vigilance required to sustain anything new dwindles without ongoing attention. Supervision can come in many forms, including group and peer supervision, but there has to be ongoing follow-up and follow-through. Supervision offers the most direct method of ensuring PCOMS reaches the front lines and stays there. (More on supervision below.)
- *The infrastructure (e.g., support staff, IT, computer hardware, software) to support the collection, analysis, and dissemination of PCOMS data at the individual consumer, therapist, program, and agency levels.* Everything is based on the data. The use of the ORS and SRS as clinical tools to facilitate conversations with clients about progress and the alliance undoubtedly enhances outcomes. But unless there is a way to collect the data in a reliable way that ensures data integrity and dissemination, PCOMS will not serve its primary function. Unless the data are used to identify clients who are not benefiting, then PCOMS is not going to enhance outcomes at an organizational level. This leads us to the second secret to successful implementation.

Love Your Data

For a long time, I implemented PCOMS with the belief that data collection would happen organically, that using the ORS would lead folks to see the value of the numbers and ultimately to systematically enter scores into some kind of aggregate database. What was I thinking?! While some people intuitively see the benefits of data collection, the overwhelming majority of folks don't. It fact, many people hate numbers and cannot see the relationship between what they do and numbers on a spreadsheet or scores on a graph.

The fact of the matter is that you don't know how implementation is progressing unless you have data. The data tell all, conveying rapid information not only about who is using the measures but also about whether the measures are being used properly, thus allowing data integrity. Data indicators of correct and incorrect use are easily taught and integrated into the supervisory process (see below) allowing supervisors to monitor and build therapist skill level. Until there is data integrity, PCOMS will not do its job of identifying nonresponding clients to enable new directions and better outcomes.

An important part of successful implementation, therefore, involves building a culture around numbers and data that help people get rid of their reluctance to embrace them. In fact, the goal has to be not only for people to see data as their friend, but for them to actually love their data. Keep in mind, when I say numbers, I am not reducing clients to statistics. Far from it. The numbers represent clients' own assessments of progress and their alliance with a helper. The measures, in short, amplify client voice. Without them, clients' views do not stand a chance to be part of the real record—that is, critical information that guides moment-by-moment, week-by-week treatment decisions or evaluates eventual outcomes. Numbers on the measures, as concrete representations of client perspectives, offer a direct way to describe client benefit at individual therapist and agency levels.

The data, of course, offer an organization the ability to demonstrate its effectiveness to funders, a major motivation for many agencies to consider PCOMS in addition to the benefits of improved effectiveness and efficiency. For example, Barbara L. Hernandez, chief operating officer of the Center for Family Services (CFS) in West Palm Beach, Florida, negotiated with a funder, Palm Beach County Children Services, to use PCOMS as the primary outcome data in a program for expectant mothers. Similarly, Dave Hanna, certified trainer and CEO of Bluegrass CMHC in Kentucky, is using PCOMS data to negotiate the waiving of initial authorization of services with one of the center's managed care entities.

Inspire the Frontline Clinician

The benefits are clear when considering organizational goals, but what about the benefits of data collection for the frontline therapist? Implementation also requires an attention to the in-the-trenches practitioner and a more "inspire" versus "mandate" organizational mentality. Although some may ultimately need to be mandated, and everyone must know that the organization is totally committed to this direction, most can be inspired to give it a shot. A recent study by Ionita (2013) of Canadian psychologists provides some insight into some of the barriers that prevent therapists from embracing outcome management. For some who have been in the field for a while, outcome management might be a totally foreign concept. Ionita reported that the longer a person was out of graduate school, the less likely it was that he or she had heard of measuring outcomes. Among those who had heard of it, the top three barriers to the task were limited knowledge of measures, lack of training, and limited accessibility to training on outcome management.

So, to state the obvious, initial and ongoing training is essential to implementation. Therapists need to feel comfortable and supported with something that may initially seem quite alien. As anyone who has attended a workshop knows, enthusiasm quickly dissipates and readily lapses into frustration if continued support is unavailable.

Still others have been turned off by cumbersome measures that seem far removed from their day-to-day work with clients. Ionita (2013) reported that the reasons people stopped using outcome measures were worries that the measures were burdening clients, they added too much work, and clinicians were not convinced of the benefits. All of the barriers exemplified in Ionita's study can be easily addressed with PCOMS. If you are with me to this point, you know that the burden on clients is minimal to none, that the work of doing the measures is folded into the clinical process itself, and that using PCOMS results in better outcomes at both the individual and organizational levels. But clinicians are more likely to be convinced of the benefits by their own clinical experience than by cited studies. That is where the inspiration really comes in. When clinicians experience the conversation they have never had before, or recapture a client who was headed nowhere, then the benefits of PCOMS provide motivation to continue. Getting therapists to that point is the challenge. Don Rogers, clinical director of Bluegrass and a Certified Trainer says that you have to drag some folks to this point, but once they get there, the feedback process provides its own motivation. Converts are good for implementation.

Still others are fearful that P4P or "pay for performance," or what I call "punish for performance" (more on this next chapter), or similarly motivated strategies will be used to malign those who do not measure up to some arbitrary standard. This is essentially an issue of trust and requires that the management mantra be that the measures will never be used in punitive ways against therapists. The sole purpose of PCOMS is to improve client outcomes. I recommend that organizations put this in writing to convince the skeptical. I also inform folks in my implementation trainings that if PCOMS is used punitively toward therapists I will remove the agency's license to use it. The point is that everyone must know that PCOMS isn't about nailing therapists or no one will do it—management needs to be adamant that the only purpose is to use data to improve the quality of care that clients receive. Given that most therapists improve their outcomes with feedback, a positive, noncompetitive approach goes a long way to assuage therapists' fears.

Even with these concerns that measuring outcomes tend to stir in clinicians, the large-scale study of therapist development described in Chapter 5 suggested three things practitioners bring to the table that help implementation: therapists want to make a meaningful difference in the lives of those they serve; therapists want to improve over the course of their careers; and therapists need to grow to avoid burnout. So implementation is enhanced when PCOMS is connected to the work that the overwhelming majority of therapists deeply value and when it appeals to their best side—their nearly universal desire to do good work and get better. In an attempt to motivate practitioners to consider the benefits of feedback, the implementation process of the Project also includes an attention to (a) the common factors, (b) a nuanced clinical process, and (c) therapist development. Of course, these are the issues that have been emphasized throughout this book.

The common factors, those elements of psychotherapy running across all models that account for change (see Chapter 1), provide an overarching framework for PCOMS. Integrating the use of PCOMS within the larger literature about what works in therapy promotes therapist understanding of the feedback process and adherence to the feedback protocol. As detailed in this book, PCOMS is presented as the tie that binds these healing components together, allowing the factors to be expressed one client at a time.

Although the more than 400,000 administrations of the ORS/SRS have yielded invaluable information regarding the psychometrics of the measures, trajectories, algorithms, etc., PCOMS remains a clinical intervention embedded in the complex interpersonal process called *psychotherapy*. For successful implementation and ongoing adherence, PCOMS must appeal to therapists at a clinical level. Consequently, PCOMS is described as the clinical process that it is—one that requires skill and nuance to achieve the maximum feedback effect. PCOMS speaks to therapists "where they live" by providing a methodology to address those clients who do not benefit from their services. Implementation in many ways rests on getting therapists to make it their own so they will realize the benefits.

Similarly, a focus on therapist development provides a positive motivation for therapists to invest time and energy in PCOMS. There will always be organizational motivations for PCOMS in terms of improved outcomes and reduced costs—the language of "return on investment" and "proof of value." But there is also the personal motivation of the therapist, the very reason most got into this business in the first place: to make a difference in the lives of those served. PCOMS appeals to the best of therapist intentions and encourages therapists to collect ORS data so that they can track their development and implement strategies to improve their effectiveness, as discussed in Chapter 5.

Including these additional aspects allows therapists to see that the intentions of PCOMS go well beyond management or funder objectives. Client-based outcome feedback is about consumer privilege and benefit and about helping therapists get better at what they do.

Supervision for a Change (in Both Clients and Therapists)

If there is any one thing that must be in place for the successful implementation of PCOMS, it is supervision. Client feedback increases in value exponentially, and consumer involvement becomes a reality when ORS scores extend past the clinical session to supervision and are used to identify those who are not responding. In the Orlinsky and Rønnestad (2005) study of therapist development, supervision was also rated highly as a positive influence on current growth. Recall that 97% of therapists in that study ranked learning from clients to be the most beneficial, with 84% rating it as highly beneficial. Supervision was rated as beneficial by 95% of therapists and as highly beneficial by 79%. So supervision is not a hard sell to therapists. Ongoing supervision is integral to positive work morale. It is often what holds agencies together in the face of pressures for production and the stress of hearing the heartaches of people struggling at the worst times of their lives. Supervision provides a context for camaraderie and support—it fosters an esprit de corps that both buffers burnout and stimulates rapid learning. And it is about change for both clients and therapists.

A four-step supervisory process (Duncan & Sparks, 2010) that focuses first on ORS-identified clients at risk and then on individual clinician effectiveness and how improvement can occur strengthens the possibility of successful implementation. This supervisory process is a bit different—it is based on outcome data instead of theoretical explanations or pontifications about why clients are not changing. It is aimed at identifying clients who are not benefiting so that services can be modified in the *next* session. This type of supervision is a big departure from business as usual because, rather than the therapist choosing who is discussed, the clients are choosing themselves by virtue of their ORS scores and lack of change. So the ORS allows clients to have a voice in supervision as well.

There is no inherently correct way to conduct supervision, and it can be accomplished in individual, group, or peer formats. Many agencies combine group and individual supervision, doing three 2-hour groups per month that cover clients at risk and one 1-hour individual session to address the development of the therapist.

1. *Supervisees bring graphs of all clients who are not benefiting; and until data integrity is ensured, graphs of all clients or a spreadsheet of all client scores.* The

first order of business is to ensure data integrity. If this is not done, then PCOMS will not do its job of identifying clients at risk and will not result in improved outcomes. A big red flag occurs when therapists say their clients refuse to do the measures. Given the infrequent nature of client refusal, this is almost always more about the therapist than the client. This can be solved by demonstrating the use of the measures with these very clients or simply asking the therapist to role-play his or her introduction with the supervisor playing the client.

There are three things to look for in the data to ensure integrity. There is a learning curve here, so don't freak out if you have to dump some of your data. For example, in the SBHS implementation led by Bob Bohanske, 31% of the data had to be dumped the first year, dropping to 5% in the last (a span of 5 years). The first data indicator is the percentage of intake scores that are over the clinical cutoff. If more than 30% of intakes are over the cutoff, it is likely that the therapist is not introducing the ORS so that the client understands it and/or is not connecting it to the work of therapy. Of course, if the therapist works primarily with mandated clients or kids, then the percentage over the cutoff will be higher.

Second, scores 35 and higher are rarely valid. Even those not receiving services rarely score this high. People tend to see that their lives are not perfect and generally leave some room for improvement on the ORS. Recall from Chapter 2 that there are generally two reasons that clients score so high: They either don't understand the measure or they are blowing it off. Both are training issues. Again, the supervisor has to make sure that the therapist knows how to introduce the ORS and integrate it into the work. And the therapist needs to know how to follow up on a high score to make sure that it matches the client's descriptions of his or her experience of life. Connecting clients' marks to their reasons for service provides assurance that the scores will be a valid representation of client distress.

Finally, the third scenario that quickly reflects improper use of PCOMS is the seesaw pattern, where client scores go up and down. This typically means that the client doesn't understand that the measure is designed to monitor progress about the reasons for service and not how his or her life is going; in other words, the ORS has become an emotional thermometer. This, of course, requires that the therapist integrate the ORS into the work, and that the client view the measure as a reflection of how therapy is addressing, for better or worse, the reasons for service. Emotional thermometer graphs are easily spotted and handled.

The data quickly highlight these training needs so that the supervisor can focus on the skills necessary for data integrity. Exhibit 8.2 lists the competencies required of therapists and a measure of fidelity or adherence that

EXHIBIT 8.2
Partners for Change Outcome Management System (PCOMS) Therapist Competency Checklist and Adherence Scale

1. Administer and score the Outcome Rating Scale (ORS) each session or unit of service.
2. Ensure that the client understands that the ORS is intended to bring his or her voice into the decision-making process and will be collaboratively used to monitor progress.
3. Ensure that the client gives a good rating, i.e., a rating that matches the client's description of his or her life circumstance.
4. Ensure that the client's marks on the ORS are connected to the described reasons for service.
5. Use ORS data to develop and graph individualized trajectories of change.
6. Plot ORS on individualized trajectories from session to session to determine which clients are making progress and which are at risk for a negative or null outcome.
7. Use ORS scores to engage clients in a discussion in every session about how to continue to empower change if it is happening and change, augment, or end treatment if it is not.
8. Administer and score the Session Rating Scale (SRS) each session or unit of service.
9. Ensure that the client understands that the SRS is intended to create a dialogue between therapist and client that more tailors the service to the client—and that there is no bad news on the measure.
10. Use the SRS to discuss whether: the client feels heard, understood, and respected, the service is addressing the client's goals for treatment, and whether the service approach matches the client's culture, preferences worldview, or theory of change.

PCOMS Therapist Adherence Scale
The PCOMS Therapist Adherence Scale uses the above PCOMS Checklist and scores it with the following scale:

Never	Sometimes	Often	Regularly	Always
1	2	3	4	5

Out of a total possible 50 points, adherence is considered acceptable at 40 or above at the 6-month mark and 45 or above at 1 year after implementation. High adherence is ensured by the PCOMS supervisory process and attention to data integrity.

---

some find helpful. Supervision that holds therapists accountable on these data validity parameters allows PCOMS to do what it was designed to do.

2. Supervisor reviews graphs, spends most time on at-risk clients, shapes discussion, and brainstorms options. Once data integrity is consistent, the focus in supervision turns to those clients who are not benefiting from services. To use the data to full advantage, supervisors will need to get over any squeamishness about trajectories, expected treatment response (ETR) curves, or reading graphs in general. It is not really that complicated, and after you do it a few times, it will be old hat. If you are using an electronic system, the ETR or mean trajectory of a given intake score is what you aiming for. It tells you at a quick glance if the client is progressing according to expectation and your hopes for them in treatment. If you are not using an electronic system, you are aiming for reliable change or 6 points on the ORS.

Start with the clients who have been in the system the longest without benefit. As supervision progresses over time, such clients will decrease, allowing at-risk clients to be identified and dealt with earlier. Each at-risk client is discussed and options are developed to present to clients, including the possibility of consultation with or referral to another counselor or service. This is perhaps the most traditional role of supervision, but here you have objective criteria to identify at-risk clients, as well as subsequent ORS scores to see if the changes recommended in the supervisory process have been helpful to the client.

To maximize efficiency and enable multiple consumers to be addressed, it is helpful for the supervisor to shape the way that therapists present non-responding clients. The goal is for therapists to leave supervision with a plan to do something different with the clients in question. Steering the conversation away from why clients aren't changing to what can be done differently instead is harder than it sounds. We have made a profession of explaining why clients don't change (usually related to client psychopathology), and we are very good at it. The supervisory process, when based on outcome data, eschews such explanations in favor of the questions discussed in Chapter 3:

- What does the client say about the lack of change?
- Is the client engaged in purposive work to address the problems at hand in ways that resonate? In other words, what does the SRS say about the alliance?
- What have you done differently so far?
- What can be done differently now? Have you exhausted your repertoire?
- What other resources can be rallied now, both from your support system and the client's?
- Is it time to fail successfully?

When therapists come prepared to answer these questions, many clients can be discussed. It takes only encouragement and follow-through to implement—and, of course, holding therapists accountable for knowing the above information.

This process is intended to be the antidote for blaming clients or therapists for negative outcomes. It strives for an end to explaining why clients are not changing while simultaneously continuing them with the same clinician or program despite a lack of progress. At the same time, it helps us stop ascribing any lack of benefit to therapist inadequacies while allowing the same unhelpful services to persist. Not all clients benefit from services. No therapist serves all clients. Lack of client response to a given clinician is the reality of providing services. If we accept that without blame to the client or therapist, we can move on to the more productive conversation of what needs to happen next to enable the client to benefit.

This acceptance includes the ability to transfer clients from one therapist to another without shame or blame. Once such transfers, those due to client lack of benefit, are a part of agency culture, another milestone of implementation has been reached. Certified Trainer Barbara L. Hernandez, in her experience at the Center for Family Services, reports that therapists welcome this process after initial concerns of vulnerability are assuaged. In addition, she noted that recognizing that clients will ultimately benefit from the transfer appeals to therapists' best intentions. Once they see that these transfers most often conclude with client benefit, both those they transfer and those they receive, the benefits of "failing successfully" become manifest and therapists can settle in to helping clients in a different way—by firing themselves. Finally, Hernandez added that, given that these failing-successfully and transfer situations are often breaking new ground for therapists, they provide many opportunities for therapist growth via the supervisory process.

While reviewing graphs, supervisors can also discuss overutilization, building a culture of recovery, and the iatrogenic effects of keeping people in therapy when they are not benefiting or have reached maximum benefit, as discussed in Chapter 3.

3. *Supervisor reviews therapist stats, discusses ways to improve, and encourages action.* Although most of the individual supervision hour applies to our primary directive, improving services to clients, the final two steps shift attention from the client to the therapist, drawing upon Orlinsky and Rønnestad's (2005) sources of development. Attending to counselor growth helps prevent burnout and encourages continued vital engagement in the work in spite of all the pressures that lead us toward mediocrity. The focus here is on the therapist's sense of career development—improvement in clinical skills, increasing mastery, and gradual surpassing of past limitations. ORS data provide an objective way to know whether career development is actually happening as well as the impetus for the therapist to take charge of it. Supervision provides the structure and encouragement to incorporate the Chapter 5 suggestions regarding monitoring and accelerating therapist development via PCOMS.

Supervision then, promotes the open discussion of stats with the intent of codeveloping a plan for improvement. It starts with helping the supervisee to understand the stats, the key performance indicators, and how they will be used to monitor effectiveness and the therapist's development over time. Recall that perhaps the easiest stat to consider is the percentage of clients who attain reliable or clinically significant change, or who achieve ETR, if you are using an electronic system. Using this stat to compare with a previous period of time or closed cases, as discussed in Chapter 5, gives a quick look at how things are going. It is important to remind supervisees of the realities of practice and that, first, the very best clinicians in some studies achieve about 46% reliable and clinically significant change rates, and, second, that wherever he or she starts, it is just that, a beginning point. By discussing the stats transparently, supervisors encourage therapists to use the data for their specific benefit. In so doing, therapists will get over their fear of numbers and looking at their performance. Over time, therapists will monitor their own stats and use the information to the greatest advantage.

From the frank discussion of therapist stats and his or her ideas about improvement, a plan is formed for the counselor to be proactive about his or her development. The plan is then implemented, monitored in supervision, and modified if outcomes are not improving. As discussed in Chapter 6, encouraging therapists to learn models and techniques is fine, but a focus on the heart and soul of change also makes good clinical sense. Encourage supervisees to enlist what clients bring and to practice well the skills of our craft, the alliance.

4. *Supervisor mentors via skill building, harvests client teachings, and encourages ongoing reflection about the work and therapist identity.* This final component brings the supervisor more actively into the process of accelerating therapist development. Supervision can provide the context for skill building in a variety of areas that are identified in the therapist's improvement plan, from specific models to alliance skills to understanding clients from a variety of conceptual vantage points (the concept of theoretical breadth). Here, any number of ways to build skills can be used, from focused video reviews to role-playing to article discussions.

Perhaps more important, this aspect of supervision sets the stage for harvesting client teachings and enhancing the most powerful influence on development identified by Orlinsky and Rønnestad (2005): the therapist's sense of current growth. Again, Step 4 of the supervisory process provides the structure and encouragement for the suggestions made in Chapters 5 and 7 regarding learning from clients and reflecting about one's identity. Here the supervisor inquires about what has been learned from successful and unsuccessful clients, about anything that happened that was new or different, and about the therapist's thoughts about his or her identity—helping the therapist experience current growth, value the daily work with clients and the opportunities for development and replenishment they offer, and stay invested in the work he or she loves.

As noted, it is important to incorporate discussion/reinforcement of what the supervisee is doing right with clients who are progressing. Such an inclusion promotes development by encouraging supervisees to understand what their role is in the client's improvement. This can stimulate confidence and can help supervisees discover their approach/style in therapy. As discussed in Chapter 5, the process begins with these questions about clients who are progressing:

- What is working with these clients?
- What is client feedback telling you about progress and the alliance?
- How are you interacting with these clients in ways that are stimulating, catalyzing, or crystallizing change?
- What are these benefiting clients telling you that they like about your work with them?
- What are they telling you about what works?

And questions about the clients who are not benefiting:

- What is working in the conversations about the lack of progress?
- What is client feedback telling you about progress and the alliance?
- How are you interacting with these clients in ways that open discussion of other options, including referral?
- What are these not-benefiting clients telling you that they like about how you are handling these tough talks?
- What are they telling you about what works in these discussions?
- What have you done differently with these not-benefiting clients? How have you stepped out of your comfort zone and done something you have never done?

The idea here, of course, is not punitive in any way but rather to promote professional reflection and encourage therapists' continued growth.

The concept of parallel process (Searles, 1955) or isomorphism (Liddle & Saba, 1983) in supervision weighs heavily on all the steps of supervision as well as on the three sources of development identified by Orlinsky and Rønnestad (2005). First, having supervisees track their career development is akin to therapists engaging clients to monitor benefit. Both are about tracking one's progress and involving oneself in a real way. Second, collaborating with therapists about potential plans to enhance their development is parallel to the egalitarian conversation that is hoped for with clients regarding the tasks of therapy. Helping supervisees expand their theoretical breadth, in turn, helps them to be more responsive to clients' idiosyncratic theories and cultural preferences. Finally, supervisor curiosity about the lessons that clients teach, the therapist's sense of current growth, helps therapists make the best of their continued reflections and further enhances curiosity for and appreciation of what can be learned from day-to-day work with clients.

CONCLUSION

The person who says it cannot be done should not interrupt the person who is doing it.

—Chinese proverb

This chapter presented the results of our study (Reese et al., 2014) of effectiveness in a large PBH setting. Our investigation came on the heels of the 50th anniversary of the Community Mental Health Act of 1963, signed into law on October 31, 1963, by President John F. Kennedy. It was the last piece of legislation JFK signed before his assassination. For millions of Americans, this legislation opened the door to a new era of hope and recovery—to a life in the community. As we remember the landmark legislation, our study presents a more hopeful picture of outcomes in PBH. Our results are reassuring to those who receive, provide, or pay for services in the public sector, suggesting that therapists in a PBH setting are effectively treating not only depression but also a range of other psychological problems. And we believe it is because of PCOMS. Routine collection of outcome data and consistent involvement of consumers in decisions about their care hold promise to not only inform us about the effectiveness of PBH care and the classic question of what works for whom, but also to improve those services and ensure quality to those who are often not considered in discussions of psychotherapy.

This chapter also presented the four secrets of successful PCOMS implementation: In it for the long haul (it's a marathon, not a 100-yard dash); Love your data (more than a friend, your data are the core of what improves outcomes at all levels and demonstrates your effectiveness to funders); Inspire the frontline clinician (implementation fundamentally happens at the therapist level, and consequently clinicians need reassurance about management intentions, must understand PCOMS in a clinical context, and need to experience its benefits to clients and their own development); and Supervision for a change (in both clients and therapists).

CLIENTS ARE THE BEST TEACHERS: THEIR STORIES DOCUMENT OUR DEVELOPMENT

Of all tyrannies, a tyranny sincerely exercised for the good of its victims may be the most oppressive.

—C. S. Lewis

Shortly after my stint in the state hospital, in addition to my next practicum I began working in a residential treatment center for troubled adolescents to help ends meet. So "disturbed" were these kids that everyone "required" at least two diagnoses and two psychotropic medications. One time, when the psychiatrist was on vacation and the center director was unable to cover him, a 16-year-old, Dawn, was admitted to the center.

Dawn was like many of the kids, abused in all ways imaginable, drop-kicked from one foster home to another, with periodic suicide attempts and trips to hospitals and runaway shelters. I was assigned her case and saw her frequently in individual therapy as well as nearly every day in the groups I conducted. She was very angry at times and uncooperative with staff, but I figured she had good reason, a perspective that has served me well. In spite of all that, Dawn was a pure delight—creative, funny, and hopeful for a future far different from her childhood. She told me she just wanted to do her time there and get out on her own as soon as she was 18. So we talked about what would need to happen for her to gain emancipation. I liked her a lot, and I admired the spunk of this worldly street kid. The therapy went great: We hit it off famously, and Dawn settled in and started attending high school for the first time in several months. Our shared love of heavy metal seemed to seal the bond.

As time went on, I felt increasingly protective toward her. Her whole life she had been betrayed if not abused by so many adults, and I didn't want to join their ranks in any way, shape, or form. Three weeks later, the psychiatrist returned and conducted a diagnostic interview (with me present) in which he, unbelievably, started massaging her neck. Didn't he have a clue what these kids had experienced in their lives? Dawn told him to get his f—king hands off her. He responded with a lecture about adhering to treatment and prescribed an antidepressant and lithium for Dawn.

She angrily and adamantly opposed taking the medications—she said she had been down that path already. Dawn told him that she would run away if they made her take meds. But her voice went unheard. More accurately, she had no voice at all in her own treatment. After Dawn left the room, I protested to the psychiatrist, citing evidence of how well she was doing, but to no avail. I was only a mental health grunt and a student to boot. I argued that forcing meds on Dawn could be harmful, but he did not listen. Instead, he lectured me about countertransference and how I was being manipulated into splitting—a sure sign of her psychopathology and my naïveté. He asked me if I thought patients should decide what treatment they get and told me that it was clear that I was way too involved. I responded that we were talking about Dawn, not me. You can imagine how that went over.

Dawn became a different person—sullen, hostile, and combative. Soon thereafter, she went to school and, true to her word, bolted. Days went by, and I grew very worried and increasingly angry at what I was coming to learn: "Treatment" consisted primarily of overmedication and control. I later found out that Dawn went on a 3-day binge of alcohol and drugs. A carload of men picked her up while she was hitchhiking and ended the ride with a gang rape. Adding insult to injury, Dawn was forcefully injected with an antipsychotic when the police brought her back to the center. When Dawn described this experience, she saw the horror on my face and reassured me that she had suffered far worse indignities than being forcefully tranquilized. It was little solace for either of us. I just held back tears of frustration and anger. Here was this kid just raped, and then suffering the indignity of a forced injection, trying to console me!

Dawn persisted in her ardent protests against the medication and did everything she could to sabotage taking meds. She had an undefeatable spirit. I felt weak in comparison. I encouraged her to talk to the center director. Rather than listening, however, the director admonished me for putting ideas into Dawn's head and told me to drop it. But I couldn't. Instead, fueled by Dawn's spirit and my frustration, I spent days researching the literature. What I found surprised me. In contrast to what most clients were told, little was known about how psychotropic drugs actually worked. Moreover, there was no empirical support for prescribing these drugs to children—let alone multiple drugs. I couldn't find one study. Figuring this wasn't possible, given the way they were given to kids on the unit, I asked for library assistance and—guess what?—not one study addressed the use of tricyclics, lithium, or antipsychotics with adolescents. Finally, I was shocked to find that the very helpfulness of medication with adults was suspect. It seemed that everything I had been told about the rationale for using these medications for youth "mental illness" was simply not true and not based on any evidence.

I organized my findings into a brief report and made an appointment to see the psychiatrist, who was less than happy to see me. I presented the information respectfully and included my astonishment over not being able to find one study demonstrating the effectiveness of the medications with kids.

How did he respond?

He fired me on the spot, yelling that I had 5 minutes to clear out.

I managed to see Dawn before I left, and she said with a smile that at least one of us was getting out. She told me not to worry about her, and I did know that she was indeed a survivor. Dawn also thanked me for supporting her about the whole med thing and added that no one had ever done anything like that before for her.

I left demoralized and confused, but this was the defining moment of my career. Nothing was the same for me after this. I lost my job and my innocence. I no longer believed the things I had been told just because they came from authority. This experience taught me never to be complacent or complicit again as a function of ignorance—that I had to look at things myself and draw my own conclusions. From that point on, I questioned things, much to the chagrin of some teachers and supervisors. Until this point I had believed that being a therapist, and therapy in general, were based in only helpful assumptions. I now understood that "helping" with good intentions can also hurt quite substantially and be downright oppressive. This was the precursor to my passion for privileging client perspectives about their own care.

And Dawn was inspirational. Here was this 16-year-old kid able to stand up to this arrogant doctor and an entire system that completely ignored her perspective in the name of "helping." She had been horribly abused, and yet she found a way to fight back without losing hope or her dignity. Dawn really believed that she could transcend all the unpleasantness and prevail, and she did. She taught me that if someone like her, who had been through so much, could overcome this level of adversity, then anyone could. This led me down the path of being aware of and trusting in client resources and resiliencies to lead the way in therapy.

I eventually heard from Dawn years later when she saw my private practice announcement in the newspaper. She sent me a postcard of a picture of the Eiffel Tower, and opened her note in true Dawn form: "No, dumbshit, I am not really in Paris." She wrote that she was taking classes at the community college and had a new baby. Life was challenging, but she was doing well. In the brief note she sent, on that postcard, without a return address, she said that she wanted me to know that she was still grateful for all I had done for her. I wish I could have told her all that she had done for me.

9

FOR THE LOVE OF THE WORK

You need to claim the events of your life to make yourself yours.
—Anne Wilson-Schaef

I am not doing direct client work nowadays, beyond consultation and demonstration sessions, which I enjoy immensely. But I miss the ongoing client contact. At some point, I will return to my first passion, psychotherapy, but in the meantime I am on a mission to help therapists be better at what they do: to spread the word about what works and how to deliver it, to get clinicians to incorporate the Partners for Change Outcome Management System (PCOMS) in their everyday practice, and to encourage counselors to give significant attention to their development. My motivation comes from the love of the work because I believe, like you, that despite the bureaucratic downsides to our job, there is nothing that quite matches the feelings that come from client change. I am also trying to influence third-party payers that it is in their best interest to help therapists to become more efficient and effective—to do good work. I'll talk about one of those efforts below.

In this book, I have suggested that you step up to the plate with two things: attaining systematic client feedback via PCOMS and taking your development

http://dx.doi.org/10.1037/14392-009
On Becoming a Better Therapist, Second Edition: Evidence-Based Practice One Client at a Time, by B. L. Duncan
Copyright © 2014 by the American Psychological Association. All rights reserved.

as a therapist to heart. Integrating these two critical aspects can open new vistas for therapists wishing to rapidly impact the quality of their work with clients. PCOMS was presented as a simple but clinically nuanced process of collaborating with clients, forming true partnerships, and enhancing the factors known to affect outcomes. It helps us know we are on track, enables us to empower change, and provides an early warning system for clients at risk for dropout or other negative outcomes. PCOMS also paves the way for your development as a therapist.

Accelerating your development is a five-step process, but the prerequisite is your understanding that you are a primary figure in each client's ultimate outcome. The client is certainly central, but, as the old saying goes, it takes two to tango. Your view of your growth influences your ability to be vitally involved in the therapeutic process. The first step is to track your career development and take it on as a project. Proactively monitor your effectiveness in implementing strategies to improve your outcomes. Practice the skills of your craft and monitor your results. Second, pay close attention to your current growth. Take a step back, review your current clients, and consider the lessons you are learning. Empower yourself, as you would your clients, to enable the lessons to take hold and add meaning to your development as a therapist. Articulate how client lessons have changed you and your work and what it means to your identity as a helper and how you describe what it is that you do. Next, deliberately expand your theoretical breadth—loosen your grip on the inherent truth value of any given approach. Take multiple vantage points on your journeys with clients while you search different understandings of client dilemmas. Fourth, reflect about your identity and construct a story of your work that captures what you do as a helper. Continue to edit and refine your identity and your accounts of what constitutes the essence of your work: Evolve a description that you can have allegiance to but that doesn't lead to dead ends.

This closing chapter discusses the fifth and final step to keep your development in the viewfinder: collecting client notes, cards, and letters about your work with them, as well as client stories that mark significant events in your growth as a psychotherapist—what I call the "Treasure Chest." Then, this chapter presents my parting thoughts about the major controversies of the day as they pertain to your identity as a helper. Finally, I discuss what I think it takes to become a "master" therapist.

TREASURE CHEST

A box without hinges, key, or lid, yet golden treasure inside is hid.
—J. R. R. Tolkien

The Treasure Chest is a way to buffer burnout, a momentary sanctuary from the downsides of the work when the requirements of the system bring you down, or when you see several clients in a row who aren't benefiting much, or when a client story hits home in a painful way. The Treasure Chest is the place to go to escape tough times and reconnect to the work, to why you became a therapist in the first place. It is also where you can add your own narrative accounts of the clients who influenced your development as a therapist.

It started simply as a file labeled "Treasure Chest" into which I put clients' unsolicited communications about the work I did with them—their feedback, usually well after therapy had ended. The letter from Maria in Chapter 2 is an example of the kind of communication that I held on to over the years. Sometimes it was a long letter or sometimes it is was a brief postcard like the one that Dawn, in Chapter 8, sent. Sometimes clients talked about something specific that happened in the therapy—something I said or did—and sometimes they gave a general overview of the time we spent together. Sometimes the letter described the changes they had made, and sometimes it was about their belief that God was working through me. Sometimes it was about their further reflections on their journey in life, and sometimes it was just telling me how things were going well. Sometimes the letters were deep and evocative, and sometimes they were light and breezy. Invariably, though, as the research indicates, client comments addressed relational factors. They were not about what I knew, but about our relational connection and who I am. Here are just two examples; although they are different in about all ways you can think of, they both convey why reading such things recharges our batteries.

Sixteen-year-old Carrie attended therapy with her mom, Janice. Carrie was distressed about her father's rapid remarriage and decision to move far away. Carrie was very close with her dad and understandably felt betrayed. This was a one-session encounter (Carrie was leaving the next day for a summer-abroad study experience), and I did what you likely would have done: I listened and I validated. I didn't think much else about it until I received a thank-you note from Janice:

> Dear Dr. Duncan:
>
> Just wanted to thank you for the hour you spent with us on January 23. Carrie's father has apparently decided to continue his current course of action, and Carrie has decided to simply avoid him as much as possible for the time being. Very sad, but the assurance and acceptance you gave to Carrie and me left us with a wonderful sense of relief and security that no money can buy. I see many changes in her—happiness and self-confidence—that I credit to you. I cannot thank you enough.

And then there was Adam, a young man who spent his 18th birthday in prison for gang violence. Released soon afterward as part of an early parole program, he was mandated to therapy, and I saw him as a favor to his probation officer, who had been a student of mine. Adam was a long-time member of the skinheads as well as a local gang. I wasn't sure I could work with Adam, not because of his record or gang status or because he was a scary-looking dude, but rather because he was openly racist and regularly spewed hate-filled comments. In amazing ways I had never heard before, Adam strung together obscenities and slurs with an alarming passion—about me (I was a lackey for the other side), the PO (an African American woman), and about everyone else who wasn't dedicated to white supremacy. But, somehow, therapy worked its magic with Adam and me. Over time, Adam's intellect and compassion pulled him out of the indoctrination of hate that had dominated his life. He became curious about my attitudes about African Americans, Jews, and Hispanics when he learned that I grew up not far from where he did—a serendipitous shot in the arm for our work. Our conversations deepened and ultimately challenged the lies embedded in hate and prejudice. Adam, an introspective man, took these discussions to heart and began to let go of his racist background and understand how poverty and despair set the context for his beliefs. He moved out of the neighborhood where the specter of gang life was inescapable and moved on in other ways as well.

About 6 months after I had written a letter in support of Adam's enlistment in the army, I received this:

> Hi Barry,
>
> I wanted to write you and let you know what was happening and to say thanks. As you know I fulfilled the obligations of my parole and joined the army (Thanks for the letter!). I just made corporal and things are going well for me. I am told that I am sergeant material, and I intend to take college courses when I get stationed after infantry training. But what I really wanted to tell you about was my barracks. The army has lots of different kinds of people. In fact, I am the minority here. Most of the guys in my unit are black or Hispanic. And that's the thing I wanted to tell you. I see their uniform first before I notice whether they are white or not. I see them as my team, and I will watch their backs like I know they will watch mine. My best friend in my unit is a Mexican-American guy from Texas. We have had some great discussions about racism and he came from a real poor background, probably even worse than me. He has gone through some real hard times with white people.
>
> So, thanks, Barry. Thanks for not giving up on me, for putting up with my bullshit, and for seeing that I was capable of something different. I see now that you didn't (pre) judge me just the way that I now don't prejudge others.

These unsolicited notes, letters, and cards have sustained me in tough moments as a therapist. Over the years, I added another dimension to my Treasure Chest file—my reflections about the clients who taught me the most about being a psychotherapist, a narrative account of my development told through my experiences with clients. Many of those stories are included in this book.

PARTING THOUGHTS

I long to accomplish great and noble tasks, but it is my chief duty to accomplish humble tasks as though they were great and noble. The world is moved along, not only by the mighty shoves of its heroes, but also by the aggregate of the tiny pushes of each honest worker.

—Helen Keller

There is a dark side of the force, things about our field that do not represent why we became therapists in the first place, things far afield of our desire to help. Dawn, from Chapter 8, for example, showed me how "helping" could be abusive and oppressive. I bring up these thorny issues here because they are potential threats to the work that we love, to our identities as therapists—each creates a particular story about our identity. It is my hope to stimulate your reflection, and I also hope that my propensity, at times, to strongly state my deeply held beliefs doesn't diminish my main message: Be informed, dig a little deeper, and rely on your own analysis of the issues—not those of professors, supervisors, professional organizations, policy wonks, or this book—to create your identity as a therapist.

Third-Party Payers and P4P

For just about forever, therapists have complained about managed care and third-party payers, and our professional organizations have heartily joined the whiner chorus. It's funny how things are always relative. I remember when CHAMPUS (the Civilian Health and Medical Program of the Uniformed Services, today known as TRICARE) first attempted to monitor what happened behind the closed doors of psychotherapy. There was such outrage. They paid less than other payers at the time and had the audacity to require a review and treatment plan at the 24th session! As a new private practitioner I often received referrals from others who would not work for such measly pay or acquiesce to such unreasonable demands. To any therapist today, what CHAMPUS paid then, combined with such limited oversight, would be to die for.

Unfortunately, we didn't work with third-party payers to address costs, but instead we and our professional organizations demonized them. Don't get me wrong, some payers definitely deserve their Darth Vader status, and as a private practitioner, I have bemoaned their existence on many occasions. But we haven't offered many alternatives and, as a profession, haven't addressed their legitimate concerns regarding the efficiency of services. But managed care, accountability, and measurable outcomes are not going away and will only increase in scope with the Affordable Care Act and the movement to integrated care systems. Instead of fighting third-party payers, we need to join them at the table and have influence.

Collecting data and managing outcomes can allow therapists, agencies, and professional organizations to become players at the reimbursement table. But we have to be conversant in the language (e.g., proof of value, return on investment) and take responsibility for the cost and effectiveness of the services we provide. It's high time. As the last chapter demonstrated, PCOMS, in addition to improving outcomes, can document improvements in efficiency in terms of cancellations, no-shows, length of stay, etc. These advantages, in turn, can be bargaining chips when negotiating with third-party payers. Increased effectiveness and efficiency should increase the value of our services.

But there could be dangers as well. Some managed care organizations, both public and private, have implemented outcome management systems. How will they use the data? Will outcome data be folded into so-called pay for performance (P4P) initiatives? P4P started in medical care and describes payment models that offer financial rewards to providers who achieve specified quality benchmarks using performance measures related to the structure, process, and outcome of providing services. The intentions are good here— P4P programs are designed to improve access, quality of care, consumer experience, and provider participation and to decrease health care costs. The incentives include higher capitation rates, increased reimbursement rates, and bonuses to provider networks that meet or exceed performance standards.

P4P makes some sense. For example, it is understandable that payers would like clinicians who average fewer sessions per client when data reveal that most clients attend fewer than eight sessions, or who get clients in service within 3 days of the initial call given the increases in follow-through when there is a rapid response. But when it comes to performance measures related to outcome, things get a bit dicey. One way that P4P has been implemented is by using outcome data to steer referrals to providers who get better results (see Brown & Minami, 2010) or to pay those providers higher rates. The darker side here is that the data are used to profile clinicians, resulting in removing therapists from provider panels or limiting referrals based on their reported outcomes. No wonder therapists are afraid of measuring outcomes! Using outcome data in this way could lead to a focus on looking good rather than providing good care. For example, therapists or agencies may select clients who are likely to do well in treatment, may avoid taking more challenging referrals, and may be tempted to leave out the data reflecting poor outcomes—or even fudge their data. When one's livelihood is involved, who knows?

Client welfare is invoked as the justification for steering clients toward the most effective therapists, thereby giving them the best chance for success. Yes, it makes some sense, but it is not that simple. Recall that even the best therapists don't benefit a substantial portion of their clients. P4P only monitors performance (on those data that are submitted) and does not address those significant numbers of clients who are not benefiting. So, regardless of a clinician's or agency's success rates, many clients go without benefit, and there is no infrastructure, support, or incentive to do anything about them. All you have to do is send your accurate (?) outcome data to meet some arbitrary performance standard. If this strategy were designed to improve outcomes, it would provide immediate feedback identifying clients who were not responding so that something different could be done for them. Monitoring without feedback has little worth for consumers receiving the service *now*—and seems far more about profiling than raising the quality of everyone's performance.

A far better idea is another kind of P4P, "pay for participation." This initiative rewards providers who use their data to identify nonresponding clients and participate in a proactive process to recapture those consumers and improve outcome. This P4P incentivizes a commitment to nonresponding clients early in therapy so that they do not languish in treatment or drop out. It encourages clinicians to acknowledge and be comfortable with what we all know (i.e., that not everyone benefits)—and to open the discussion to any alternative that would better serve the client, including consultation and referral. The purpose here is not to profile clinicians according to their outcomes but rather to assist them in providing better care via outcome feedback and support. Serving clients and therapists in this way will ultimately improve outcomes, increase efficiency, and decrease costs.

New Directions (great name) Behavioral Health, a managed care company serving over 8 million members, is piloting such a program now with clients who have not been successful in previous attempts at therapy. They provided PCOMS training to a group of therapists as well as a web-based data system to track outcomes so that therapists and consumers could keep their fingers on the pulse of progress and the alliance. An incentive of a value-based bonus (beyond the incentives of training, the data system, and ongoing support to improve outcomes) is awarded to those practitioners who demonstrate data integrity and actively participate in a system of care that openly acknowledges the realities of practice—that not all clients benefit and that therapists cannot benefit all clients—and proactively does something about it to better serve consumers. The goal is to build a sustainable value-based collaborative with providers to improve outcomes for members.

In short, provider profiling and incentive practices based on outcome, without feedback and the opportunity to improve, pit us against each other. Such policies risk turning therapists against measuring outcomes and could perhaps encourage us to "cheat the system" to ensure referrals and a competitive edge. The therapist identity created by a pay-for-performance mentality is a competitive one that measures success by the defeat of fellow therapists. Pay for *participation*, on the other hand, proactively addresses outcome and cost via the identification of clients at risk; it incentivizes a more realistic view of clinical practice and also creates an infrastructure to truly improve the quality of care.

> **Bottom Line:** *Become a player at the reimbursement table. Collect data, take responsibility for costs, learn the language of business, and negotiate for higher rates of reimbursement. Oppose the collection of data without feedback and join the conversation about P4P to ensure that it is aligned with sound clinical practice. Voice your concerns that referral steerage or other incentives will kill the spirit of outcome management. Insist on safeguards about the misuse of outcome data.*

Diagnosis and the Medical Model

The medical model of psychotherapy remains the dominant paradigm. The late George Albee (2000) suggested that psychology made a Faustian deal with the medical model at the famed Boulder conference in 1949, where psychology's bible of training was developed with a fatal flaw, namely: "the uncritical acceptance of the medical model, the organic explanation of mental disorders, with psychiatric hegemony, medical concepts, and language" (p. 247). Later, in the 1970s, with the passing of freedom-of-choice legislation guaranteeing parity with psychiatrists, psychologists (and later others) learned to collect from third-party payers solely on the basis of a psychiatric diagnosis. Thereafter, drowning any possibilities for other psychosocial systems of understanding human challenges, the National Institute of Mental Health (NIMH), the leading source of research funding for psychotherapy, decided to apply the same methodology used in drug research to evaluate psychotherapy (Goldfried & Wolfe, 1996)—the randomized clinical trial requiring both diagnosis and manualized treatments. Diagnosis reached its pinnacle. Now, both reimbursement and research funding depended on it. Since then, it has remained a fixed part of graduate training programs, a prominent feature of evidence-based treatments (EBTs), and a prerequisite for funding in most mental health and substance abuse delivery systems—all of which engenders an illusion of scientific aura and clinical utility that far overreaches the deeply flawed infrastructure of the *Diagnostic and Statistical Manual of Mental Disorders* (DSM; Sparks, Duncan, & Miller, 2007).

Diagnosis in mental health is not correlated with outcome or length of stay, and given the dodo verdict, cannot provide reliable guidance to clinicians or clients regarding the best approach to resolving a problem. Recall that our benchmark study reported in Chapter 8, like other research, found no relationship between diagnosis and outcome. And of course, it has long been known that diagnosis is neither reliable nor valid (Carson, 1997; Duncan, Miller, & Sparks, 2004; Kirk & Kutchins, 1992); the very authors of the *DSM* acknowledge this. Regarding reliability, Robert Spitzer, the architect of the *DSM-III*, admitted:

> To say that we've solved the reliability problem is just not true . . . if you're in a situation with a general clinician it's certainly not very good. There's still a real problem, and it's not clear how to solve the problem. (Spiegel, 2005, p. 63)

Regarding validity, Allen Frances, lead editor of the fourth edition of the *DSM*, confessed that "there is no definition of a mental disorder. It's bullshit. I mean, you just can't define it" (Greenberg, 2010, p. 1). This candid admission merely confirms what has been known for many years, in fact, since its inception. In the first edition of his classic 1961 book, Jerome Frank wrote, "Psychotherapy is the only form of treatment which, at least to some extent, appears to create the illness it treats" (p. 7), a statement that still rings true today. Finally, in an amazing turn of irony, NIMH, the organization that almost single-handedly catapulted its use, recently withdrew support from the *DSM*, just before the release of the new fifth edition. Thomas Insel, MD, the director of NIMH, said, "The weakness of the manual is its lack of validity" (http://www.nimh. nih.gov/about/director/2013/transforming-diagnosis.shtml).

Diagnosis as a starting point for treatment or reimbursement is empirically and clinically bankrupt. Collection of outcome data on a large scale could help usher it out once and for all. It could supply the impetus for reevaluating funding parameters and the medical-model assumptions that support them. As more and more evidence is collected that shows the lack of relationship between diagnoses, EBTs, length of stay, and improvement, the real predictors of progress may come to light (like the alliance and early change) and a different set of assumptions, like those of recovery, individually tailored treatment, and so on can be implemented.

Moreover, we could escape the medicalization of our identity. Psychotherapy is not a medical endeavor; it is a relational one. You have probably noticed that I haven't described clients as patients with illnesses who require treatment from an expert administering powerful interventions. Instead, I have hopefully demonstrated an empirically based account of psychotherapy in proportion to the amount of variance attributed to the different common factors, and I have characterized clients in ways other than the Killer *D*s— their diseases, disorders, deficits, disabilities, or dysfunctions. My identity as a psychotherapist lies outside of the language of diagnosis, prescriptive treatment, and cure and seeks to reflect the interpersonal nature of the work, as well as the consumer's perspective of therapeutic process, the benefit and fit of the services.

These are thorny topics to be sure, and in the current zeitgeist of integrated care, they will increasingly come to light. The issues are complex, and I encourage you to investigate and draw your own conclusions about them and the other identity-threatening topics discussed. Collaboration with and respect for medical professionals are essential, as is retention of our own separate identity as behavioral health practitioners. Integrated primary care offers a unique opportunity to provide quality behavioral health services to people who do not seek mental health services for any number of reasons. Given that up to 70% of primary care visits have mental health/behavioral components (Hunter, Goodie, Oordt, & Dobmeyer, 2009), there is a huge potential for positive impact. Our objective is to be a valued member of a collaborative team that respects the medical model without being assimilated, while keeping our relational model and the factors that account for behavioral change central to our work.

Brian DeSantis, director of Behavioral Health at Peak Vista Community Health Centers, project leader, and veteran of integrated care, suggests that a successful "marriage" of medical and behavioral health is challenging but certainly attainable. He currently applies PCOMS in his integrated setting and believes that it not only brings evidence-based accountability to the partnership but also aligns well with medicine's movement toward collaborative patient-centered care and an emphasis on both medical and patient-rated outcomes.

> **Bottom Line:** *Diagnosis and the medical model are valid ways to approach physical problems, but their assumptions do not hold up well in application to behavioral health. With the rise of integrated care, increased opportunities for providing quality behavioral services and pressures to assimilate into the medical model will happen together. Respectfully educate medical professionals about the shortcomings of diagnosis, help them understand the factors that account for change in behavioral health, and demonstrate your accountability with PCOMS.*

Psychotropic Medication

Medication treatment, like all others, offers a myth and ritual for the client's consideration, and it occurs in the context of a client, helper, their alliance, and both of their beliefs in the restorative capabilities of the selected rationale and remedy. The common factors loom large here, as they do in psychotherapy (recall from Chapter 1 the psychiatrists in the Treatment of Depression Collaborative Research Program [Elkin et al., 1989] demonstrating therapist effects, as well as how the alliance predicted outcome across conditions, including medication). Perhaps because of the widespread cultural acceptance of medical myths and rituals or the continual barrage of pharmaceutical marketing, to many this is a bitter pill to swallow. Everyone knows someone who has benefited from drug treatments or even someone whose life has been "saved" by medication. Clients do benefit from medication, as they do from almost anything they believe in, but as Saul Rosenzweig (1936) wrote over 75 years ago, that says nothing about the truth value or broad applicability of the method at hand. That leaves us with the data, and an obligation to discern science from science fiction. This requires some effort.

Given the infiltration of industry influence, discerning good science from good marketing requires a willingness to engage primary source material (see Sparks, Duncan, Cohen, & Antonuccio, 2010, for tips about what to look for), as I did after my experience with Dawn (Chapter 8). Despite its vaunted status as a favored treatment, a critical examination of the evidence regarding the safety and efficacy of psychotropic medication leads to the conclusion that psychosocial options should be considered a first-line intervention, especially with children. The very studies purporting to support the use of the major classes of drugs reveal the limited efficacy of antidepressants over placebo as well as a high side effect and relapse profile (Kirsch, 2011; Sparks & Duncan, 2013), the underwhelming results of antipsychotics, their pervasive intolerability, and better recovery rates without them (Sparks & Duncan, 2012; Wunderink, Nieboer, Wiersma, Sytema, & Nienhuis, 2013), and a lack of meaningful benefit of combining psychotherapy and medication (Forand, DeRubeis, & Amsterdam, 2013), with psychotherapy alone making the most sense most of the time, especially considering long-term results.

Sparks et al. (2010) concluded:

> Knowing that there is no irresistible scientific justification to medicate, therapists are free to put other options on the table and draw in the voices of their clients—to engage in an informed risk/benefit analysis to help clients choose treatments in concert with their values, preferences, and cultural contexts. (p. 224)

All this, of course, doesn't mean that clients are not helped by psychotropics or that those who prescribe them are evil but, rather, that medication treatment should not be privileged, nor should psychotherapy considered a secondhand service. Nevertheless, the use of psychotherapy alone and in combination with medication has decreased while the use of medications alone has increased (Olfson & Marcus, 2010). Psychotherapy, despite robust evidence of effectiveness and the unfavorable risk/benefit profile of psychotropics, appears to have been demoted to a lower-tier way to help clients in distress. Good marketing trumps bad data every time—but not my identity as a psychotherapist, and I hope not yours. My identity is embedded in the fact that psychotherapy is an evidence-based, stand-alone, effective treatment for the wide variety of concerns, problems, and issues—both catastrophic and everyday—that human beings encounter in life.

> **Bottom Line:** *There is nothing wrong with FDA-approved medication treatment (not polypharmacy or off-label concoctions) when prescribed in line with consumer preferences and with full informed consent of the risks and benefits, and when patient-rated measures of outcome are used (see Duncan & Antonuccio, 2011, for a list of patient rights for psychotropic prescription). But know and be proud that the data say psychotherapy is a better choice most of the time in the long run. Challenge assumptions and practices that privilege medication over psychotherapy as a first-line intervention.*

BECOMING A MASTER THERAPIST

Nobody can go back and start a new beginning, but anyone can start today and make a new ending.

—Maria Robinson

I was recently asked four questions (Kottler & Carlson, in press) about what made my work effective (assuming that it is). Here I use those questions to summarize the major points of this book.

1. What is it that you do (or who you are) that you believe is most important in contributing to your effectiveness as a master therapist, meaning a professional who produces consistently good outcomes and feels reasonably confident in his or her work?

First I must say something about the term *master therapist*. The notion itself is troublesome because it seems to connote that an elite group of "masters" possesses something special that others do not have. I don't possess anything that others don't have or can't develop. There are two parts to this question: What I do and who I am. What I do that is the most important in contributing to my effectiveness is that I routinely measure outcome and the alliance (via PCOMS) with every client to ensure that I don't leave either issue to chance. This allows me to deal directly and transparently with clients, involving them in all decisions that affect their care and keeping their perspectives the centerpiece of everything I do. In addition, it serves as an early warning device that identifies clients who are not benefiting so that the client and I can chart a different course, which, in turn encourages me to step outside my therapeutic business-as-usual (see Question 4), do things I've never done before, and therefore continue to grow as a therapist. Finally, PCOMS improves my focus (see Question 4) on what matters most to the client, in terms of what needs to change outside of therapy as well as during the hour. It allows me to focus every session with every client on the alliance so that I tailor what I do to the client's expectations. Although it sounds like hyperbole, identifying clients who are not benefiting is the single most important thing a therapist can do to improve outcomes—11 randomized clinical trials now support this assertion.

As for who I am as a therapist, let me first remind the reader that the client is the engine of change. I believe that, as therapists develop, they learn that their best ally for successful psychotherapy is not the books on their shelves touting the latest miracle cure but rather the person in the room with them right now. After what the client brings to the table of change, the therapist is the most potent influence on outcome—not *what* model or technique he or she is wielding but *who* the therapist is. Therapists account for most of the variance of change of any treatment delivered. What I bring to the therapeutic endeavor is that I am a true believer. I believe in the client, in the power of relationship and psychotherapy as a vehicle for healing and change, and I believe in myself, my ability to be present, fully immersed in the client, and dedicated to making a difference.

There is an old story about two apprentice Zen monks who are discussing their respective masters while cleaning their temple. The first novice proudly tells his companion about the many miracles that he has seen his famous master perform. "I have watched," the young novice says, "as my master has turned an entire village to the Buddha, has made rain fall from the sky, and has moved a mountain so that he could pass."

The other novice listens attentively and then demonstrates his deeper understanding by responding, "My master also does many miraculous things. When he is hungry, he eats. When he is thirsty, he drinks. When he is tired, he sleeps."

Like the first monk, many have become too enamored of "miracles" touted by the masters. My experience with thousands of clients, and the research about change, however, have taught me to discard the claims of the gurus and snake-oil salesmen, and instead honor more simple but enduring acts: believing in clients, the power of partnership, and my ability to show up in full. These simple but magical acts are the eating, drinking, and sleeping of effective therapy.

2. What do you think is most important in identifying or defining an extraordinary therapist, one who stands out from her or his peers?

I mentioned above that the therapist accounts for most of the variance of any treatment offered. Therapists vary significantly in their ability to bring about positive outcomes. The big question, of course, is what makes one therapist better than another. No need to hire a detective here. The answer is the therapeutic alliance. Therapists who form strong alliances across more clients get better results, period. The alliance engages the person in purposeful work and is the fuel of all change.

In the 1980s and 1990s, I used to direct a training institute that also housed a big group practice. I was very fortunate to witness the work of several very talented therapists. We regularly consulted with therapists and agencies having trouble with a client. We took turns being the therapist in the room with the client while the team and the primary therapist watched behind a one-way mirror. It was the most enriching learning experience of my career and one that I will always look back on with great fondness. Although all the therapists on the team were very good, Greg Rusk stood out. He stood out because of his remarkable ability to engage clients from all walks of life, facing all kinds of despair and destitution, in this thing we call psychotherapy.

Peg was a particularly memorable client of his. She was referred to us by her psychiatrist/therapist and was taking max doses of two antidepressants as well as pain medication. Peg suffered severe pain as a result of a fall in an elevator shaft 2 years prior, and she had not been able to return to her job as a night cleaning person in a large office building. She was "profoundly depressed" and "perpetually suicidal," and the referring therapist wanted an opinion about electroconvulsive therapy and involuntary hospitalization because many changes in medications had been tried and she refused hospitalization. In addition, the psychiatrist reported that Peg didn't make eye contact, gave barely audible one sentence replies to questions, and seemed to punctuate every utterance with "I have no reason to live."

Greg greeted both Peg and her husband, Wayne, in the waiting room, and asked Peg if it was okay if Wayne joined them. True to form, Peg never looked up and responded in a low voice that it was okay. On the way back to the consultation room, Greg started chatting with Wayne about his "Hooked on Fishing" hat, and Wayne shared that actually Peg was the true fisherman of the family. They arrived in the therapy room, and Greg, while ushering Peg and Wayne to the couch, asked Peg if she remembered the first fish she ever caught. And Peg looked Greg right in the eye, and told him the story of her first fish, a sun granny, and moreover, about her very special relationship with her father who taught her not only about fishing but also about life. She spoke of her father's death as a blessing after his horrible bout with cancer, which happened right after her accident, and Wayne added that many in Peg's family compared Peg's gentle parenting style and overall compassion with her father's. Wayne proudly said that Peg was the rock of the family, and he told about how she stood by him when he was struggling with alcohol and ongoing unemployment (Wayne said that he was now sober and, on an ironic note, that he was employed as truck driver of a beer distributor).

It was a very touching conversation, and Greg, visibly moved, commented on his heartfelt admiration for this couple, as well as the difficulty of the situation. From there, it emerged that Peg felt useless to the family, that she was unable to contribute financially or, more important, to parenting their two daughters. Wayne chimed in to say that both their daughters were honor roll students because of Peg. In essence, Greg said, it was no wonder that Peg believed she had no reason to live, given that her identity had been stolen by the accident. From there, a lively discussion ensued about how Peg could recapture her usefulness and identity. The couple outlined ways that Peg could start to contribute more to the family, which included a frank discussion about the merits of the medications and their effects on her ability to function. The beginnings of a plan surfaced and, even better, so did hope. This was Greg Rusk. He engaged people, even those who seemed impossible to engage, in meaningful conversations about how their lives could be better.

The research about what differentiates one therapist from another, as well as my personal experience, suggests that the ability to form alliances with people who are not easy to form alliances with—to engage people who don't want to be engaged—is what separates the best from the rest.

3. What do most people, and even most professionals, not really understand about what it takes to be really accomplished in our field?

There are two things (in addition to the alliance). First, although proponents of different models and EBTs would like you to think otherwise, the truth of the matter is that we don't know ahead of time what model or technique will be helpful with the client who is in our office now. In other words, there is a lot of uncertainty that accompanies the work of psychotherapy. To be accomplished, I believe, is to *embrace* uncertainty. It is the place of unlimited possibilities for change, the space for new directions and insights to occur to both the client *and* the therapist.

A recent consult I did illustrates the possibilities in not knowing what to do next, when things don't go as planned. Rosa, who was 7, had gone to live with her foster parents—her aunt and uncle, Margarita and Enrique—because the parental rights of her birth parents had been terminated. Both her father and mother were addicts with long criminal records; the father was in jail, and the mother was still using. Rosa clearly had been born with two strikes against her: parents missing in action and her development impaired by drugs.

Although much psychopathological gobbledygook accompanied her, it was safe to say that Rosa was a "difficult" child, to say the least—prone to tantrums that included kicking, biting, and throwing anything she could find. I began the session by asking Rosa if she was going to help me today, and she immediately yelled, "NO!" and leaned back, with her arms folded across her chest. As I turned to speak with Enrique and Margarita, Rosa began having a tantrum in earnest—screaming at the top of her lungs and flailing around, kicking me in the process.

With Rosa's tantrum escalating, Margarita, who'd first tried to soothe her, dropped a bombshell. In a disarmingly quiet voice, she announced that she didn't think she could continue foster-parenting Rosa. The tension in the room immediately escalated; the only sound was Rosa's yelling, which had become more or less rote at that point. I felt as if I'd been kicked in the gut. I'd expected to be helping foster parents contain and nurture a tough child. Now it felt like participating in a tragedy. Here was a couple, after trying their best to do the right thing by taking in a troubled kid with nowhere else to go, who now seemed ready to give up. The situation was obviously wrenching for Margarita and Enrique, but it was potentially catastrophic for Rosa. In this rural setting, they were her last hope, not only of living with family but of living nearby at all, because the next closest foster-care placement was at least 100 miles away. I contemplated Rosa's life unfolding in foster care with strangers who'd encounter the same difficulties and likely come to the same impasse—resulting in a nightmare of ongoing home placements.

What's the correct diagnosis for Margarita? Is there an EBT for feeling overwhelmed, hopeless, and not knowing whether you can go on parenting a tough kid? Enter uncertainty, and not knowing what the hell will happen next, let alone what to *do* next.

Margarita continued explaining why she couldn't go on, speaking softly while tears rolled down her cheeks. Not only did she feel she couldn't handle Rosa, she also worried about the child's attachment to her. As Margarita expressed her doubts in a near whisper, Enrique's eyes began to tear up and a feeling of despair permeated the room. At that moment, I felt helpless to prevent a terrible ending to an already bad story and didn't have a clue about what to do. Meanwhile, Margarita began gently caressing Rosa's head and speaking softly to her—the Spanish equivalent of "there, there, little one"—until the little girl started to calm down. With her tantrum at an end, Rosa turned to face Margarita, and then reached up and wiped the tears from her aunt's face. "Don't cry, Auntie," she said warmly, "don't cry."

Witnessing these actions was yet another reminder to me of how new possibilities can emerge at any moment in a seemingly hopeless session and the uncertainty of what will happen next. "It's tough to parent a child who's been through as much as Rosa has," I said. "I respect your need to really think through the long-term consequences here. But I'm also impressed with how gently you handled Rosa when she was so upset, and with how, you, Rosa, comforted your Auntie, when you saw her crying. Clearly there's something special about the connection between you two."

Margarita replied that Rosa definitely had a "sweet side." When she saw that she'd upset either Margarita or Enrique, she quickly became soft, responsive, and tender. I began to talk with Margarita and Enrique about what seemed to work with Rosa and what didn't. While Rosa snuggled with

Margarita, we talked about how to bring out Rosa's sweet side more often. As ideas emerged, I was in awe, as I often am, of the fortitude clients show when facing formidable challenges. Here was a couple in their late 40s, who'd already raised their own two children, considering taking on the responsibility of raising another one who had such a difficult history.

By now, the tension and despair present a few moments before had evaporated. The decision to discontinue foster parenting, born of hopelessness, had lost its stranglehold, though nothing had been said explicitly about that. Now all smiles and bubbly, Rosa was bouncing up and down in her chair. She scored all 10s on the Child Session Rating Scale and wrote "very good" across all the scales. Somewhat out of the blue, Margarita announced that she was going to stick with Rosa. "Great," I said quietly. Then, as the full meaning of what she'd said washed over me, I repeated it a bit louder, and then a third time with enthusiasm—"Great!" I asked Margarita if anything in particular had helped her come to this decision. She answered that although she'd always known it, she'd realized in our session, even more than before, that there was a wonderful, loving child inside Rosa, and that she, Margarita, just had to be patient and take things one day at a time. The session had helped her really see the attachment that was already there. I felt the joy of that moment then, and I still do.

In my view, the session included that intimate space in which we connect with people and their pain in a way that somehow opens the path from what is to what can be. My heartfelt appreciation of both the despair of the circumstance and their sincere desire to help this child, combined with the fortuitous "attachment" experience, generated new resolve for Margarita and Enrique. This session taught me, once again, that anything is possible—that even the bleakest sessions can have a positive outcome if you stay with the process. Just when things seemed the most hopeless, when both the family and I were surely down for the count and needed only to accept the inevitable, something meaningful and positive emerged that changed everything—including me.

Uncertainty is at the core of these occurrences, and staying in those moments requires both a comfort level with the unknown and the confidence that it might lead to something good. Embracing uncertainty requires faith—faith in the client, yourself, and psychotherapy (see Question 1).

The second thing that I think is very understated regarding doing good work is perhaps the most difficult skill for therapists to master, namely, the ability to keep sessions focused and not get lost in the sometimes confusing and nearly always complex ways that clients unfold their stories. When the conversation jumps from important topic to important topic without thematic connection or relevance to the way the client is experiencing life between sessions, it is almost a guaranteed recipe for failure. But it is not easy to change this dynamic. It can require therapists to step up their involvement and steer the conversation toward ensuring that some meaningful difference is accomplished in the client's day-to-day life.

It doesn't have to be heavy-handed and it can, of course, be collaborative. For example, I ask clients whether they think it is better for us to continue talking about the topic at hand or whether we should return to what they are most concerned about. I also ask if it is okay with them if I return us to task from time to time. But it can be tricky to follow the client's lead while simultaneously never losing sight of where the client wants to go—to balance being empathic with the sometimes overwhelming presentation of topics and concerns with ensuring that these topics and concerns are tied to making a meaningful difference in the client's experience of life. It is much easier to meander across a myriad of worthwhile topics and legitimate concerns and not connect the conversation to what the client will actually do in between sessions. The unfortunate result is a therapy that represents an ongoing commentary of the client's life and never leads to any real change. I have been there and done that. Often I used to write in my progress notes, "Get some focus!"

But PCOMS really helps here. Monitoring benefit on the Outcome Rating Scale, after ensuring that the client's reasons for service are represented, enables the focus to start and remain on what the client would like to see happen. It helps the therapist stay on task and take charge of channeling the conversation and complexities of clients' lives toward something tangible that will make a difference.

4. What advice would you give someone who aspires to be a master therapist?

First, of course, measure your outcomes to improve your effectiveness and track your development. The research literature offers strong evidence that therapists aren't good judges of their own performance. It's not that we're naïve or stupid; it's simply impossible to assess our effectiveness without a quantitative standard as a reference point. PCOMS offers a feasible way to cut through the ambiguity of therapy and discern your clinical development without falling prey to wishful thinking. The systematic collection of outcome feedback will improve your outcomes by identifying that pool of clients (that we all have) who are not responding, so that you can collaboratively forge new directions. It also allows you to track your effectiveness over time (your career development) and proactively implement strategies to improve your outcomes (like your alliance skills—have I said this before?).

Second, treasure the clients who do not respond to your therapeutic business as usual. Clients provide the opportunity for constant learning, but tracking outcomes takes the notion that "the client is the best teacher" to a more immediately practical level. Tracking outcomes with clients focuses us more precisely on the here-and-now of sessions, and it provides an in vivo training ground to expand our theoretical and technical repertoires. From our openness to client reactions and reflections and our authentic search for new possibilities, we step out of our comfort zone and do things we have never done before. Tracking outcomes enables your clients—especially those who aren't responding well to your usual fare—to teach you how to work better.

And when the chips are down, remember what I learned from Tina, my very first client: Authenticity matters, and when in doubt or in need of help, ask the client, because you are in this thing together.

CONCLUSION

> Between stimulus and response there is a space. In that space is our power
> to choose our response. In our response lies our growth and our freedom.
> —Viktor E. Frankl

This final chapter addressed what I called the "Treasure Chest," a collection of client comments about your work with them and your own articulations of the experiences that meant the most to your development. Helping you re-remember why you became a therapist, opening this file enables an escape from the pressures and disappointments of the daily grind of being a therapist. This chapter also presented my parting thoughts and, hopefully, in the process encouraged you to investigate the controversial issues of the day and take a stand to protect the aspects of your identity as a therapist that you hold dear. Finally, I shared my thoughts about what it takes to become a master therapist.

I hope that this book has encouraged you to continue your commitment to this work that we love. I also hope that it reaffirmed why you became a therapist to begin with and your belief in psychotherapy as a healing endeavor. On becoming a better therapist: If you got into this business, like me and the majority of therapists I meet, because you wanted to help people, you already have what it takes to become a better therapist. It boils down to two things: One is your commitment to forming partnerships with clients to monitor the alliance you have with them and the outcome of the services you are providing. The second is your investment in yourself, your own growth and development. PCOMS provides the method for both.

Recall Yolanda from Chapter 6, the courageous young woman who overcame crack addiction and a violent partner to protect her children and make a better life. Here is what she said to me after I administered the final Session Rating Scale (SRS), which was a 38.7:

> I didn't think much of you or coming to therapy when we started. And I had been to a few others like you about my addiction and the kids during the whole violence thing and I didn't think much of them either. They were okay mostly, but this was different. I like this SRS and the other form you do. It made me feel a part of this—that this was about me. You were always so interested in whether I was on the right track and that we were doing what I thought we needed to be doing. So thanks for that and thanks for helping me get my kids.

That's what I am talking about. And that's why I am a therapist. And that's why I am a therapist who collaboratively monitors the alliance and outcome. And that's why I'll always have my compass close at hand.

REFERENCES

Ackerman, S. J., & Hilsenroth, M. J. (2003). A review of therapist characteristics and techniques positively impacting the therapeutic alliance. *Clinical Psychology Review, 23*, 1–33. doi:10.1016/S0272-7358(02)00146-0

Albee, G. W. (2000). The Boulder model's fatal flaw. *American Psychologist, 55*, 247–248. doi:10.1037/0003-066X.55.2.247

American Psychological Association Commission on Accreditation. (2011). *Commission on Accreditation Implementing Regulations.* Retrieved from http://www.apa.org/ed/accreditation/about/policies/implementing-guidelines.pdf

American Psychological Association Presidential Task Force on Evidence-Based Practice. (2006). Evidence-based practice in psychology. *American Psychologist, 61*, 271–285. doi:10.1037/0003-066X.61.4.271

Anderson, T., Lunnen, K. M., & Ogles, B. M.(2010). Putting models and techniques in context. In B. L. Duncan, S. D. Miller, B. E. Wampold, & M. A. Hubble (Eds.), *The heart and soul of change: Delivering what works in therapy* (2nd ed., pp. 143–166). Washington, DC: American Psychological Association. doi:10.1037/12075-005

Anker, M. G., Duncan, B. L., & Sparks, J. A. (2009). Using client feedback to improve couples therapy outcomes: A randomized clinical trial in a naturalistic setting. *Journal of Consulting and Clinical Psychology, 77*, 693–704. doi:10.1037/a0016062

Anker, M. G., Owen, J., Duncan, B. L., & Sparks, J. A. (2010). The alliance in couple therapy: Partner influence, early change, and alliance patterns in a naturalistic sample. *Journal of Consulting and Clinical Psychology, 78*, 635–645. doi:10.1037/a0020051

Anker, M. G., Sparks, J. A., Duncan, B. L., Owen, J. J., & Stapnes, A. K. (2011). Footprints of couple therapy: Client reflections at follow-up. *Journal of Family Psychotherapy, 22*, 22–45. doi:10.1080/08975353.2011.551098

Ariely, D. (2008). *Predictably irrational: The hidden forces that shape our decisions.* New York, NY: HarperCollins.

Asay, T. P., & Lambert, M. J. (1999). The empirical case for the common factors in therapy: Quantitative findings. In M. A. Hubble, B. L. Duncan, & S. D. Miller (Eds.), *The heart and soul of change: What works in therapy* (pp. 23–55). Washington, DC: American Psychological Association. doi:10.1037/11132-001

Baldwin, S. A., Berkeljon, A., Atkins, D. C., Olsen, J. A., & Nielsen, S. L. (2009). Rates of change in naturalistic psychotherapy: Contrasting dose-effect and good-enough level models of change. *Journal of Consulting and Clinical Psychology, 77*, 203–211. doi:10.1037/a0015235

Baldwin, S. A., & Imel, Z. (2013). Therapist effects. In M. J. Lambert (Ed.), *Bergin and Garfield's handbook of psychotherapy and behavioral change* (6th ed., pp. 258–297). Hoboken, NJ: Wiley.

Baldwin, S. A., Wampold, B. E., & Imel, Z. E. (2007). Untangling the alliance–outcome correlation: Exploring the relative importance of therapist and patient variability in the alliance. *Journal of Consulting and Clinical Psychology, 75,* 842–852. doi:10.1037/0022-006X.75.6.842

Ballard, R. (1992). Short forms of the Marlowe-Crowne Social Desirability Scale. *Psychological Reports, 71,* 1155–1160.

Barber, J. P. (2009). Towards a working through of some core conflicts in psychotherapy research. *Psychotherapy Research, 19,* 1–12. doi:10.1080/10503300802609680

Baskin, T. W., Tierney, S. C., Minami, T., & Wampold, B. E. (2003). Establishing specificity in psychotherapy: A meta-analysis of structural equivalence of placebo controls. *Journal of Consulting and Clinical Psychology, 71,* 973–979. doi:10.1037/0022-006X.71.6.973

Baum, L. F. (1900). *The wonderful wizard of Oz.* Chicago, IL: George M. Hill.

Benish, S. G., Imel, Z. E., & Wampold, B. E. (2008). The relative efficacy of bona fide psychotherapies for treating post-traumatic stress disorder: A meta-analysis of direct comparisons. *Clinical Psychology Review, 28,* 746–758. doi:10.1016/j.cpr.2007.10.005

Berg, I. K. (1994). *Family based services: A solution-focused approach.* New York, NY: Norton.

Berg, I. K., & de Shazer, S. (1993). Making numbers talk: Language in therapy. In S. Friedman (Ed.), *The new language of change* (pp. 5–24). New York, NY: Guilford Press.

Beutler, L. E., Malik, M., Alimohamed, S., Harwood, T. M., Talebi, H., Noble, S., . . . Wong, E. (2004). Therapist variables. In M. J. Lambert (Ed.), *Bergin and Garfield's handbook of psychotherapy and behavior change* (5th ed., pp. 227–306). New York, NY: Wiley.

Bohanske, R., & Franczak, M. (2010). Transforming public behavioral health care: A case example of consumer directed services, recovery, and the common factors. In B. L. Duncan, S. D. Miller, B. E. Wampold, & M. A. Hubble (Eds.), *The heart and soul of change: Delivering what works in therapy* (2nd ed., pp. 299–322). Washington, DC: American Psychological Association. doi:10.1037/12075-010

Bohart, A., & Tallman, K. (2010). Clients: The neglected common factor in psychotherapy. In B. L. Duncan, S. D. Miller, B. E. Wampold, & M. A. Hubble (Eds.), *The heart and soul of change: Delivering what works in therapy* (2nd ed., pp. 83–111). Washington, DC: American Psychological Association. doi:10.1037/12075-003

Bordin, E. (1979). The generalizability of the psychoanalytic concept of the working alliance. *Psychotherapy: Theory, Research & Practice, 16,* 252–260. doi:10.1037/h0085885

Bringhurst, D. L., Watson, C. W., Miller, S. D., & Duncan, B. L. (2006). The reliability and validity of the Outcome Rating Scale: A replication study of a brief clinical measure. *Journal of Brief Therapy, 5*(1), 23–30.

Brown, G. S., Jones, E., Lambert, M. J., & Minami, T. (2005). Evaluating the effectiveness of psychotherapists in a managed care environment. *The American Journal of Managed Care, 11*(8), 513–520.

Brown, J., Dreis, S., & Nace, D. K. (1999). What really makes a difference in psychotherapy outcomes? Why does managed care want to know? In M. A. Hubble, B. L. Duncan, & S. D. Miller (Eds.), *The heart and soul of change: What works in therapy* (pp. 389–406). Washington, DC: American Psychological Association. doi:10.1037/11132-012

Brown, J., & Minami, T. (2010). Outcomes management, reimbursement, and the future of psychotherapy. In B. L. Duncan, S. D. Miller, B. E. Wampold, & M. A. Hubble (Eds.), *The heart and soul of change: Delivering what works in therapy* (2nd ed., pp. 267–297). Washington, DC: American Psychological Association. doi:10.1037/12075-009

Burckhardt, C. S., & Anderson, K. (2003). The Quality of Life Scale (QOLS): Reliability, validity, and utilization. *Health and Quality of Life Outcomes, 1*, 60. doi:10.1186/1477-7525-1-60

Burlingame, G. M., Mosier, J. I., Wells, M. G., Atkin, Q. G., Lambert, M. J., Whoolery, M., & Latkowski, M. (2001). Tracking the influence of mental health treatment: The development of the Youth Outcome Questionnaire. *Clinical Psychology & Psychotherapy, 8*, 361–379. doi:10.1002/cpp.315

Campbell, A., & Hemsley, S. (2009). Outcome Rating Scale and Session Rating Scale in psychological practice: Clinical utility of ultra-brief measures. *Clinical Psychologist, 13*, 1–9. doi:10.1080/13284200802676391

Carey, B. (2005, December 27). Psychotherapy on the road . . . to where? *New York Times*. Retrieved from http://www.nytimes.com/2005/12/27/science/27ther.html

Carroll, L. (1962). *Alice's adventures in wonderland*. Harmondsworth, Middlesex, England: Penguin. (Original work published 1865)

Carson, R. C. (1997). Costly compromises: A critique of *The Diagnostic and Statistical Manual of Mental Disorders*. In S. Fisher & R. P. Greenberg (Eds.), *From placebo to panacea: Putting psychiatric drugs to the test* (pp. 98–112). New York, NY: Wiley.

Castonguay, L., Barkham, M., Lutz, W., & McAleavey, A. (2013). Practice-oriented research: Approaches and applications. In M. J. Lambert (Ed.), *Bergin and Garfield's handbook of psychotherapy and behavior change* (6th ed., pp. 85–133). Hoboken, NJ: Wiley.

Chambless, D. L., & Crits-Christoph, P. (2006). The treatment method. In J. C. Norcross, L. E. Beutler, & R. F. Levant (Eds.), *Evidence-based practices in mental health* (pp. 191–199). Washington, DC: American Psychological Association.

Clement, P. W. (1994). Quantitative evaluation of more than 26 years of private practice. *Professional Psychology: Research and Practice, 25*, 173–176. doi:10.1037/0735-7028.25.2.173

Cooper, M., Stewart, D., Sparks, J., & Bunting, L. (2013). School-based counseling using systematic feedback: A cohort study evaluating outcomes and predictors of change. *Psychotherapy Research, 23*, 474–488. doi:10.1080/10503307.2012.735777

Crethar, H. C., & Winterowd, C. L. (2012). Values and social justice in counseling. *Counseling and Values, 57,* 3–9. doi:10.1002/j.2161-007X.2012.00001.x

Crits-Christoph, P., Connolly Gibbons, M., & Mukherjee, D. (2013). Process-outcome research. In M. J. Lambert (Ed.), *Bergin and Garfield's handbook of psychotherapy and behavioral change* (6th ed., pp. 298–340). Hoboken, NJ: Wiley.

Crits-Christoph, P., Connolly Gibbons, M. B. C. Crits-Christoph, K., Narducci, J., Schamberger, M., & Gallop, R. (2006). Can therapists be trained to improve their alliances? A preliminary study of alliance-fostering psychotherapy. *Psychotherapy Research, 16,* 268–281. doi:10.1080/10503300500268557

Crits-Christoph, P., Gallop, R., Temes, C., Woody, G., Ball, S., Martino, S., & Carroll, K. (2009). The alliance in motivational enhancement therapy and counseling as usual for substance use problems. *Journal of Consulting and Clinical Psychology, 77,* 1125–1135.

de Jong, K., Van Sluis, P., Annet Nugter, M., Heiser, W. J., & Spinhoven, P. (2012). Understanding the differential impact of outcome monitoring: Therapist variables that moderate feedback effects in a randomized clinical trial. *Psychotherapy Research, 22,* 464–474. doi:10.1080/10503307.2012.673023

de Jong, P., & Berg, I. K. (2008). *Interviewing for solutions* (3rd ed.). Belmont, CA: Thomson Higher Education.

Dennis, M., Godley, S. H., Diamond, G., Tims, F. M., Babor, T., Donaldson, J., . . . Funk, R. (2004). The Cannabis Youth Treatment (CYT) Study: Main findings from two randomized trials. *Journal of Substance Abuse Treatment, 27,* 197–213. doi:10.1016/j.jsat.2003.09.005

Dew, S., & Riemer, M. (2003, March). Why inaccurate self-evaluation of performance justifies feedback interventions. In L. Bickman (Chair), *Improving outcomes through feedback intervention.* Symposium conducted at the 16th Annual Research Conference, A System of Care for Children's Mental Health: Expanding the Research Base, Tampa, University of South Florida, The Louis de la Parte Florida Mental Health Institute, Research and Training Center for Children's Mental Health.

Duncan, B. L. (2010a). *On becoming a better therapist.* Washington, DC: American Psychological Association. doi:10.1037/12080-000

Duncan, B. L. (2010b). Saul Rosenzweig: The founder of the common factors. In B. L. Duncan, S. D. Miller, B. E. Wampold, & M. A. Hubble (Eds.), *The heart and soul of change: Delivering what works in therapy* (2nd ed., pp. 3–22). Washington, DC: American Psychological Association. doi:10.1037/12075-000

Duncan, B. L. (2011a). *The Partners for Change Outcome Management System (PCOMS): Administration, scoring, interpreting update for the Outcome and Session Ratings Scale.* Retrieved from http://heartandsoulofchange.com

Duncan, B. L. (2011b). What therapists want: It's certainly not money or fame. *Psychotherapy Networker, May/June,* 40–43, 47, 62.

Duncan, B. L. (2012). The partners for change outcome management system (PCOMS): The heart and soul of change project. *Canadian Psychology, 53*, 93–104. doi:10.1037/a0027762

Duncan, B. L. (in press). The person of the therapist: One therapist's journey to relationship. In K. J. Schneider, J. F. Pierson, & J. F. T. Bugental (Eds.), *The handbook of humanistic psychology* (2nd ed.). New York, NY: Sage.

Duncan, B. L., & Antonuccio, D. O. (2011). A patient bill of rights for psychotropic prescription: A call for a higher standard of care. *International Journal of Clinical Medicine, 2*, 353–359. doi:10.4236/ijcm.2011.24061

Duncan, B. L., Hubble, M. A., & Miller, S. D. (1997). *Psychotherapy with "impossible" cases: Efficient treatment of therapy veterans*. New York, NY: Norton.

Duncan, B. L., & Miller, S. D. (2000a). The client's theory of change. *Journal of Psychotherapy Integration, 10*, 169–187. doi:10.1023/A:1009448200244

Duncan, B. L., & Miller, S. D. (2000b). *The heroic client: Doing client-directed, outcome-informed therapy*. San Francisco, CA: Jossey Bass.

Duncan, B. L., & Miller, S. D. (2004). *The Relationship Rating Scale*. Retrieved from http://heartandsoulofchange.com.

Duncan, B. L., & Miller, S. D. (2007). *The Group Session Rating Scale*. Retrieved from http://heartandsoulofchange.com.

Duncan, B. L., Miller, S. D., & Sparks, J. A. (2003a). *The Child Outcome Rating Scale*. Retrieved from http://heartandsoulofchange.com.

Duncan, B. L., Miller, S. D., & Sparks, J. A. (2003b). *The Child Session Rating Scale*. Retrieved from http://heartandsoulofchange.com.

Duncan, B. L., Miller, S. D., & Sparks, J. A. (2004). *The heroic client: A revolutionary way to improve effectiveness through client-directed outcome-informed therapy* (Rev. ed.). San Francisco, CA: Jossey-Bass.

Duncan, B. L., Miller, S. D., Sparks, J. A., Claud, D. A., Reynolds, L. R., Brown, J., & Johnson, L. D. (2003). The Session Rating Scale: Preliminary psychometric properties of a "working" alliance measure. *Journal of Brief Therapy, 3*(1), 3–12.

Duncan, B. L., Miller, S. D., Sparks, J. A., & Higgins, A. (2003). *The Young Child Outcome Rating Scale*. Retrieved from http://heartandsoulofchange.com.

Duncan, B. L., Miller, S. D., Sparks, J. A., & Murphy, J. (2011). *The Child Group Session Rating Scale*. Retrieved from http://heartandsoulofchange.com.

Duncan, B. L., Miller, S. D., Wampold, B. E., & Hubble, M. A. (Eds.). (2010). *The heart and soul of change: Delivering what works in therapy* (2nd ed.). Washington, DC: American Psychological Association. doi:10.1037/12075-000

Duncan, B. L., & Moynihan, D. W. (1994). Applying outcome research: Intentional utilization of the client's frame of reference. *Psychotherapy: Theory, Research, Practice, Training, 31*, 294–301. doi:10.1037/h0090215

Duncan, B. L., Parks, M. B., & Rusk, G. S. (1990). Strategic eclecticism: A technical alternative for eclectic psychotherapy. *Psychotherapy: Theory, Research, Practice, Training, 27*, 568–577. doi:10.1037/0033-3204.27.4.568

Duncan, B. L., & Reese, R. J. (2012). Empirically supported treatments, evidence based treatments, and evidence based practice. In G. Stricker & T. Widiger (Eds.), *Handbook of psychology: Clinical psychology* (2nd ed., pp. 977–1023). Hoboken, NJ: Wiley. doi:10.1002/9781118133880.hop208021

Duncan, B. L., & Reese, R. J. (2013). Clinical and scientific considerations in progress monitoring: When is a measure too long? *Canadian Psychology/Psychologie canadienne, 54*, 135–137. doi:10.1037/a0032362

Duncan, B. L., Solovey, A. D., & Rusk, G. S. (1992). *Changing the rules: A client-directed approach.* New York, NY: Guilford Press.

Duncan, B. L., & Sparks, J. (2002). *Heroic clients, heroic agencies: Partners for change.* Fort Lauderdale, FL: Nova Southeastern University.

Duncan, B. L., & Sparks, J. (2007). *Heroic clients, heroic agencies: Partners for change* (Rev. ed.). Retrieved from http://heartandsoulofchange.com.

Duncan, B. L., & Sparks, J. (2010). *Heroic clients, heroic agencies: Partners for change* (2nd ed.). Retrieved from http://heartandsoulofchange.com.

Duncan, B. L., Sparks, J., Miller, S., Bohanske, R., & Claud, D. (2006). Giving youth a voice: A preliminary study of the reliability and validity of a brief outcome measure for children. *Journal of Brief Therapy, 5*(1), 5–22.

Elkin, I., Shea, T., Watkins, J. T., Imber, S. D., Sotsky, S. M., Collins, J. F., . . . Parloff, M. B. (1989). National Institute of Mental Health Treatment of Depression Collaborative Research Program: General effectiveness of treatments. *Archives of General Psychiatry, 46*, 971–982. doi:10.1001/archpsyc.1989.01810110013002

Elkin, I., Yamaguchi, J., Arnkoff, D., Glass, C., Sotsky, S., & Krupnick, J. (1999). "Patient-treatment fit" and early engagement in therapy. *Psychotherapy Research, 9*, 437–451.

Elliott, R., Bohart, A. C., Watson, J. C., & Greenberg, L. S. (2011). Empathy. *Psychotherapy, 48*, 43–49. doi:10.1037/a0022187

Erickson, M., & Rossi, E. (1979). *Hypnotherapy: An exploratory casebook.* New York, NY: Irvington.

Farber, B. A., & Doolin, E. (2011). Positive regard. *Psychotherapy, 48*, 58–64. doi:10.1037/a0022141

Fisch, R., Weakland, J., & Segal, L. (1982). *The tactics of change: Doing therapy briefly.* San Francisco, CA: Jossey-Bass.

Flückiger, C., Del Re, A. C., Wampold, B. E., Symonds, D., & Horvath, A. O. (2012). How central is the alliance in psychotherapy? A multilevel longitudinal meta-analysis. *Journal of Counseling Psychology, 59*, 10–17. doi:10.1037/a0025749

Forand, N., DeRubeis, R., & Amsterdam, J. (2013). Combining medication and psychotherapy in the treatment of major mental disorders. In M. J. Lambert (Ed.), *Bergin and Garfield's handbook of psychotherapy and behavioral change* (6th ed., pp. 735–774). Hoboken, NJ: Wiley.

Frank, J. (1961). *Persuasion and healing: A comparative study of psychotherapy.* Baltimore, MD: Johns Hopkins University Press.

Frank, J. (1973). *Persuasion and healing: A comparative study of psychotherapy* (2nd ed.). Baltimore, MD: Johns Hopkins University Press.

Frank, J. D., & Frank, J. B. (1991). *Persuasion and healing* (3rd ed.). Baltimore, MD: Johns Hopkins University Press.

Franklin, C., Corcoran, J., Nowicki, J., & Streeter, C. (1997). Using client self-anchored scales to measure outcomes in solution-focused therapy. *Journal of Systemic Therapies, 16,* 246–265.

Gassmann, D., & Grawe, K. (2006). General change mechanisms: The relation between problem activation and resource activation in successful and unsuccessful therapeutic interactions. *Clinical Psychology & Psychotherapy, 13,* 1–11. doi:10.1002/cpp.442

Gaston, L. (1990). The concept of the alliance and its role in psychotherapy: Theoretical and empirical considerations. *Psychotherapy: Theory, Research, Practice, Training, 27,* 143–153. doi:10.1037/0033-3204.27.2.143

Geller, J. D., Norcross, J. C., & Orlinsky, D. E. (Eds.). (2005). *The psychotherapist's own psychotherapy: Client and clinician perspectives.* New York, NY: Oxford University Press.

Gillaspy, J. A., & Murphy, J. J. (2011). The use of ultra-brief client feedback tools in SFBT. In C. W. Franklin, T. Trepper, E. McCollum, & W. Gingerich (Eds.), *Solution-focused brief therapy* (pp. 73–93). New York, NY: Oxford University Press.

Goldfried, M. R., & Wolfe, B. E. (1996). Psychotherapy practice and research: Repairing a strained alliance. *American Psychologist, 51,* 1007–1016. doi:10.1037/0003-066X.51.10.1007

Greenberg, G. (2010). Inside the battle to define mental illness. *Wired Magazine.* Retrieved from www.wired.com/magazine/2010/ff_dsmv.

Halstead, J., Youn, S. J., & Armijo, I. (2013). Scientific and clinical considerations in progress monitoring: When is a brief measure too brief? *Canadian Psychology, 54,* 83–85. doi:10.1037/a0031324

Hanlon, P. (2005). PacifiCare screening tool, policies raise concerns. *New England Psychologist, 13,* 11–12.

Hannan, C., Lambert, M. J., Harmon, C., Nielsen, S. L., Smart, D. W., Shimokawa, K., Sutton, S. W. (2005). A lab test and algorithms for identifying clients at risk for treatment failure. *Journal of Clinical Psychology, 61,* 155–163. doi:10.1002/jclp.20108

Hansen, N., Lambert, M., & Forman, E. (2002). The psychotherapy dose-effect and its implications for treatment delivery services. *Clinical Psychology: Science and Practice, 9,* 329–343. doi:10.1093/clipsy.9.3.329

Harmon, S. C., Lambert, M. J., Smart, D. W., Hawkins, E. J., Nielsen, S. L., Slade, K., & Lutz, W. (2007). Enhancing outcome for potential treatment failures: Therapist/client feedback and clinical support tools. *Psychotherapy Research, 17,* 379–392. doi:10.1080/10503300600702331

Hatcher, R. L., & Barends, A. W. (1996). Patient's view of psychotherapy: Exploratory factor analysis of three alliance measures. *Journal of Consulting and Clinical Psychology, 64,* 1326–1336. doi:10.1037/0022-006X.64.6.1326

Hatcher, R. L., & Barends, A. W. (2006). How a return to theory could help alliance research. *Psychotherapy, 43,* 292–299. doi:10.1037/0033-3204.43.3.292

Hatfield, D. R., & Ogles, B. M. (2004). The use of outcome measures by psychologists in clinical practice. *Professional Psychology: Research and Practice, 35*(5), 485–491. doi:10.1037/0735-7028.35.5.485

Hawkins, E. J., Lambert, M. J., Vermeersch, D. A., Slade, K., & Tuttle, K. (2004). The effects of providing patient progress information to therapists and patients. *Psychotherapy Research, 14,* 308–327. doi:10.1093/ptr/kph027

Hill, C., & Knox, S. (2013). Training and supervision in psychotherapy. In M. J. Lambert (Ed.), *Bergin and Garfield's handbook of psychotherapy and behavior change* (6th ed., pp. 775–812). Hoboken, NJ: Wiley.

Horvath, A. O., & Bedi, R. P. (2002). The alliance. In J. C. Norcross (Ed.), *Psychotherapy relationships that work* (pp. 37–69). New York, NY: Oxford University Press.

Horvath, A. O., Del Re, A. C., Flückiger, C., & Symonds, D. (2011). Alliance in individual psychotherapy. *Psychotherapy, 48,* 9–16. doi:10.1037/a0022186

Horvath, A. O., & Greenberg, L. S. (1989). Development and validation of the Working Alliance Inventory. *Journal of Counseling Psychology, 36,* 223_233.

Howard, K. I., Kopta, S. M., Krause, M. S., & Orlinsky, D. E. (1986). The dose–effect relationship in psychotherapy. *American Psychologist, 41,* 159–164. doi:10.1037/0003-066X.41.2.159

Howard, K. I., Moras, K., Brill, P. L., Martinovich, Z., & Lutz, W. (1996). Evaluation of psychotherapy: Efficacy, effectiveness, and patient progress. *American Psychologist, 51,* 1059–1064. doi:10.1037/0003-066X.51.10.1059

Hunter, C. L., Goodie, J. L., Oordt, M. S., & Dobmeyer, A. C. (2009). *Integrated behavioral health in primary care: Step by-step guidance for assessment and intervention.* Washington, DC: American Psychological Association. doi:10.1037/11871-000

Ionita, G. (2013). Canadian psychologist's attitudes and behaviors about outcome management. Doctoral dissertation in progress. McGill University.

Jacobson, N. S., & Truax, P. (1991). Clinical significance: A statistical approach to defining meaningful change in psychotherapy research. *Journal of Consulting and Clinical Psychology, 59,* 12–19. doi:10.1037/0022-006X.59.1.12

Johnson, L. (1995). *Psychotherapy in the age of accountability.* New York, NY: Norton.

Kaiser Commission on Medicaid and the Uninsured. (2011). *Mental health financing in the United States: A primer.* Menlo Park, CA: The Henry J. Kaiser Family Foundation. Retrieved from http://www.kff.org

Kim, D. M., Wampold, B. E., & Bolt, D. M. (2006). Therapist effects in psychotherapy: A random effects modeling of the NIMH TDCRP data. *Psychotherapy Research, 16,* 161–172. doi:10.1080/10503300500264911

Kirk, S. A., & Kutchins, H. (1992). *The selling of DSM: The rhetoric of science in psychiatry.* New York, NY: Aldine.

Kirsch, I. (2005). Placebo psychotherapy: Synonym or oxymoron? *Journal of Clinical Psychology, 61,* 791–803. doi:10.1002/jclp.20126

Kirsch, I. (2011). *The emperor's new drugs: Exploding the antidepressant myth.* New York, NY: Basic Books.

Kolden, G. G., Klein, M. H., Wang, C. C., & Austin, S. B.(2011). Congruence/genuineness. *Psychotherapy, 48,* 65–71. doi:10.1037/a0022064

Kottler, J., & Carlson, J. (in press) *Becoming a master therapist.* New York, NY: Wiley.

Kraus, D. R., Castonguay, L., Boswell, J. F., Nordberg, S. S., & Hayes, J. A. (2011). Therapist effectiveness. *Psychotherapy Research, 21,* 267–276. doi:10.1080/105 03307.2011.563249

Krupnick, J. L., Sotsky, S. M., Simmens, S., Moyer, J., Elkin, I., Watkins, J., & Pilkonis, P. A. (1996). The role of the therapeutic alliance in psychotherapy and pharmacotherapy outcome: Findings in the National Institute of Mental Health Treatment of Depression Collaborative Research Project. *Journal of Consulting and Clinical Psychology, 64,* 532–539. doi:10.1037/0022-006X.64.3.532

Lambert, M. J. (1986). Implications of psychotherapy outcome research for eclectic psychotherapy. In J. C. Norcross (Ed.), *Handbook of eclectic psychotherapy* (pp. 436–462). New York, NY: Brunner/Mazel.

Lambert, M. J. (2010a). *Prevention of treatment failure: The use of measuring, monitoring, and feedback in clinical practice.* Washington, DC: American Psychological Association. doi:10.1037/12141-00

Lambert, M. J. (2010b). Yes, it is time for clinicians to routinely monitor treatment outcome. In B. L. Duncan, S. D. Miller, B. E. Wampold, & M. A. Hubble (Eds.), *The heart and soul of change: Delivering what works in therapy* (2nd ed., pp. 239–266). Washington, DC: American Psychological Association. doi:10.1037/12075-008

Lambert, M. J. (2013). The efficacy and effectiveness of psychotherapy. In M. J. Lambert (Ed.), *Bergin and Garfield's handbook of psychotherapy and behavior change* (6th ed., pp. 169–218). Hoboken, NJ: Wiley.

Lambert, M. J., Bergin, A. E., & Garfield, S. L. (2004). Introduction and overview. In M. J. Lambert (Ed.), *Bergin & Garfield's Handbook of psychotherapy & behavior change* (5th ed., pp. 3–15). New York, NY: Wiley.

Lambert, M. J., Hansen, N. B., Umphress, V., Lunnen, K., Okiishi, J., & Burlingame, G., . . . Reisinger, C. (1996). *Administration and scoring manual for the OQ 45.2.* Stevenson, MD: American Professional Credentialing Services.

Lambert, M. J., & Shimokawa, K. (2011). Collecting client feedback. *Psychotherapy, 48,* 72–79. doi:10.1037/a0022238

Lambert, M. J., Whipple, J. L., Smart, D. W., Vermeersch, D. A., Nielsen, S. L., & Hawkins, E. J. (2001). The effects of providing therapists with feedback on client progress during psychotherapy: Are outcomes enhanced? *Psychotherapy Research, 11,* 49–68. doi:10.1080/713663852

Lambert, M. J., Whipple, J. L., Vermeersch, D. A., Smart, D. W., Hawkins, E. J., Nielsen, S. L., & Goates, M. K. (2002). Enhancing psychotherapy outcomes via providing feedback on client progress: A replication. *Clinical Psychology & Psychotherapy*, 9, 91–103. doi:10.1002/cpp.324

Lese, K. P., & MacNair-Semands, R. R. (2000). The Therapeutic Factors Inventory: Development of a scale. *Group*, 24, 303–317. doi:10.1023/A:1026616626780

Liddle, H., & Saba, G. (1983). On context replication: The isomorphic relationship of training and therapy. *Journal of Strategic & Systemic Therapies*, 2, 3–11.

Linehan, M. M., Comtois, K. A., Murray, A. M., Brown, M. Z., Gallop, R. J., Heard, H. L., . . . Lindenboim, N. (2006). Two-year randomized controlled trial and follow-up of dialectical behavior therapy vs. therapy by experts for suicidal behaviors and borderline personality disorder. *Archives of General Psychiatry*, 63, 757–766. doi:10.1001/archpsyc.63.7.757

Littell, J. (2010). Evidence based practice: Evidence or orthodoxy? In B. L. Duncan, S. D. Miller, B. E. Wampold, & M. A. Hubble (Eds.), *The heart and soul of change: Delivering what works in therapy* (2nd ed., pp. 167–198). Washington, DC: American Psychological Association. doi:10.1037/12075-006

Lovibond, P. F., & Lovibond, S. H. (1995). The structure of negative emotional states: Comparison of the Depression Anxiety Stress Scales (DASS) with the Beck Depression and Anxiety Inventories. *Behaviour Research and Therapy*, 33, 335–343. doi:10.1016/0005-7967(94)00075-U

Luborsky, L., Barber, J., Siqueland, L., Johnson, S., Najavits, L., Frank, A., & Daley, D. (1996). The revised Helping Alliance Questionnaire (HAQ–II). *The Journal of Psychotherapy Practice & Research*, 5, 260–271.

Lutz, W., Stulz, N., & Köck, K. (2009). Patterns of early change and their relationship to outcome and follow-up among patients with major depressive disorders. *Journal of Affective Disorders*, 118, 60–68. doi:10.1016/j.jad.2009.01.019

MacKenzie, K. R. (1983). The clinical application of group measure. In R. R. Dies & K. R. MacKenzie (Eds.), *Advances in group psychotherapy: Integrating research and practice* (pp. 159–170). New York, NY: International Universities Press.

Marcus, D. K., Kashy, D. A., & Baldwin, S. A. (2009). Studying psychotherapy using the one-with-many design. *Journal of Counseling Psychology*, 56, 537–548. doi:10.1037/a0017291

McDonagh, A., Friedman, M., McHugo, G., Ford, J., Sengupta, A., Mueser, K., . . . Descamps, M. (2005). Randomized trial of cognitive–behavioral therapy for chronic posttraumatic stress disorder in adult female survivors of childhood sexual abuse. *Journal of Consulting and Clinical Psychology*, 73, 515–524. doi:10.1037/0022-006X.73.3.515

McFadzean, D. (2010). Therapist. In B. Duncan & J. Sparks (Eds.), *Heroic clients, heroic agencies: Partners for change* (2nd ed., p. 199). Retrieved from http://heartandsoul ofchange.com.

Miller, S. D., & Duncan, B. L. (2000). *The Outcome Rating Scale*. Retrieved from http://heartandsoulofchange.com.

Miller, S. D., Duncan, B. L., Brown, J., Sorrell, R., & Chalk, B. (2006). Using outcome to inform and improve treatment outcomes. *Journal of Brief Therapy, 5*, 5–22.

Miller, S. D., Duncan, B. L., Brown, J., Sparks, J., & Claud, D. (2003). The Outcome Rating Scale: A preliminary study of the reliability, validity, and feasibility of a brief visual analog measure. *Journal of Brief Therapy, 2*, 91–100.

Miller, S. D., Duncan, B. L., & Johnson, L. (2002). *The Session Rating Scale*. Retrieved from http://heartandsoulofchange.com.

Miller, W. R., & Rollnick, S. (2012). *Motivational interviewing: Helping people change* (3rd ed.). New York, NY: Guilford Press.

Minami, T., Davies, D. R., Tierney, S. C., Bettmann, J. E., McAward, S. M., Averill, L. A., . . . Wampold, B. (2009). Preliminary evidence on the effectiveness of psychological treatments delivered at a university counseling center. *Journal of Counseling Psychology, 56*, 309–320. doi:10.1037/a0015398

Minami, T., Wampold, B. E., Serlin, R. C., Hamilton, E. G., Brown, G. S., & Kircher, J. C. (2008). Benchmarking the effectiveness of psychotherapy treatment for adult depression in a managed care environment: A preliminary study. *Journal of Consulting and Clinical Psychology, 76*, 116–124. doi:10.1037/0022-006X.76.1.116

Murphy, J. J., & Duncan, B. L. (2007). *Brief intervention for school problems: Outcome informed strategies* (2nd ed.). New York, NY: Guilford Press.

Neimeyer, G. J., Taylor, J. J., & Wear, D. M. (2009). Continuing education in psychology: Outcomes, evaluations, and mandates. *Professional Psychology: Research and Practice, 40*, 617–624. doi:10.1037/a0016655

Norcross, J. C. (Ed.). (2002). *Psychotherapy relationships that work: Therapist contributions and responsiveness to patient needs*. New York, NY: Oxford University Press.

Norcross, J. C., & Goldfried, M. R. (2005). *Handbook of psychotherapy integration* (2nd ed.). New York, NY: Oxford University Press.

Nyman, S. J., Nafziger, M. A., & Smith, T. B. (2010). Client outcomes across counselor training level within a multitiered supervision model. *Journal of Counseling & Development, 88*, 204–209. doi:10.1002/j.1556-6678.2010.tb00010.x

Okiishi, J., Lambert, M. J., Nielsen, S. L., & Ogles, B. M. (2003). In search of supershrink: Using patient outcome to identify effective and ineffective therapists. *Clinical Psychology & Psychotherapy, 10*, 361–373. doi:10.1002/cpp.383

Okiishi, J. C., Lambert, M. J., Eggett, D., Nielsen, L., Dayton, D. D., & Vermeersch, D. A. (2006). An analysis of therapist treatment effects: Toward providing feedback to individual therapists on their clients' psychotherapy outcome. *Journal of Clinical Psychology, 62*, 1157–1172. doi:10.1002/jclp.20272

Olfson, M., & Marcus, S. (2010). National trends in outpatient psychotherapy. *The American Journal of Psychiatry, 167*, 1456–1463. doi:10.1176/appi.ajp.2010.10040570

Orlinsky, D. E., Rønnestad, M. H., Gerin, P., Davis, J. D., Ambühl, H.,Willutzki, U., . . . Schröder, T. A. (2005). The development of psychotherapists. In D. E. Orlinsky and M. H. Rønnestad (Eds.), *How psychotherapists develop: A study of therapeutic work and professional growth* (pp. 3–13). Washington, DC: American Psychological Association. doi:10.1037/11157-001

Orlinsky, D. E., & Rønnestad, M. H. (2005). *How psychotherapists develop: A study of therapeutic work and professional growth*. Washington, DC: American Psychological Association. doi:10.1037/11157-000

Orlinsky, D. E., Rønnestad, M. H., & Willutzki, U. (2004). Fifty years of process-outcome research: Continuity and change. In M. J. Lambert (Ed.), *Bergin and Garfield's handbook of psychotherapy and behavior change* (5th ed., pp. 307–390). New York, NY: Wiley.

Owen, J., Duncan, B., Anker, M., & Sparks, J. (2012). Initial relationship goal and couple therapy outcomes at post and six-month follow-up. *Journal of Family Psychology, 26*, 179–186. doi:10.1037/a0026998

Owen, J., Duncan, B. L., Reese, J., Anker, M. G., & Sparks, J. A. (in press). Accounting for therapist variability in couple therapy: What really matters? *Journal of Sex & Marital Therapy*.

Pesale, F. P., & Hilsenroth, M. J. (2009). Patient and therapist perspectives on session depth in relation to technique during psychodynamic psychotherapy. *Psychotherapy: Theory, Research, Practice, Training, 46*, 390–396. doi:10.1037/a0016999

President's New Freedom Commission on Mental Health. (2002). Interim report (DHHS Pub. No. SMA-03-3932). Retrieved from http://www.mentalhealthcommission.gov/reports/interim_toc.htm

Project MATCH Research Group. (1997). Matching alcoholism treatments to client heterogeneity: Project MATCH posttreatment drinking outcomes. *Journal of Studies on Alcohol, 58*, 7–29.

Quirk, K., Miller, S., Duncan, B., & Owen, J. (2013). Group Session Rating Scale: Preliminary psychometrics in substance abuse group interventions. *Counselling & Psychotherapy Research, 13*, 194–200. doi:10.1080/14733145.2012.744425

Reese, R. J., Duncan, B., Bohanske, R., Owen, J., & Minami, T. (2014). *Benchmarking outcomes in a public behavioral health setting: Feedback as a quality improvement strategy*. Manuscript submitted for publication.

Reese, R. J., Gillaspy, J. A., Owen, J. J., Flora, K. L., Cunningham, L. E., Archie, D., & Marsden, T. (2013). The influence of demand characteristics and social desirability on clients' ratings of the therapeutic alliance. *Journal of Clinical Psychology, 69*, 696–709. doi:10.1002/jclp.21946

Reese, R. J., Norsworthy, L. A., & Rowlands, S. R. (2009). Does a continuous feedback system improve psychotherapy outcome? *Psychotherapy, 46*, 418–431. doi:10.1037/a0017901

Reese, R. J., Toland, M. D., Slone, N. C., & Norsworthy, L. A. (2010). Effect of client feedback on couple psychotherapy outcomes. *Psychotherapy, 47*, 616–630. doi:10.1037/a0021182

Reese, R. J., Usher, E. L., Bowman, D. C., Norsworthy, L. A., Halstead, J. L., Rowlands, S. R., & Chisholm, R. R. (2009). Using client feedback in psychotherapy training: An analysis of its influence on supervision and counselor self-efficacy. *Training and Education in Professional Psychology, 3*, 157–168. doi:10.1037/a0015673

Rogers, C. R. (1957). The necessary and sufficient conditions of therapeutic personality change. *Journal of Consulting Psychology, 21*, 95–103. doi:10.1037/h0045357

Rønnestad, M. H., & Skovholt, T. M. (2013). *The developing practitioner: Growth and stagnation of therapists and counselors.* New York, NY: Routledge.

Rosenberg, M. (1989). *Society and the adolescent self-image* (Rev.ed.). Middletown, CT: Wesleyan University Press.

Rosenzweig, S. (1936). Some implicit common factors in diverse methods of psychotherapy. *American Journal of Orthopsychiatry, 6*, 412–415. doi:10.1111/j.1939-0025.1936.tb05248.x

Rusk, G. (2010). Wizard, humbug, or witch. In B. Duncan & J. Sparks (Eds.), *Heroic clients, heroic agencies: Partners for change* (2nd ed., pp. 151–253). Ft. Lauderdale, FL: HSCP Press.

Safran, J. D., Muran, J. C., & Eubanks-Carter, C. (2011). Repairing alliance ruptures. *Psychotherapy (Chicago, Ill.), 48*, 80–87. doi:10.1037/a0022140

Saleeby, D. (2006). *The strengths perspective in social work practice* (4th ed.). New York, NY: Pearson/Allyn and Bacon.

Schuman, D., Slone, N., Reese, R. J., & Duncan, B. (in press). Using client feedback to improve outcomes in group psychotherapy with soldiers referred for substance abuse treatment. *Psychotherapy Research.*

Searles, H. (1955). The informational value of the supervisor's emotional experience. *Psychiatry, 18*, 135–146.

Sharf, J., Primavera, L. H., & Diener, M. J. (2010). Droput and the therapeutic alliance: Meta-analysis of adult individual psychotherapy. *Psychotherapy: Theory, Research, Practice, Training, 47*, 637–645. doi:10.1037/a0021175

Shimokawa, K., Lambert, M. J., & Smart, D. W. (2010). Enhancing treatment outcome of patients at risk of treatment failure: Meta-analytic and mega-analytic review of a psychotherapy quality assurance system. *Journal of Consulting and Clinical Psychology, 78*, 298–311. doi:10.1037/a0019247

Slade, K., Lambert, M. J., Harmon, S. C., Smart, D. W., & Bailey, R. (2008). Improving psychotherapy outcome: The use of immediate electronic feedback and revised clinical support tools. *Clinical Psychology & Psychotherapy, 15*, 287–303. doi:10.1002/cpp.594

Slone, N. C., Reese, R. J., Mathews-Duvall, S., & Kodet, J. (2014). *Evaluating the efficacy of client feedback in group psychotherapy.* Manuscript submitted for publication.

Sotsky, S. M., Glass, D. R., Shea, M. T., Pilkonis, P. A., Collins, J. F., Elkin, I., . . . Oliveri, M. E. (1991). Patient predictors of response to psychotherapy and pharmacotherapy: Findings in the NIMH Treatment of Depression Collaborative Research Program. *The American Journal of Psychiatry, 148*, 997–1008.

Sparks, J. A. (2013). *Just talk: The Partners for Change Outcome Management System as political action.* Manuscript submitted for publication.

Sparks, J. A., & Duncan, B. L. (2012). Pediatric antipsychotics: A call for ethical care. In S. Olfman & B. D. Robbins (Eds.), *Drugging our children: How profiteers are pushing antipsychotics on our youngest, and what we can do to stop it* (pp. 81–98). Westport, CT: Praeger.

Sparks, J. A., & Duncan, B. L. (2010). Couple and family therapy and the common factors: Have all won prizes? In B. L. Duncan, S. D. Miller, B. E. Wampold, & M. A. Hubble (Eds.), *The heart and soul of change: Delivering what works in therapy* (2nd ed., pp. 357–391). Washington, DC: American Psychological Association. doi:10.1037/12075-012

Sparks, J. A., & Duncan, B. L. (2013). Outside the black box: Re-assessing pediatric antidepressant prescription. *Journal of the Canadian Academy of Child and Adolescent Psychiatry, 22,* 240–246.

Sparks, J. A., Duncan, B. L., Cohen, D., & Antonuccio, D. O. (2010). Psychiatric drugs and common factors: An evaluation of the risks and benefits for clinical practice. In B. L. Duncan, S. D. Miller, B. E. Wampold, & M. A. Hubble (Eds.), *The heart and soul of change: Delivering what works in therapy* (2nd ed., pp. 199–235). Washington, DC: American Psychological Association. doi:10.1037/12075-007

Sparks, J. A., Duncan, B. L., & Miller, S. D. (2007). Common means to uncommon outcomes. In J. Lebow (Ed.), *21st century psychotherapies* (pp. 453–497). New York, NY: Wiley & Sons.

Sparks, J. A., Kisler, T. S., Adams, J. F., & Blumen, D. G. (2011). Teaching accountability: Using client feedback to train effective family therapists. *Journal of Marital and Family Therapy, 37,* 452–467.

Sparks, J. A., & Muro, M. L. (2009). Client-directed wraparound: The client as connector in community collaboration. *Journal of Systemic Therapies, 28,* 63–76. doi:10.1521/jsyt.2009.28.3.63

Spiegel, A. (2005). The dictionary of disorder: How one man redefined psychiatric care. *The New Yorker, January 3,* 56–63.

Stiles, W. B., Barkham, M., Mellor-Clark, J., & Connell, J. (2008). Effectiveness of cognitive-behavioural, person-centred, and psychodynamic therapies in UK primary-care routine practice: Replication in a larger sample. *Psychological Medicine, 38,* 677–688. doi:10.1017/S0033291707001511

Stricker, G., & Gold, J. (Eds.). (2006). *A casebook of psychotherapy integration.* Washington, DC: American Psychological Association. doi:10.1037/11436-000

Swift, J. K., Callahan, J. L., & Vollmer, B. M. (2011). Preferences. In J. C. Norcross (Ed.), *Psychotherapy relationships that work: Evidence-based responsiveness* (2nd ed., pp. 301–315). New York, NY: Oxford University Press. doi:10.1093/acprof:oso/9780199737208.003.0015

Task Force on Promotion and Dissemination of Psychological Procedures, Division of Clinical Psychology of the American Psychological Association. (1995).

Training and dissemination of empirically-validated psychological treatments: Report and recommendations. *Clinical Psychologist, 48*, 3–23.

Thomas, F., & Cockburn, J. (1998). *Competency-based counseling*. Minneapolis, MN: Fortress Press.

Tracey, T. J., & Kokotovic, A. M. (1989). Factor structure of the Working Alliance Inventory. *Psychological Assessment: A Journal of Consulting and Clinical Psychology, 1*, 207–210. doi:10.1037/1040-3590.1.3.207

Truax, C. B., & Carkhuff, R. R. (1967). *Toward effective counseling and psychotherapy*. Chicago, IL: Aldine.

Tryon, G. S., & Winograd, G. (2011). Goal consensus and collaboration. *Psychotherapy, 48*, 50–57. doi:10.1037/a0022061

Vasquez, M. J. T. (2012). Psychology and social justice: Why we do what we do. *American Psychologist, 67*, 337–346. doi:10.1037/a0029232

Walfish, S., McAlister, B., O'Donnell, P., & Lambert, M. J. (2012). An investigation of self-assessment bias in mental health providers. *Psychological Reports, 110*, 639–644.

Wampold, B. E. (2001). *The great psychotherapy debate: Models, methods, and findings*. Mahwah, NJ: Erlbaum.

Wampold, B. E. (2007). Psychotherapy: The humanistic (and effective) treatment. *American Psychologist, 62*, 855–873. doi:10.1037/0003-066X.62.8.857

Wampold, B. E., & Brown, G. S. (2005). Estimating therapist variability in outcomes attributable to therapists: A naturalistic study of outcomes in managed care. *Journal of Consulting and Clinical Psychology, 73*, 914–923. doi:10.1037/0022-006X.73.5.914

Watzlawick, P., Weakland, J. H., & Fisch, R. (1974). *Change: Principles of problem formation and problem resolution*. New York, NY: Norton.

Weersing, V. R., & Weisz, J. R. (2002). Community clinic treatment of depressed youth: Benchmarking usual care against CBT clinical trials. *Journal of Consulting and Clinical Psychology, 70*, 299–310. doi:10.1037/0022-006X.70.2.299

Wierzbicki, M., & Pekarik, G. (1993). A meta-analysis of psychotherapy dropout. *Professional Psychology: Research and Practice, 24*, 190–195. doi:10.1037/0735-7028.24.2.190

Whipple, J. L., Lambert, M. J., Vermeersch, D. A., Smart, D. W., Nielsen, S. L., & Hawkins, E. J. (2003). Improving the effects of psychotherapy: The use of early identification of treatment failure and problem solving strategies in routine practice. *Journal of Counseling Psychology, 50*, 59–68. doi:10.1037/0022-0167.50.1.59

Wunderink, L., Nieboer, R. M., Wiersma, D., Sytema, S., & Nienhuis, F. J. (2013). Recovery in remitted first-episode psychosis at 7 years of follow-up of an early dose reduction/discontinuation or maintenance treatment strategy: Long-term follow-up of a 2-year randomized clinical trial. *JAMA Psychiatry, 70*, 913–920.

Zuroff, D. C., Kelly, A. C., Leybman, M. J., Blatt, S. J., & Wampold, B. E. (2010). Between-therapist and within-therapist differences in the quality of the therapeutic relationship. *Journal of Clinical Psychology, 66*, 681–697.

INDEX

age range for use, 120
assisting clients with, 120
development of, 45
and PCOMS with families, 99–100
Chronic clients, 91–92
Churchill, Winston, 71
Cicero, Marcus Tullius, 72
Civilian Health and Medical Program
of the Uniformed Services
(CHAMPUS), 221
Clarification, about ORS ratings, 51–52
Clement, Paul, 130, 131
Clemmer, Jim, 68
Client(s). *See also* Nonresponding clients
abilities of, 95–98
angry, 61, 166–170
asking for help from, 3–5, 61
believing, 171–173
benefits of tracking treatment
response for, ix
chronic, 91–92
collaboration with, 164, 186–189
communications from, 218–220
doing something different with,
80–82
as element in psychotherapy, vii–viii
empowering change with, 74–77,
155–158
as engine of change, 229
experience of, 36, 58–61
goals of, 58–59, 79–80
heroic stories of, 150–155
insight from conversations with,
31–33
long-term work with, 38, 39, 85
mandated, 56–57, 119, 166–169
model/technique preferences
of, 165
as primary agents of change, 150
privileging perspectives about care
from, 212–215
probability of success by a given
session for, 93–94
reasons therapists are unsuccessful
with, 71–72
refusal to use PCOMS by, 205
resources of, 149–158
as "rites of passage," 4
strengths of, 150–155

tailoring approach to ideas of,
141–142
as teachers, 136–137, 236
view of therapeutic alliance by, 68–70
Client benefit, monitoring, 41–44, 134,
136–137
Client deterioration, 9, 13
Client-directed, outcome-informed
(CDOI) approach, 182–184
Client-directed approach to therapy,
xi, 182
Client-directed perspective on common
factors, 19–20
Client expectancy, 25–26
Client/life factors, 19–21
Client's theory of change, 82–83, 165
Clinical cutoff
for adults, 53–58, 112
for children, 112–113, 118
and data integrity, 205
Clinical management, 21
Clinical trials, vii–viii
Clinicians, frontline, 201–204
CMHCs (community mental health
centers), 192, 194
Cognitive behavioral therapy (CBT), 8,
10, 21, 25
Cognitive therapy without exposure, 10
Coherence dimension (CSRS), 45
Collaboration
and alliance, 102
with clients in psychotherapy, 164,
186–189
confident, 46
with families, 111–112
with medical professionals, 226
in PCOMS, 49
on tasks of therapy, 164
Collaborative goal formation, 163
Collateral raters, 109
Commission on Accreditation
(APA), 131
Commitment, to PCOMS, 197–200
Common factors, 8, 18–27
alliance, 23–24
client expectancy, 25–26
client/life factors, 19–21
feedback effects, 26–27
as framework for PCOMS, 203

and PCOMS with couples, 100–103
and PCOMS with youth/families,
103
termination in, 77
Nyman, S. J., 7

O'Donnell, P., 17, 131
Ogles, B., 131, 141
Okiishi, J. C., 135
Olsen, J., 195
"On the other hand" game, 143
OQ. *See* Outcome Questionnaire 45.2
Orientation, for ORS ratings, 52
Orlinsky, D. E., xv, 7, 21, 73–74,
128–130, 135–136, 139, 176,
204, 208–211
Orr, Bobby, 144
ORS. *See* Outcome Rating Scale
ORS scores. *See* Outcome Rating
Scale scores
Orwell, George, 8
Outcome(s). *See also* Tracking outcomes
and diagnosis, 224–225
and early change/therapeutic
alliance, 37–40
and length of stay, 39–40
positive, 7, 9–10, 65–66
as proof of effectiveness, 130
therapists' measurements of, 16–17
Outcome management systems, 130,
131, 201–202, 222–223
Outcome Questionnaire 45.2 (OQ), 37
in CMHC study, 194, 195
and development of ORS, 40–41
and development of PCOMS, xiv
as measure of effectiveness, 135
in ORS validity studies, 43
randomized clinical trials of, 13–14
Outcome Rating Scale (ORS), 13, 14
development of, 41
dimensions on, 41–43
as emotional thermometer, 205, 206
function of, 49
and goals of couples in therapy,
102–103
indications of reason for service
on, 114
introducing, 49–52, 109–111
maintaining focus with, 234

monitoring client benefits with, 134,
136–137
reliability and validity of, 41, 43–44
scoring, 52, 111
for teenagers, 105
tracking outcomes with, 72–74
tracking professional development
with, 132–135
Outcome Rating Scale (ORS) scores
accuracy of, 60–61, 205, 206
agreement on, 114–116
calculating probability of success
with, 93–94
and change, 122
for children from parents/caregivers,
106, 109
and client's experience/reasons for
service, 58–61
clinical cutoff for, 53–58, 111–112
contextualizing, 53–58, 111–112
disagreement on, 116–118
graphing, 72–73, 122
increases in, 74–77
life events as reasons for, 77, 84
non-increasing, 77–87
plateaus in, 76–77
precipitous drops in, 83–84
reconsidering approach due to, 141
supervisory process based on,
204–211
tracking outcomes with, 72–74
Outcome research, clinical trials in,
vii–viii
Outpatients, intake scores of, 53–55, 134
Overall dimension (ORS), 42
Overall dimension (SRS), 45
Overutilization, 77, 208
Owen, J., 24, 101–103

P4P (pay for performance) initiatives,
202, 221–224
Palm Beach County Children
Services, 201
Paperwork, 37, 192–193
Parallel process, 211
Parents
change for youth and, 109
clinical cutoff for child's scores
from, 112

ABOUT THE AUTHOR

Barry L. Duncan, PsyD, a therapist, trainer, and researcher with 17,000 hours of clinical experience, is director of the Heart and Soul of Change Project (https://heartandsoulofchange.com). Dr. Duncan has published, as author or coauthor, more than 100 articles in various publications, as well as 16 books, addressing client feedback, consumer rights and involvement, the power of relationship, and a risk/benefit analysis of psychotropic medications. Because of his self-help books (the latest is *What's Right With You*), he has appeared on *Oprah* and several other national TV programs.

His work regarding consumer rights and client feedback, the Partners for Change Outcome Management System (PCOMS), is included in the Substance Abuse and Mental Health Services Administration's National Registry of Evidence-Based Programs and Practices and has been implemented across the United States and in 20 other countries. He codeveloped PCOMS to give clients the voice they deserve as well as to provide clients, clinicians, administrators, and payers with feedback about the client's response to services, thus enabling more effective care tailored to client preferences. He is the developer of the clinical process of PCOMS.

Dr. Duncan implements PCOMS in small and large systems of care and conducts agency trainings, workshops, and keynote presentations on all of the topics listed above. Drawing upon his extensive clinical experience and passion for the work, his trainings speak directly to the frontline clinician about what it means to be a therapist and how each of us can re-remember and achieve our original aspirations to make a difference in the lives of those we serve.

Barry L. Duncan may be reached at barrylduncan@comcast.net.